The Songs of Robert Schumann

by the same author

The Songs of Hugo Wolf

to my mother
and father

THE SONGS OF ROBERT SCHUMANN

ERIC SAMS

Foreword by
GERALD MOORE

W · W · NORTON & COMPANY · INC · NEW YORK

Printed in Great Britain

CONTENTS

Foreword by Gerald Moore

Eric Sams's *The Songs of Hugo Wolf* has proved of such immeasurable help to lovers of this composer, a source of such inspiration to those of us who sing and play his songs, that we can only be grateful that the author has now performed a similar service for Robert Schumann.

These two books are necessary; for surely, after the unparalleled Franz Schubert, Wolf and Schumann share second place in the hierarchy of the Lied.

Ardent Wolfians will protest at my honouring both equally, and indeed they have an argument; for undeniably the Austrian seemed able to feel the words as the poet felt them – to transform them into music as the poet would have transformed them. Thus, we believe that Goethe, if he could, would have sung *Anakreons Grab* as Wolf sang it. This composer was the poet's medium and inhabited his world as completely as he inhabited the very different worlds of Eichendorff, Mörike and the Italian Songbook of Heyse.

On the contrary – and as we can find in the following pages – Schumann was apt to regard poetry as an inferior art-form, while Wolf held it of prime importance; he often recited the lyric before performing his songs. Schumann held that the poem was 'an orange from which the juice should be crushed'; or that 'it must wear the music like a wreath'. The difference, for instance, between Wolf's and Schumann's approach to Mörike's *Das verlassene Mägdlein* is revealing. To use Wolf's words, it had been 'set to heavenly music by Schumann'; and yet he felt impelled to set it himself. Sams truly says of the Schumann version, 'For most hearers the beauty and intuitive perception will remain *behind* the music rather than *part* of it.' But in two words he sums up for Wolf: he 'goes deep'. It would be utterly misleading and presumptuous to postulate that Schumann was superficial; but he did occasionally, if only occasionally, fail to penetrate deeply beneath the surface.

Comparisons of this nature are irresistible and desirable. When Sams suggests that Schumann's setting of Goethe's *Philine* is arguably preferable to Wolf's we, while not necessarily agreeing whole-heartedly with the author, are glad to see Schumann even up the score. Speaking personally, I find Hugo's *Er ist's*, though enjoyable to perform and thrilling to hear, too flamboyant when compared with Schumann's version, with its shy fragrant 'Veilchen träumen schon' and the maiden modesty of 'Dich hab ich vernommen, ja du bist's'.

Wolf, be it understood, is far too precious to me for me to disparage his genius. Yet (magician though he unquestionably is) I fancy one is able to perceive, not infrequently, how he arrives at his breath-taking dénouements. We are not perhaps so mystified as we should be. Whereas hearing *Der Leiermann* or *Der du von dem Himmel bist* we kiss Schubert's hand, and not only because these songs are close to God: their simplicity and purity defeat us and hold us, eternally hold us, through our inability to explain *why* or *how* they are so sublime.

Robert Schumann has something of this mysterious quality. It can be seen in the last song of *Frauenliebe und -leben*. The writing is bare and attenuated, the two pages look commonplace; yet, in some inexplicable way, they catch at the heart. *Auf einer Burg* ('the very music of a ruined castle in a timeless heat-haze') – *Auf das Trinkglas eines verstorbenen Freundes* ('an impressive sense of the ceremonial mourning rituals of white magic'), which invariably fills me with awe at the words 'Leer steht das Glas! Der heil'ge Klang tönt nach in dem kristallnen Grunde' – *Stirb, Lieb und Freud* ('the inward eye sees in the great cathedral one small figure; the inward ear hears among the chanting and the carillon one lonely cry') – *Du bist wie eine Blume* ('the laying on of hands is made to seem a ritual gesture of consecration)' – all these are just a handful of songs that are typically and disarmingly simple; and it can be seen by the parenthetical quotations to what eloquence our author has been moved by them.

The reader turns again and again with excitement to see if his love for such simple creations is echoed by a writer of such authority and it is an added delight to find his enthusiasm shared.

I have purposely refrained from putting too much emphasis on the piano parts in Schumann's song writing, but perhaps I may be permitted one paragraph on this subject.

'The prelude has the play of an April wind. The slight texture and the piano interludes let air and space into the music.' Thus, on page 75 we find this fascinating reflection on *Aus den 'Östlichen Rosen'*. Of all composers none had more magic than Schumann in making us forget the percussive quality of the pianoforte. We find this again and again in such songs as *Mondnacht* ('the bridal of the earth and sky') – *Der Nussbaum*, where the fingers scarcely brush the keys, and from *Dichterliebe*, one of the world's supreme song cycles, the pianoforte becomes almost de-materialized in *Im wunderschönen Monat Mai*, *Hör ich das Liedchen klingen* and *Am leuchtenden Sommermorgen* ('the piano's preluding arpeggios express a wind-stirred movement of tall flowers nodding, painting a picture in which the opening harmony is mysteriously bright and alien to the key into which it instantly fades and vanishes'). Schumann's accompaniments certainly did not have such independence, such glorious freedom from the vocal line, as we find in *Geh, Geliebter* (Wolf's apotheosis) but no composer whatsoever had a more intimate knowledge of the pianoforte as an instrument. He made it breathe upon the air.

To me this is the most exciting publication of its kind since the Sams book on Wolf. So felicitous is the writing that one is hardly conscious of the erudition and profound thought that have gone into the making of it. Occasionally controversial perhaps, it is invariably stimulating and authoritative and most obviously inspired by deep affection.

Once more Eric Sams has produced a work that will be read and read again as long as Robert Schumann's songs are loved.

PREFACE

This book, like *The Songs of Hugo Wolf* (Methuen, 1961 and Faber & Faber, 1969), gives a date, translation, commentary and notes on points of detail for the 246 songs in the Peters Edition, arranged as nearly as possible in order of composition.

Definite dates come mainly from Schumann's own fair copies[1] or diaries;[2] others are modified in the light of the evidence. On occasion I have suggested reasons for dating or re-dating.

In the translations, Schumann's repetitions are not normally shown unless they occur out of context, e.g. where a first verse is repeated at the end, and then in square brackets.

The textual notes include the major changes[3] that Schumann made in the words of the songs as inferred from comparison of their first editions with the known or probable sources of the poems (see Appendix III).

The other notes are mainly a gloss on Schumann's musical language[4] (see pp. 8–26) as inferred from the relation between the poem and the music.

Two of the 'Clara-themes' in the songs (see pp. 22–25) have already been described in the piano music.[5,6] Readers interested in these themes and the evidence they offer for Schumann's use of cipher-systems as a device of composition may like to consult my *Musical Times* articles.[7] A book on these and kindred topics is in preparation.[8]

[1] Wolff, V. E., *Schumanns Lieder in ersten und späteren Fassungen*, (1914).

[2] Jansen, G., *Briefe von Robert Schumann*, (1904) and Bötticher, W., *Robert Schumann in seinen Briefen und Schriften*, (1942).

[3] See also, Friedländer, M., *Textrevision zu Schumanns Liedern*, (ND).

[4] See also, Bötticher, W., *Robert Schumann in Persönlichkeit und Werk*, (1941).

[5] Schauffler, R., *Florestan*, (1945).

[6] Fiske, R., 'A Schumann mystery', *Musical Times*, August 1964.

[7] 'Did Schumann use ciphers?', August 1965, (trans. *Neue Zeitschrift für Musik*, June 1966); 'The Schumann ciphers', May 1966; 'The Schumann ciphers, a coda', December 1966 (trans. *Musica*, July–August 1967); 'Politics, Literature and People', February 1968.

[8] To be published by Faber & Faber.

Lastly I should like to thank all those who have helped me.

I am obliged to the late Max Hinrichsen for permission to quote and refer to the Peters Edition of Schumann's songs.

Andrew Porter was generous with his time and his advice, both of which are valuable; I am indebted to him for a number of corrections, and for some suggestions on points of substance which I have been glad to adopt or adapt for my own purposes.

I am also most grateful to Julian Armitage-Smith, Edward Greenfield, David Lloyd-Jones and Robert Moberly for similarly generous and helpful comment and criticism.

My thanks are due to Miss Margaret Barton for timely help with the manuscript.

SCHUMANN AS A SONG WRITER

Songs were among Schumann's first works, at seventeen (in 1827); they were among his last (in 1852). All his life, most of his music was associated with words, whether as texts, titles or programmes. Well over half of it is for voice; well over three-quarters is for (or with) piano. His inspiration ebbed and flowed in ten-year cycles,[1] with crests of activity in 1840 and 1849; so each of those waves of music broke in song for voice and piano.

These songs mirror the life of the man and his music. They tell a life story of genesis, growth, maturity and decline; they have an unchanging spirit that animates them still. Most of this book follows the vital process through two decades of life and song; this chapter tries to define the vital principles.

Schumann himself defines his music for us. 'Everything that happens in the world affects me, politics, literature, people; I think it all over in my own way, and then it has to find a way out through music.' In a review he writes:

> Improvise at the keyboard, hum a melody, weave that melody into the piano texture; thus – if you are a Mendelssohn – you can write the most beautiful songs without words.

He might have added – sing that melody to words by (say) Heine and then you can – if you are a Schumann – write the most beautiful songs. The songs are an extension of the piano-music; and they too express Schumann's own world of feeling.

By 1840 he had spent ten years in perfecting his unique mastery of the lyric piano piece. Of course he would continue to write what came naturally and what he knew best. The long expressive postludes are especially characteristic; they are piano solos. The best known of all

[1] The letters and journals confirm what this pattern of composition suggests; Schumann's innate temperament was markedly cycloid, with upswings of elation, downswings of depression (often with hypochondria or actual illness: see Appendix II).

(in *Dichterliebe*) reappears in the piano concerto. Some of the boyhood songs (Appendix I) were later adapted as piano-music. Conversely, Schumann tells us how he turns his piano-music into song (see *Ich wandre nicht*). *Mit Myrthen und Rosen* is like a re-reading of the first Novellette; *Zum Schluss* rounds off the songs of Op. 25 just as *Zum Beschluss* rounds off a piano-cycle (Op. 20); *Sitz' ich allein* even has an optional Da Capo.

The two genres have not only common titles (e.g. *Abendlied*, *Intermezzo*) but common form. Both can be simple and repetitive (i.e. in so-called song-form). But this is rare; more usually they are varied or extended with climax and coda. Schumann thought those features very apt for the end of a song (as also for the piano piece *Ende vom Lied*, Op. 12) and he often repeats words in order to achieve a peroration.

Finally the songs, just like the piano works, are organized into groups or cycles. This reflects his passion for verbal expressiveness, order and symmetry. In his daily life, everything goes into books; a day-book, a project-book, a song-book, a correspondence-book, a note-book, a marriage-book, and a cash-book. The piano-music appears as Novellettes, Albums, and so on, complete with titles and headings. Among the songs, the cycles are the most famous (the two *Liederkreise*, *Dichterliebe*, *Frauenliebe* etc.) as they are the most characteristic (about four-fifths of all the songs form part of some group). Most are musically integrated, whether by key-sequence or by motto-themes, again just as in the piano music. Sometimes it is the same theme in both, as in the *Davidsbündler*, Op. 6, and the *Liederkreis*, Op. 24. The typical vocal lines:

like the themes mentioned on pp. 22–25, are fully as typical of Schumann's purely instrumental melodies. Indeed, he habitually speaks of 'vocal works' or 'works for voice', much as one might speak of works for piano; never as if the words, or even the vocal timbre or compass, were significant as such.

This explains the indifferent accentuation found throughout the songs. It explains such odd directions as 'for soprano or contralto'. It explains the alternative vocal lines that Schumann was always ready to write if he found his piano tunes straying beyond what he thought was a reasonable vocal compass, as in the well-known example of *Ich grolle nicht* (in such cases the rule is to sing the piano line if possible). Above all it explains why voice and piano so often share the melody. This trait has been criticized on the ground that the piano only echoes the voice, which is a 'weakness'. But on the contrary; since the piano concept is primary, it is the voice that borrows the piano melody, and this sharing is the heart and strength of Schumann song. Sometimes the shared melody is the same in voice and piano, as in *Die Nonne*; sometimes it is varied or decorated in the piano part, often very subtly, as in *Aufträge* or *Resignation*. But from Schumann's first song to his last the melody is essentially the piano's. If all the voice parts were lost we could deduce from the piano part and the words what the vocal line must be. This may seem exaggerated or over-simplified; but it will be found verifiably true of most of the songs, and not irrelevant to the rest.

If then the piano is primary, and if the music expresses the composer rather than the poet, it follows that both voice and verse are subordinate. Yet the music is all shapely melody, singable and beautiful; and Schumann is often acclaimed as among the most literary of all composers, sensitively attuned to the least poetic nuance, with a special affinity for the poems of Heinrich Heine. However, this is a myth, as we can discover from the Heine settings themselves.

Their source was the first edition of the *Buch der Lieder* – thirteen years, two editions, and several revisions out of date. Schumann's selection of poems was indiscriminate. He foisted his own meaning on them, and not only repeated words or lines or whole verses for this purpose but added and altered and miscopied and omitted at will. He rarely offers any equivalent for Heine's obvious irony or innuendo, and mostly seems not to understand them. Out of twenty-five years of composing he devoted some twenty-five days, spread over a year or two at most, to setting a few pages of one single volume; there is no evidence that he even so much as glanced at another Heine lyric for the rest of his life.

Schumann himself implied that he believed poetry to be an inferior art-form.[1] Nothing suggests that he ever changed his mind. On the contrary, all his recorded comments on the relation of words to music instinctively award pride of place to the latter. The poem, he said, must be crushed and have its juices expressed like an orange; it must

[1] See, e.g., his letter to Hermann Hirschbach, June 1839.

wear the music like a wreath, or yield to it like a bride. For him there was no contradiction, no problem; nor is there, unless one is created. His own music, as he very well knew, is expressive of ideas just as words are. In his songs (as in most songs) the meaning of the music takes precedence. Sometimes the two are in phase, so that the expression is enhanced; sometimes they are out of phase, so that new patterns and tensions are created from the interaction of music and words. The latter is the typical Schumann; original, rewarding, infinitely expressive of the composer, his life and his world.

Even his choice and treatment of poets and poems was self-expressive. He liked the poets to be known to him personally (most of them were) and to share his liberal and agnostic views (most of them did).[1] The settings responded to some need of the moment. 'Bring the Kerner volume', he writes to Clara; 'lend me the Geibel', to a friend. From the volumes he chose poems which either directly mirrored his own feelings or could be adjusted to reflect them. Thus Eichendorff's devotional *Mondnacht* is steeped in love-music until it takes on a different colour of devotion. Similarly, words or phrases or verses are repeated or altered to remould their meaning nearer to the composer's mood. This treatment is typical of Schumann; and his prevailing moods and themes are typical of the Romantic movement.

In his own person he expresses a whole universe of life and feeling; the one becomes the infinite. The surest way is by self-abnegation, by losing oneself and being reborn in the love of another. His life as well as his work was dedicated to his wife, Clara. There are no more deeply-felt declarations in music than his love-songs for her in their marriage year (*Liederkreis*, *Myrthen*, *Dichterliebe*, the best of him). Indeed, many songs transcend even this degree of exaltation by identifying the music with Clara herself; by sharing the writing with her (as in Op. 47), or by seeing life through her eyes (some of *Myrthen*, all *Frauenliebe und -leben*) as well as by the continuous use of meaningful motto-themes signifying Clara (see pp. 22–25). Of course there are other, more light-hearted, ways of losing one's own identity, such as assuming various guises or disguises, a theme very dear to Schumann.[2] He masquerades in

[1] See Appendix III.

[2] Thus not only the founding but the entire membership of the League of David (Davidsbund) was his own idea; he was the only one to use such names as 'Felix Meritis' for Mendelssohn, and the many others including his own Florestan and Eusebius, and of course David (because the war was against the Philistines). Among other *noms de guerre* mentioned in the letters, note-books and articles are: 2; 4; 6; 12; XII; 13; 14; 22; 32; 39; A.L.; Chiara; Die Dblr;

the songs, with evident relish, as a Spanish grandee (*Der Hidalgo*), a smuggler (*Der Contrabandiste*), a clown (*Schlusslied*), and so on. Often Clara is brought into the masquerade (as in *Myrthen* and *Die Kartenlegerin*) as she was into *Carnaval*.

However, such flights from reality take no one very far. The disguise becomes the man too well or too often; Schumann *in propria persona* wears the frowning mask of tragedy. Thus a recurring theme is tragic isolation. Very many songs are about lost love (*Die Nonne, Stirb, Lieb' und Freud'*) and jealousy (*Die Löwenbraut, Die feindlichen Brüder*), while in song after song the central figure is a rejected suitor, often at the wedding-feast (*Der Spielmann, Der arme Peter, Das ist ein Flöten*, etc). This music is often so intense as to compel the conclusion that some very powerful personal emotion went into its making – no doubt Schumann's own estrangement from Clara in 1835–6.

The feelings of guilt and unworthiness which haunted him all his life are also expressed in the songs (e.g. *Mein schöner Stern*). The symbolism of rejection or guilt becomes so obsessional with the later Schumann that it motivates all his larger-scale vocal works; *Manfred, Faust, Genoveva, Paradise and the Peri* and others. The linking theme is the idea of isolation, difference, otherness; and almost all his chosen texts express it directly or indirectly. Next to a striving to be someone else, for example, comes a longing to be elsewhere.

Very often Schumann sings of the open road (*Freisinn, Wanderung*), travel abroad (*Wanderlied*), the wide world (*Sehnsucht*). There is a strong undercurrent of a wish for freedom in the political sense (*Des Knaben Berglied*). But there is an air of diffidence about his travel songs, and his sense of social satire is far from keen (*Abends am Strand, Vom Schlaraffenland*). The vision is always that of the lone idealist and dreamer endlessly questing for new worlds of the spirit, and the universal brotherhood of the outsider's dream. So there are translations of verse from all over the world; from England (Byron), Ireland (Moore),

---

E; E–s; Euseb.; Eusebius; F; F–n; Flor.; Florestan; F und E; Florestan und Eusebius; Faust; Fust; Fridolin; Gustav; Jeanquirit; Jonathan; Julius; Meister Raro; R–o; Robert an der Mulde; Serpentin; Serpentinus; Skülander; K. Schumann; R.S.; R.Sch.; Voigt; R.W.; W.Z.; and, on occasion, Robert Schumann.

Clara was at various times e.g. Ambrosia; Beda; Chiara; Chiarina; Cilia; Clärchen; Peri; Zilia.

The two together were imagined as e.g. Egmont and Clärchen; Hermann und Dorothea; Hero and Leander; Sarazen und Sarazene; Pantalon et Colombine; and so on.

Scotland (Burns), Denmark (Hans Andersen), France (Béranger), Spain (the many Geibel translations), and Greece (via Chamisso). Of other poets, many were strongly liberal: Hoffmann was persecuted, Heine and Kinkel were exiled, for their politics. But Schumann's longing for some other country or some other society remained unstilled. As he grew older his vision moved from horizons in space to horizons in time; to classical antiquity (*Requiem*); to the golden age of legend or ballad (*Die feindlichen Brüder*, *Ballade*); to later history (*Blondels Lied*, the *Maria Stuart Lieder*); or to childhood (*Liederalbum für die Jugend*), a favourite domain.

So the creative Romantic mind ranges over all space, all time, all feeling, all humanity. The true ideal is not just to be someone else, but to be everyone; not just somewhere else, but everywhere; not just another time but all time. This progress from the one to the infinite culminates in the passionate identification of man with Nature, a feeling stronger in the Romantic than in any other era, and stronger perhaps in Schumann than in any other Romantic composer. His own music is at one with sky and springtime (*Im wunderschönen Monat Mai*, *Der Nussbaum*, *Jasminenstrauch*). True, he is more at home in the little world of leaves, rainfall, and birdsong, just as he is most at home in the little world of love, marriage, and children. But his own feeling unites both realms; roadside and hearthside, starlight and firelight, in ways which often give the music great range and power. Nor is Schumann without a certain dark grandeur of his own when he sings of the depths of night or sea (*Abends am Strand*, *Frühlingsfahrt*).

There seems to be a reason for this in the depths of the subconscious mind. Over the years, it is as if his need to find another personality led to the loss of his own; as if his desire for another world led to the negation of this world. 'Between 1830 and 1850 the Romantic faith in love and the future turned into a longing for nothingness' as Nietzsche wrote. Schumann's mind turns to poems about madness (*Der Spielmann*, *An die Türen*) and finally death (*Der Einsiedler*, *Requiem*, *Abschied von der Welt*). And both ways of escape lead through the depths of despair. One late song (*Herzeleid*) is about suicide and death by drowning; and it is eerie to hear, over the years, the hidden themes of burial and submersion. A ship is sunk (*Frühlingsfahrt*); a coffin is sunk (*Die alten bösen Lieder*). Treasure is buried in the womb of earth (*Der Schatzgräber*) and in the bed of the river (*Auf dem Rhein*). There lurk death and night (*Berg und Burgen*); there under the waves dwells the enchantress (*Lorelei*), singing and calling 'Remember me'. Over and over again in Schumann's songs we can hear the Rhine appealing to him, long before his own despairing leap from the bridge at Düsseldorf (*Im Rhein; Auf einer Burg; Berg und Burgen; Auf dem Rhein; Sonntags am Rhein;* and then the Rhenish symphony).

This flows into a great theme which unites all we have so far heard. It is not obvious; it could not in the nature of things be that. It hides at the heart of all Schumann's music. It is the common characteristic of love, disguise, elsewhere, beyond, long ago, far away, Nature, death. It is the theme of mystery. The choice of poem faithfully reflects this theme down to the last detail of code (*Liebeslied*) and cipher (*Rätsel*).[1]

There is a sense then in which Schumann is indeed the most lettered of composers. The verbal, the conceptual, the semantic, are of overwhelming importance in his music; and it follows that the words of his songs, though secondary, exert a profound influence of their own. We have seen the resemblance between the song-music and the piano-music. Now we must consider in detail the differences; and these can be explained only by the presence of words.

First, as Schumann himself explained, the songs are more tuneful and more direct. He was among the world's greatest melodists; even the piano-music sings; and words sang themselves into tunes in his mind as naturally and inevitably as in Schubert's. *Du meine Seele, du mein Herz, Im wunderschönen Monat Mai,* and scores of other phrases are best remembered as melodies patterned in the stresses of speech and verse. The new directness in the music matches the supposed simplicity of lyric poetry. Just as with Beethoven, the songs sound many opus numbers earlier than the other music. The rhythmic quirks and experiments of the piano works are ironed out; their favourite three-four time now yields place to the duple and quadruple time-signatures that correspond with usual German scansion and metre. Similarly we return from the tonally complex world of the piano-music into the bright harmonies hardly heard since *Papillons,* with transient tonal changes in contrasting bands of dark and bright. The reason is that the short song-form hardly allows time for long-range modulation, or indeed any real key-change at all. There are only insets in related keys, notably supertonic and mediant, which are heard as relating to the home tonic.

[1] One aspect of disguise is the idea of verbal disguises such as puns, riddles, charades, enigmas, etc., in which Schumann's delight was lifelong. His known uses of musical cipher are worth recording: A, B, E, G, G (1831); A, S, C, H, As, C, H, S, C, H, A (1834); B, E, D, A (1837); E, H, E (1838, 1840); H (1840); G, A, D, E (1843); G, A, D, E, A, DE (1844); B, A, C, H (1845); A, C, H (1847); G, A, D, E (1848); F, A, E (1853).

On this small scale a real modulation is often surprising and always significant.

Most striking of all is the change in form. In the piano-music Schumann was veering towards ever darker and more labyrinthine constructions, as in *Kreisleriana*. The song music comes out of this high-hedged maze into an open flower-garden.

Finally the gaiety and excitement of discovery make the music reckless and vivid. The sheer driving impetus of it meant there was hardly time to write it down. The editorial and interpretative problems are often grave in consequence. We often have the feeling of a sketch or blueprint that requires skilled and sympathetic interpretation to make it alive and real again. Then the music is heard nascent and inchoate, quick and brilliant from its contact with words. It sees, hears, gestures, mimes, acts, reacts and speaks.

Here are some of the ways in which it does so. Many of them may derive from subconscious sources. Thus we know from an early essay that Schumann could imagine different keys as expressive of varying moods. In practice, however, he was usually ready to transpose his music for the sake of vocal compass, or to create a cyclic unity as in *Dichterliebe*; and this destroys some of the evidence for his expressive use of key. But enough is left to demonstrate the association of e.g. A major with spring or sunshine (*Jasminenstrauch*, *An den Sonnenschein*), and A flat major with a mellower quality of light (*Die Lotosblume*), and moods of reverence or dedication (*Stirb, Lieb' und Freud'; Widmung*). B flat major is the key of 22 songs of which six are directly and twelve indirectly about the open air; it seems a good choice also for a spring symphony, for the entry to the woodland scenes of Op. 82, and for the idyllic outdoor music of *Faust* No. 4. E minor has strong associations with twilight (*Zwielicht*) and the heart (*Lieb Liebchen*). D minor has a melodramatic quality (*Melancholie*); B minor may suggest estrangement, even enmity (*Die feindlichen Brüder*). E flat major has a special quality of light and shade, found in moods of mingled reverence and elation (*Lust der Sturmnacht*, *Schneeglöckchen*) while E flat minor is an unequivocally defunctive music of darkness, death and funeral (*Ich hab' im Traum geweinet*). Such a use of key, of which there are many other examples, commonly gives colour and pattern to a whole song or cycle. More rarely a tonality is illustrative, lighting up a particular word or scene, like the A flat major moonrise in *Die Lotosblume*.

The sound-effects are even clearer. They too are usually long-range or structural. Harp music resounds throughout *Requiem* and the late

Byron songs, as well as the Harper songs. We hear the lute (*Mein Herz ist schwer*); the guitar (*Flutenreicher Ebro*); the horn (*Der Knabe mit dem Wunderhorn*); the organ (*Stirb, Lieb' und Freud'*); the bagpipes (*Des Sennen Abschied*); and the drum (*Die Soldatenbraut*), among many other examples. Sometimes they stand for a central character, like the violin passages in *Der Spielmann*; more rarely they illustrate a word or thought in the poem, like the bugle-call at the end of *Da liegt der Feinde* or the bell-notes in *Die Meerfee*. There is an easy transition from sound effect to dramatic effect (the bell announces midnight in *Auf das Trinkglas* just as in the piano-music of Op. 6) or to scene-painting (e.g. from the spinning-wheel in *Die Spinnerin* to the rolling stage coach in *Mein Wagen rollet langsam*). But Schumann goes beyond this to far deeper levels of association.

No musical imagination was ever more bright or vivid; his is the music of the mind's eye and the mind's ear blending in his own inner perception of an idea or image. Indeed, he often sets the imagery rather than the verbal meaning of a poem, as Robert Franz pointed out (see Nos 67 and 95, Note 3). In song after song the music is all gesture and mime for the characters depicted, all colour and chiaroscuro for the scenes. What follows is an attempt to isolate some elements of this symbolic kinship with language. 'Motif' or 'M' is used as a convenient shorthand for a musical expression found in association with a given verbal idea. Motif 45 (M 45) for example means the basic progression II–V (sometimes IV–V) of the prevailing tonality, together with a reference in the sung text to the idea of going away, departure or disappearance. Agreed, neither the musical nor the verbal concept is rare, nor is there any obvious reason for their association. On the other hand, compare these typical supertonic-dominant progressions:

Song	*Bars*	*Words*	
Sag an, o lieber Vogel mein	4/5	*wohin die Reise?*	(whither away?)
Was will die einsame Träne?	16/17	*zerflossen*	(dispersed)
Wenn ich in deine Augen	3/4	*schwindet*	(disappears)
Heimliches Verschwinden	31/32	*floh*	(fled)

These and other examples strongly suggest some correlation in Schumann's mind. In the same way, each of the motifs and themes listed below seem to be a real and meaningful element in Schumann's composition. They occur in countless isotopes and compounds; most are difficult to isolate; some are very rare. But each can be verified by direct experience of the music. The following list is intended only to exemplify. Further instances of these and other possible correspondences will be found in the notes to the songs, though of course it is not possible to mention each motif each time it occurs.

MOTIFS

Schumann always insisted that he invented his titles to suit the music, not vice versa. Either way, he felt that his music had the closest analogy with language. When word-setting sharpens the musical expression, the piano idiom becomes more penetrative. For example *Glückes genug* (Quite contented) from *Kinderszenen* (Scenes of childhood), Op. 15, begins with the melody:

In the songs the bracketed phrase is often associated with words expressing innocent contentment (M 1).

Again, in the last movement of *Faschingsschwank aus Wien* (Carnival jest from Vienna), Op. 26, the brio of the last movement is conveyed in terms of

In the songs this simple resolution, usually in the right hand, stands for happiness (M 2), sometimes given added gaiety (M 3) by a decoration of rising notes

The essence of all three is a simple dominant-tonic movement, whether folding over in a relaxed melody for a more passive feeling or clapped together in brisk chords for a more active one.

A similar relation is also the basis of the so-called horn passage

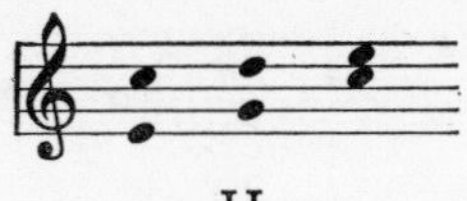

a fanfare which flourishes throughout Schumann's songs to express well-being (M 4), with clear overtones of the chase and the open air. Similarly the upper melody alone often means a call or summons, as in the opening trumpet call of the first symphony.

The ascending *minor* horn passage, however, or its melody, expresses a mood of resentment, indignation, or courage in adversity (M 5) and this in turn has a descending counterpart of indifference, disappointment or resignation (M 6):

Mein Herz ist betrübt (*Jemand*)
(My heart is sair)

These minor moods coalesce in the minor triad (M 7) which begins a song which is to be sad the whole way through, like a signpost pointing down a road of melancholy (*Die Höchlander-Witwe*, *Käuzlein*). A more acute grief (M 8) is expressed by the pang of the flattened sixth of the scale falling to the fifth. This idea is actually smuggled into a song by the composer on a monosyllable of his own devising, to symbolize a groan

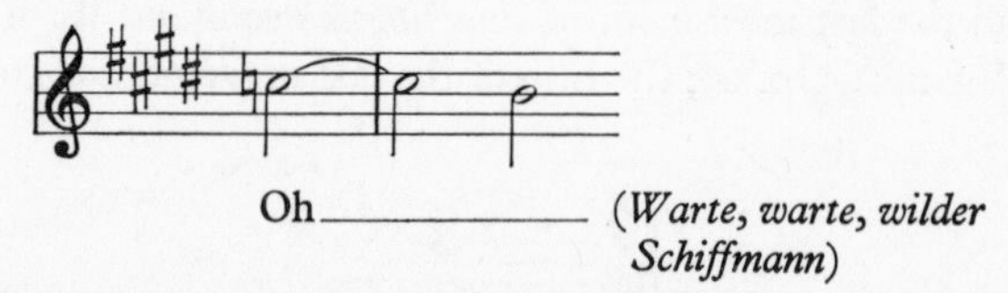

(*Warte, warte, wilder Schiffmann*)

This falling semitone is accompanied by a rising one in a resolution which meant 'tears' to Schumann (M 9), namely a diminished seventh resolving on to a supertonic (see p. 72) which recurs throughout *Was will die einsame Träne?* (The solitary tear).

One expressive element in this progression is of course the minor mode of motif 2 above. Joys and sorrows are close kin in Schumann. Indeed his most consistent and striking conflation of pleasurable with painful feelings suggests that for him the two are emotionally inseparable. For example, pleasure (M 10) is expressed by rising semitones in descending sequence, treated as a passing or inessential note in a diatonic context, thus:

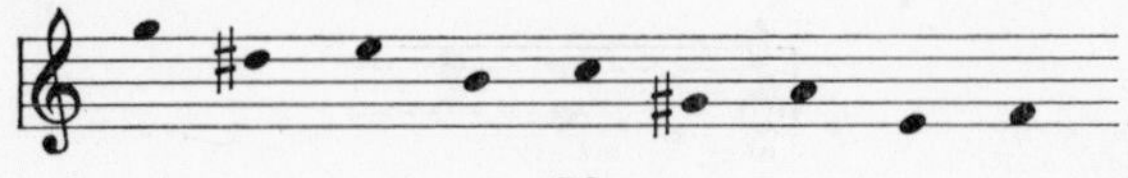

This insinuating melodic line with its oblique effect of nuzzling or wheedling can also serve on occasion as a love-theme, as in *Intermezzo*.

But when the harmony is chromatic, the tonality minor, the elision less smooth, then the music has the meaning of distress (M 11), e.g.

This expresses various shades of significance from discomfort (as in the part-song *Zahnweh*, Toothache, Op. 55, No. 2) and dismay (Faust No. 3) to dire grief when the lower semitone is stressed, as in *Einsamkeit*.

We can also separate out the expressive components of these basic motifs 10 and 11. Thus a semitone rising smoothly to a major mediant is linked with the idea of sweetness (M 12) often found in association with the word 'süss', as in *Süsser Freund*

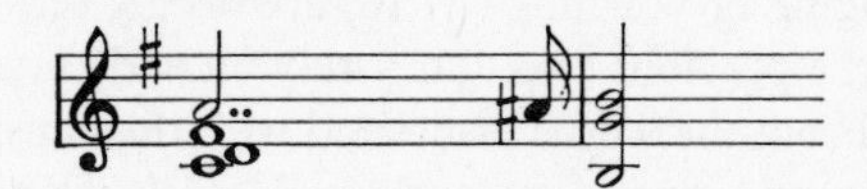

But as in motif 11A the accented rising semitone and the minor resolution give a much sharper tang of bitterness (M 13), as at the word 'Qualen' (torments) in *Was will die einsame Träne?*

In Schumann's later music the grief and asperity of these falling or rising semitones (as in M 8, 9, 11, 13), become an obsession. But they have their lighter side. The upward semitone can even be used on occasion for burlesque effects (M 14), usually with both notes staccato (for the light touch) as in Schumann's only comic song, *Der Contrabandiste*.

For the idea of actual laughter (M 15) whether in mockery, as in *Jung Volkers Lied*, or joy, as in *Intermezzo*, the equivalent is a wider falling interval, e.g. an octave or seventh.

Burlesque and amusement (M 14 and 15), combine graphically in what may have been Schumann's first song-motif, typifying Feste the clown, whose motley provokes our mirth:

True, such motifs are not plentiful in the songs. But then, Schumann was always more Jaques than Feste: and though he may not have laughed very often we can perhaps guess what it sounded like when he did.

Motifs for longing or yearning (M 16) are deeply serious, and hence the opposite of the previous two. They rely on wide intervals rising to a stressed note. From the words associated with this music we can infer a mimetic image of arms outstretched (M 16[A]) whether in offered embrace (*Im Westen*) or in supplication (*Im Rhein, im heiligen Strome*) or even, unlikely though it seems, in digging (*Der Schatzgräber*). There is a similar use of an image of arms as wings in flight (*Flügel! Flügel!*); whence it is no great stretch of the imagination to the symbolism of a striving for freedom (M 16[B]) as in the prelude to *Sitz' ich allein*

or more elaborately in the prelude and postlude of *Sehnsucht*, where title and poem unite the ideas of longing and escape.

On similar conceptual grounds these ideas provide an equivalent for dancing (M 17) (which is a repeated rising interval, e.g. an octave, as in *Der arme Peter*, about a wedding dance)

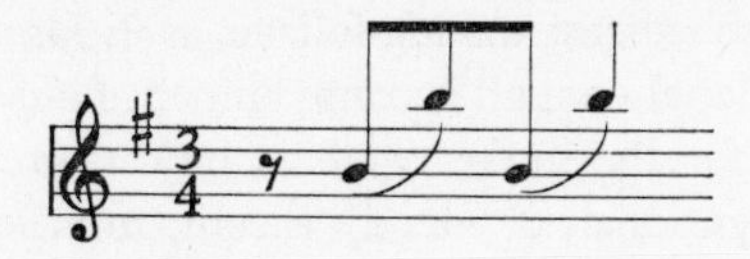

or for walking (M 18) (smaller rising intervals, as in *Morgens steh ich auf*, about walking in a daydream)

The rising interval of a sixth on its own is often heard in association with the idea of a song or singing (M 19) (*In der Fremde*, *Wehmut*). For dancing as for walking however the effect has to be a double one, as it were for the sake of stability. The idea of walking often goes with a very apt stepwise melody, d′ t l s (M 20) sometimes linked with the word 'wandeln' as in the example above, which begins and ends a song with the closing words 'wandle ich bei Tag' (I walk by day); or as in the prelude to *Ich wandelte unter den Bäumen*, where that melody steps down on to those words.

The dancing motif too is at its liveliest when partnered with other motivic ideas. Thus the prelude to *Berg und Burgen* in the bright key of A major gives a colourful reflection of the dancing of waves in spring sunshine. Indeed, Schumann has a whole cluster of musical images about the idea of movement of winds and waves in the open air and hence the feeling of kinship with Nature in changing moods.

The prototypes are the movement of leaves (M 21) whether downwards, or upwards, as in *Der Nussbaum*,

or of waves (M 21A) as in *Die Lorelei*

The latter may also suggest waving foliage, as in *Jasminenstrauch*. True, these are conventional enough accompaniment figures. But this piano-music is notable for the intensity of its lyric expression; it is hardly ever merely conventional, or merely accompaniment. And Schumann knew well enough, and described, what such figurations meant to him (see *Jasminenstrauch*, No. 41).

Another equivalent for winds (M 22), whether as breeze or storm, is a gentle tremolo, found mainly in the later songs, which even at its most vehement rarely rises above a modest force two; Schumann's prevailing wind was a gentle one, like his prevailing mood of joy in Nature (M 23). This is typically expressed by the arpeggio of motif 21 or 21^{A} used as a rising vocal melody, as in e.g. the opening of *Talismane* or *Wanderlied* or *An den Sonnenschein*. This seems to have had some strong personal significance in those examples and perhaps in others, e.g. *Er der Herrlichste von allen*, or the same melody in the finale of the Rhenish symphony (Ex. F on p. 2).

The verbal opposite of joy-in-Nature (M 23), i.e. the idea of grief and death in connexion with the open air, is an unusual concept, and only three Schumann songs express it. So it is noteworthy that each begins with the *opposite musical idea*, viz. a *downward minor* movement (M 24)

Die feindlichen Brüder *Herzeleid*

Warnung

These contrasts of major and minor, sunshine and showers, smiles and tears, day and night, are at the heart of Schumann's music. One of the most pervasive is the idea of two *major* tonalities a *minor* third apart. Thus a change from C major to E flat major, though ostensibly cheerful, contains the lingering wistfulness of an E flat remembered from the first tonality, blending the two in a pivotal C minor. This effect is elusive and not easy to define in verbal terms; but its lingering hidden hint of sadness (M 25) is a Schumannian essence that flavours song after song.

The contrast of tones provides another image-cluster of kinship with Nature, the images of peace and tranquillity, beginning with silence, evening, twilight, and gradually shading into darkness, sleep and a quiet death.

Take first the rising and falling interval which seems to have meant 'silence' to Schumann (M 26) often found in association with the word 'Stille', e.g.

Perhaps in his subconscious mind there was an association with the rise and fall of waves, as in the analogous motif 21^A; 'such a tide as moving seems asleep'. Perhaps there was the further idea of the rise and fall of breathing in sleep, since the same image animates *Kind im Einschlummern* (Child falling asleep) from Op. 15.

One component of this motif, the falling fifth, usually in voice or right hand, is associated with the idea of flowers, especially roses (M 27). Perhaps this idea is rooted in the spoken cadence of the word 'Rosen'; perhaps it stems from the previous motif and the silent contemplation of beauty (see also M 64). Like many of the motifs here listed, it is not confined to the songs; for ears attuned to this Schumannian imagery the first movement of the A major quartet opens a window on to the coloured air of high summer.

When this brightness falls lower down the keyboard it creates the converse image of increasing depth or darkness (M 28). A descending expression of this kind in the piano left hand suggests either nightfall, as in *Mondnacht*, or in a minor key a more ominous descent (compare M 24) as in *Lieb Liebchen.*

Again the metaphor is plain. The bass notes mean bed-rock firmness (M 29); and their depths have a darker shade of colour or meaning; whether as it were literally the deep sea (M 29^A) as in *Abends am Strand*, or the dark hollows of the mountains (M 29^B) as in *Die Sennin.* More figuratively they may mean a deep sleep, as in *Schöne Wiege*, or the darkening of the mind in death or madness, as in *Der Spielmann.* Finally, by further extension, repeated bass notes may symbolize a profound conviction or a blind faith (M 29^C). When they are accompanied by repeated chords or arpeggios in the right hand, the bass notes give added assurance in the further sense of protestations (M 30), of magnanimity, as in *Ich grolle nicht*, or love, as in *Widmung*. When sustained under slower chords, e.g. minims, they make an effect of awe-inspiring solemnity (M 31) whether in a verbal context of the sea (*Frühlingsfahrt*) or night (*Trost im Gesang*); or any sombre picture, such as an old castle (*Auf einer Burg*) or a great cathedral (*Im Rhein*).

In these last two examples the key of E minor links up with another subgroup of motifs of twilight and reverie and melancholy, which has the common idea of a *missing* element. Thus the Schumannian expression for dream (M 32), often found in association with the word 'Traum', is the insistent soft mezzo-staccato of a note that is only half there. This idea lends its intense inward quality to many a masterpiece, as in the prelude to *Mondnacht*, which is all about dreaming (von ihm nun *träumen* müsst'). (Here is one example among many also of the ways in which a Schumann motif, if sufficiently accredited, may help with interpretation and performance. The quality of touch required for motif 32 must be clearly distinguished from the lighter staccato of motif 14, or the martellato effects of motif 53.)

Again, there are many songs in tranquil mood where the staccato is marked only in the opening bars, to give the idea, but should surely be continued throughout, as e.g. in *Morgens steh ich auf*. There the motif is merged with motifs 18 and 20 to give the idea 'walking in a dream' which continues throughout the song. Elsewhere this dream-staccato illustrates a particular point, as in *Muttertraum*, where the only bar marked staccato is the only moment at which the word 'träumen' occurs.

Another example of the missing element is the rhythm

with no initial quaver, which is associated with an E minor mood of twilit melancholy (M 33). Similarly the idea of three-part instead of four-part harmony, i.e. a missing voice, is associated with moods of loneliness or sadness (M 34); as, predictably, in *Mädchen-Schwermut* (A girl's sorrow), also in E minor.

To return to the main idea of bass notes. The images of motifs 28–31 rest on the same foundation of calmness or inviolability; and this is a special sense of *prolonged* bass notes in Schumann (M 35). Together with a rocking movement in both hands they have the obvious meaning of lullaby or cradlesong (M 35[A]) found in association with the word 'Wiege', as in *Schöne Wiege* or *Hochländisches Wiegenlied*.

Two further equivalents for calmness are found mainly in later songs; a rocking rhythm in triplet crotchets in four-four time, (M 36), cognate with M 35[A], as in *Abendlied*; and a figure of three parallel thirds rising by step (M 37). We noted in motif 30 that the bass notes were given added meaning by added chords in the right hand. The expressive quality of repeated chords in *both* hands has the well-defined meaning of humility (M 38), often found in association with the word 'Demut', as in *Er der Herrlichste*. When slower chords are changed in gradual sequence they express feelings of passive strength or endurance (M 39), a human emotive equivalent of the scenes contemplated in motif 31.

A sharper change of harmony, where two unrelated tonalities are juxtaposed, gives the idea of mystery (M 40), as in *Auf das Trinkglas*. Similarly the diminished seventh, which Schumann considered tonally uncertain and difficult to classify, serves as his general expression of puzzlement or bewilderment (M 41). For example in *Jasminenstrauch* (q.v.) that arpeggio strays in against a diatonic background to express sudden perplexity.

When this diluted arpeggio form is concentrated into a *chord* of the diminished seventh, the effect is one of stronger perplexity or even histrionic surprise in the tone of voice (M 42), as in two rhetorical questions – 'was ist's?' in *Rätsel*, and 'Enden?' in *Lied der Braut I*.

A real question on the other hand is unaffectedly diatonic; the equivalent (M 43), is a plain dominant, e.g. in an imperfect cadence, often IV–V as at 'Kommt Feinsliebchen heut'?' in *Morgens steh ich auf*.

When this chord is altered to the dominant seventh we get the favourite effect not of a question but of a questioning or pleading expression (M 44); as at the final chord of *Im wunderschönen Monat Mai* or *Die Nonne*; or, to take another example from the piano-music, *Bittendes Kind* (Pleading child) in Op. 15.

In the context of motif 43, the dominant chord is usually preceded by any chord other than the supertonic. That progression (II–V) is, very curiously, reserved for a special meaning, namely departure or going away (M 45) (see p. 9). The even more special case of 'music dying away' is symbolized by the mediant at the end of a song, often the rising notes d r m (M 46). Perhaps Schumann could hear the reverberations of a note up to those harmonics?

A mediant key-change in the middle section of a song, a harmonic device found in Schubert, has in Schumann the added verbal sense of interpolation (M 47) almost as though the new key were in brackets, or inverted commas (as in *Ich wandelte unter den Bäumen*). The sense of speech or recitative (M 48) is conveyed by a resolution of a diminished or altered chord, e.g. the so-called French sixth, often in sequences:

This is often associated with the actual word 'sprechen' (speak); the example given comes from *Die beiden Grenadiere*, just after 'Der Eine sprach' and 'Der Andre sprach'. Cf. also *Ich kann's nicht fassen* after 'er habe gesprochen'.

Another motif which may derive from the cadence of speech is a melody typically thus:

which is heard in contexts suggesting the idea of finality, the last word (M 49).

Another group of motifs depending on tonality relates to religion or the numinous. First, there seems to have been a close link in Schumann's mind between the flattened seventh of a given key and the idea of the skies or heavens (M 50), often in association with the word 'Himmel' as in *Widmung* or *Ich sende einen Gruss*. Similarly the progression tonic–subdominant–tonic, I–IV–I, set Schumann thinking not only of higher things but of higher personages, perhaps by a similar process. There is a clear association between this progression and the idea of a royal or noble presence (M 51). For example, the princess in *Der Gärtner*, the king in *Der Handschuh*, the knight in the declaimed ballad *Schön Hedwig*, Op. 106, all receive this tribute. It is also implicit in the instrumental music, e.g. the opening bars of the finale of the D minor symphony with its air of processional panoply. The component IV–I in later Schumann expresses the idea of song or singing (M 52), as in *Der Einsiedler*, a stereotyped falling bass harmony which contrasts sadly with the rising melody of the earlier equivalent motif 19. It is as if subdominant tonality attracted various moods of reverence and solemnity; perhaps the underlying idea is the plagal or Amen cadence.

The dominant, in contrast, is a more active source of energy which powers the entire harmonic structure of some of the songs, e.g. *Die beiden Grenadiere*, and also provides smaller-scale motivic ideas. The progression tonic–dominant–tonic, I–V–I, expresses active strength (M 53) (indeed, it is often hammered out in both hands), while V–I–V on the contrary yields the idea of weakness (M 54). Giant strength or size (M 55), is suggested by a double-dotted rhythm, whether reinforced by the strength motif 53, as in the prelude to *Die alten bösen Lieder*, or on one chord, as in the overture *Julius Cäsar*, Op. 128 – perhaps because he bestrode the narrow world like a Colossus? A dotted rhythm also embodies Schumann's own favourite concept of manliness (M 56). This is a march-rhythm, typically with or 3 on the second or fourth beats of the bar. This is used as it were literally for soldiers, as in *Der Soldat*, *Soldatenlied*, *Die Soldatenbraut*, etc., or figuratively for manly endeavour, as in *Talismane* or *Wanderlied*, often with the arpeggio melody of motif 23 arranged as a march-tune.

A good example of motif 56 is found in *Frühlingsfahrt*, about young men venturing forth to seek their fortunes. This includes passages in thirds or tenths which express the idea of comradeship or togetherness (M 57). But if these two voices part, confusion ensues (M 58), as at the word 'verwirren' in *Talismane*, where the melodies insist on going astray in their separate ways. Canonic symbolism may also mean following (M 59), whether holding back (M 59^{A}) or, on the contrary, insistence, urgency (M 59^{B}) depending on which voice carries the musical emphasis. Similarly delay or the slow passage of time can be symbolized by suspensions (M 60^{A}), as in *Auf einer Burg*, or *Im Rhein* (where they are added to M 31) while anticipations obviously have the contrary effect (M 60^{B}) by urging the melody to arrive before its harmony is there to meet it, as in the postlude to *Es treibt mich hin*. The idea of urgency or impatience (M 61) may also be conveyed by the rhythm in quicker tempi, as in *Abschied vom Walde*. Similarly the form suggests agitated heartbeats (M 61^{A}) in one or two songs.

Motifs associated with virile energy and achievement, notably motif 56, correspond with the active outgoing aspect of personality which Schumann named 'Florestan'. Characteristic of this mood and march rhythm is a melody beginning on the tonic, or with a decisive rise to it from the dominant (M 62) as in *Die beiden Grenadiere*, among many others. The more dreamy or inward Eusebian mood is typified by a melody in a more yielding rhythm and lingering on a repeated mediant (M 63), as in *Widmung* or *Der Nussbaum* – a use of the mediant akin to motif 46, as Florestan's is to motif 53. Perhaps the association is with the notes F and E in their relation to C? Certainly Eusebius and Florestan have won eternal fame for their courtship of Clara; and a review of Schumann's motivic language must fittingly conclude with the guiding leitmotif of his whole mind and art, his love-music for her.

At first hearing such motifs appear to be surprisingly few. Robert Schauffler has suggested that the falling fifth which he finds used thematically in the piano-music is 'a private greeting to Clara'. We have speculated on its association with roses (M 27); and it appears at the root of Schumann's expression of affection in music (M 64), namely a chain of successive dominant sevenths, e.g.

as in *Er der herrlichste von allen*. One other motif is clearly a response to the idea of grace and beauty (M 65), often found in association with the word 'schön', as in *Es treibt mich hin*; a decoration of the tonic with grace notes, thus:

There are one or two other possible equivalents. Thus there is a vague connexion between the turn ∾ in a vocal melody and the expression of florid sentiment; there is a hint of allusion, in such melodies, to the Schubert love-song *Das Rosenband* (as in *Widmung*); there is the four-part harmony used to illustrate love in *Die Löwenbraut*; there is the falling four-note melody s m r d, or an analogue, used in a similar sense in *Ballade des Harfners* and *Märzveilchen*.

But these are rare and inconclusive; while Schumann leaves us in no doubt that his expressive love-music was as constant and clear in the songs as anywhere. Again we must look to the instrumental music for guidance. Over and over again Schumann writes that it mourns for Clara, cries for her, calls her name; or that it is Clara herself. He also tells us, though he need not have done, that the same is true of the songs written for her in their marriage year. Now, many of the works in question have an obvious five-note running theme which gives structural unity to the music.

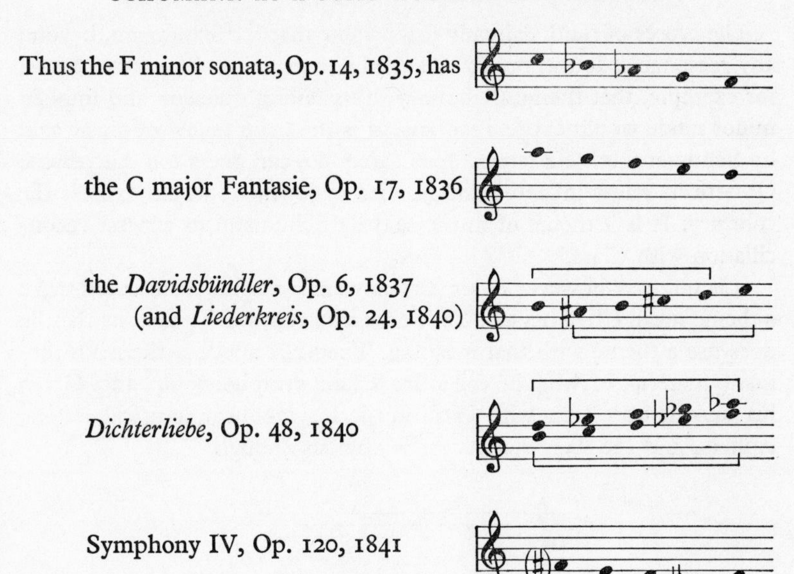

Each can of course occur transposed. But once they are all written down at the same pitch for comparison it is easy to see that they are all part of the same concept, a mine of themes meaning Clara

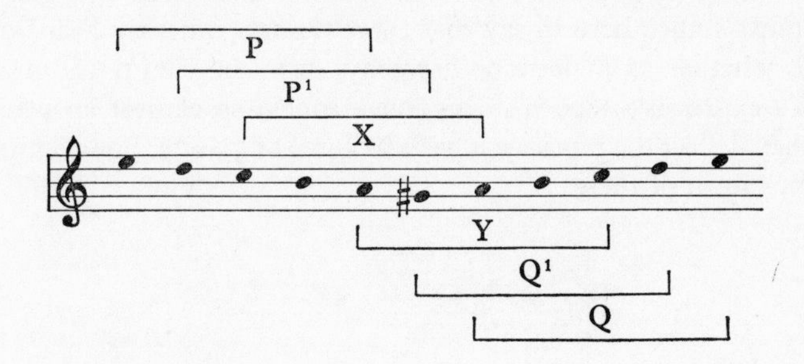

We also find the four-note forms

used equally deliberately and allusively.

The scores of motifs already listed show that for Schumann, beyond any reasonable doubt, music had symbolic meaning. So we can guess, for example, that theme P above with its falling inflexion and implied minor mode would express sadness. It is the main theme of music said by Schumann to be a lament for Clara.[1] We can guess too that theme Q^1 with its rising inflexion and implied major mode would express the contrary. It is a theme of music said by Schumann to express reconciliation with Clara.[2]

It is not easy however to see how any *musical* symbolism could make a theme mean Clara herself. Yet Schumann repeatedly suggests that he does use a theme with that meaning. Theme X above is the main thematic material of what he called his 'Clara' symphony, Op. 120. Given his known obsession with extra-musical symbolism, musical letters, ciphers, and the like, the answer is obvious enough

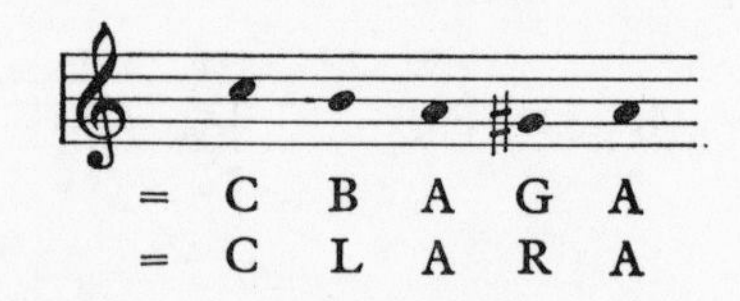

To describe all that can be inferred and demonstrated from these simple premises about Schumann's Clara-themes and the cipher system on which they are based has taken another book[3] as long as this one.

It must suffice here to say that these themes, whether heard or unheard, whether as melody or harmony, form the vital tones of Schumann's expressive speech in his finest songs; so earnest an utterance that they deflect the music as it were by force of gravity. For example the B minor form of theme Y

though unremarkable in songs which are themselves in B minor (*Es treibt mich hin; Ich will meine Seele*) loses its protective coloration in other tonalities. In D major, it tinges even joyous songs with the relative minor (*Mit Myrthen und Rosen*); in A major with the supertonic minor

[1] Op. 17: letter to Clara of March 1838.
[2] Op. 6: letter to Clara of January 1838.
[3] To be published by Faber & Faber.

(*Lied der Suleika*); in G major with the mediant minor (*Venezianisches Lied II*; the *Davidsbündler* passim). Similarly the A minor forms occur as tonic in that key (*Und wüssten's die Blumen*), as relative minor in C major (*Nichts Schöneres*), as supertonic minor in G major (*Lied der Braut*), or as mediant minor in F major (*Im Westen*), again in increasing order of clarity. These themes, as melody and harmony, are at the heart of the song-music. Their possibilites, though manifold, are not inexhaustible; and they occur mainly in orthodox diatonic harmony. So an ideally happy marriage eventually replaced them with its own music; and there was in any event little place for them within Schumann's later chromatic style.

These 'Clara' themes may seem to be among the veriest commonplaces of music. In fact they are not, as comparison with other composers will show. For example, in Beethoven's many piano sonatas we can hardly hear forms P or Q used thematically at all; while in Schumann's (Opp. 11, 14 and 22) we can hardly hear anything else. Again, in Schubert's best-known songs the X or Y forms are not common in the voice and rare in the piano; in Schumann's they are ceaseless as song and undersong. Perhaps other composers found them too featureless to use as main thematic material. But for Schumann they wore Clara's own features, and are hence recognizable in the music written for her. From 1833 (not earlier) to 1841 (rarely later) the music pours out into these moulds, although it takes many years' listening to hear them for what they are: not just musical fingerprints but gestures, signs, symbols, of as profound a feeling as any ever experienced by a composer. So passionate an obsession is admittedly strange, even eccentric. But it is not sentimental, nor uncharacteristic; in every sense the mind of the man is manifest in these themes.

They lead on directly to another mode of expression which is still closer to the level of discursive intelligence, namely the conscious and deliberate use of cipher, or quotation, in order to express some special meaning. This too has its effect on the music. Thus where Schumann writes a prelude or postlude apparently unrelated to the rest of the song (*Widmung; Ich wandelte unter den Bäumen*), it is often a sign that the conscious mind is at work. With that idea in mind the hidden meaning may leap to our ears, as when the postlude to *Der Himmel hat eine Träne* is heard singing to itself 'Caro mio ben'; or there may be another kind of meaning harder to detect, as in the postlude to *Und wüssten's die Blumen*. Conformably with the hypothesis already advanced about the essential nature of Schumann's song-writing, these procedures are exactly the same conceptually as in the piano-music, where ciphers and quotations[1] are frequent and famous.

It is no disparagement of Schumann to point out the importance of such ideas in his work. On the contrary, we disparage him if we neglect the part played in his creative imagination by the conscious intellect. The prejudice against the idea is understandable. It does at first seem invidious to suggest that, for example, the left-hand motif of the universally admired *Mondnacht* is an encipherment of the word 'Ehe' (marriage). Yet this would be wholly consistent with Schumann's known ideas and procedures, and his acknowledged stature as man and artist. If he was typically Romantic in being a dreamer and a visionary, he was no less so in being a chess-player and cryptographer. For Romantic art, good or bad, aims to deal with life in all its aspects; the abstract as well as the vital, the brain as well as the heart.

So by means of the musical imagination, the mind's eye, the mind's ear; from wordless emotion, through vague key-association via musical effects to motifs and Clara-themes, and thence to quotation and cipher; from heart to brain, thalamus to cortex, Schumann's music is heard to proceed from the whole of his personality in response to the whole of his experience, exactly as he said it did.

Thus conceived and born, the music itself has an organic structure. The external world impinges on the sensitive mind to produce a single living cell of music, the small-scale musical idea, whether as key, motif, theme, quotation or encipherment. These cells cohere and interact to form an expressive organic whole, which may in turn contain the gametes of new musical ideas (the process can be studied as it were *in vitro* in some songs, e.g. *Mit Myrthen und Rosen*). Then these organic wholes, piano works or songs, evolve into orders and sub-orders to symbolize a whole new creation of felt life.

No less than this was Schumann's declared mission as an artist; no less than this was his achievement and the measure of his greatness. So his theme was ever the mystery of all creation, the one and the infinite.

[1] E.g. from his own Op. 1 in Op. 4, from Op. 9 in Op. 6, from Op. 6 in Op. 18; from Beethoven in Op. 17, Schubert in Op. 18, Chopin in Op. 26, Marschner in Op. 13, Giordani in Op. 37, to cite only the most evident.

The Songs

I · PRELUDE

On 8th June 1810, in Saxony; 'to August Schumann, bookseller of Zwickau near Leipzig, a son'.

Nine years later there was born to Friedrich Wieck, pianist and pedagogue in Leipzig, a daughter, Clara.

When the two children met, another nine years later, it was the little girl, not the young man, who was the famous musician. All her life she was to be the greatest woman pianist in the world; and Schumann worshipped her from the first. He had himself shown great promise as a pianist (more indeed than as a composer) and Wieck was proud to have him as a pupil while still a law-student at Leipzig University. He had also shown immense aptitude for ideas; names, words, symbols, mathematics, chess, literature. But his hybrid genius for the ideas of music, the music of ideas, was unique and therefore slow to develop. A mind so unprecedented was not free to choose its influences, only to find them if it could. In the German-speaking world of the early nineteenth century there were just two creative minds that could be of service to Schumann's; and at seventeen he found them both.

The novels of Jean-Paul (J. P. F. Richter) were popular for their effusive and exalted sentiment. But connoisseurs then and later admired his rhythmic, sonorous and formal uses of language, which are wholly analogous with music.[1] For Schumann this was less an influence than a revelation. Jean-Paul became a second saint, and his home at Bayreuth a place of pilgrimage. From that moment his own writings also, in word or tone, teem with puns, quips, allusions, superscriptions, quotation and enigma (including code and cipher).[2] 'I learned more counterpoint from Jean-Paul than from my music master,' he said in later years; and so, no doubt, he did. But words were never his true creative

[1] A modern stylistic parallel is James Joyce, himself a musician and with a special appeal to musicians.

[2] All these are to be found in e.g. Schumann's favourite novel *Die Flegeljahre*. Ciphers, etc., are found also in Johann Klüber's *Kryptographik*, Schumann's use of which is a separate study; see e.g. *Musical Times* May 1966.

medium. It was even more important for him to learn that *music* could be quasi-*verbal*. Of all music ever written, Schubert's songs speak that message most clearly and profoundly; and they were just then becoming known in Germany. 'Letter to Franz Schubert in Vienna; not sent', records the diary disconsolately; at the news of his death his young devotee was heard crying all night.

The boy's mind was infinitely original and sensitive, receptive and suggestible; and it had waited many years for these twin signs. They fired him to speak music, and with tongues. His first use of this new language was to write songs[1] in the style of Schubert and send them for comments to another song-writer, long forgotten,[2] who had made some settings of Jean-Paul. His second was to write piano duets in the style of Schubert with fancy titles à la Jean-Paul.

Now these two names begin to resound together like a litany. 'My *own* Schubert; my *own* Jean-Paul' he calls them ecstatically; and 'whenever I play Schubert, I feel as though I were reading a novel by Jean-Paul turned into music'. His next work, *Papillons*, was exactly that; in it Schumann enters his own new world. His music is electric with the excitement of that discovery, which lasted all his life. So did his gratitude to his two revered masters. We recall how he later wrote of the 'heavenly length' of Schubert's great C major symphony; we may have forgotten how he added 'like a novel in four volumes by Jean-Paul'. Towards the end of his life he was comparing Bach with Jean-Paul, without any sense of incongruity; it was his way of giving thanks for his own deliverance, and praise to a light in which his own way ahead lay clearly revealed. But on that way there already lay, in the broadest daylight, strange shadows. He knew early on that his temperament was chequered in gaiety and gravity, elation and depression; the outgoing and the inward moods that he symbolized as Florestan and Eusebius.[3]

In these early years, in one of the most mysterious events in all musical history,[4] he injured his right hand. The layman may think of a self-inflicted injury in the depressive phase. Whatever the cause, the outcome was clear; he would never be called upon to be a concert virtuoso (for which he was by temperament wholly unfitted), nor to rival Clara as a pianist. Instead he became editor of the newly-founded

[1] See Appendix I.

[2] Gottlob Wiedebein (1797–1854).

[3] No doubt in homage to Clara; see *Musical Times*, February 1967.

[4] The literature contains many accounts of this, some very vivid and detailed; but the fact is that no one knows for sure what Schumann did, or how, or when.

Neue Zeitschrift für Musik in Leipzig; and before long he was beginning to make, as critic and composer, a name and fortune worthy to offer his Clara. But again the shadow fell, longer and darker than ever. Friedrich Wieck, to Schumann's distraught amazement, opposed the marriage with bitter and protracted violence. The sixteen-year-old girl was coerced into renouncing Schumann and returning his letters. There was talk of her marriage to another. There followed a time of jealous and suffering estrangement which left Schumann near madness. His music was written in blood, as he said; many of the songs flow from this hurt. His consolation was in music; the Beethoven song-cycle *An die ferne Geliebte* (To the distant beloved) acquired a special significance for him at this time, and is often quoted in his work.

In 1837 Clara shook free of parental domination and the battle in the law courts began for her right to marry the man she loved and honoured.

At about this time Mendelssohn came to live in Leipzig, as director of the famous Gewandhaus concerts and the conservatoire. He was soon enrolled in the communion of saints. His *St Paul* had also greatly impressed Schumann, whose review praises in particular the union of word and tone.

In 1838–9 came a visit to Vienna, to see whether there was any possibility of publishing the *Neue Zeitschrift* there. There was none; but Schumann found ample compensation in the discovery (at the house of Schubert's brother Ferdinand) of the score of the great C major symphony, which was sent back to Leipzig in triumph for a first performance under Mendelssohn. There was another exciting rediscovery, which we are not told about directly, but which can be clearly heard in the 1840 songs; the Schubert Nachlass or posthumous songs then being published in Vienna by Diabelli.

All the paths of Schumann's life were again converging on the inspiration that had begun his music; the love-song. In 1840 Clara would be twenty-one and free to marry.

Love of Clara; the words-and-music of Jean-Paul and Schubert; a Beethoven love-song-cycle; a Mendelssohn oratorio; a rediscovery of Schubert; all the ferments of song were at work.

One thing only was lacking; poetry. About that subject, in all Schumann's voluminous writings, in letters, diaries, critiques and notebooks, there is hardly a word. It was as though his verbal gifts and insights had all gone straight into his music, to give it a new strength and brightness and durability. It was perhaps for this reason that, as we have seen, he looked on poetry, and hence song, as an inferior art form; the addition of actual words would spoil music which had so many ideas of its own already. He needed to be shown that in fact the word was the best of catalysts for his art.

In late 1839 and early 1840 he was much in Mendelssohn's company. 'Scarcely a day passes on which he does not say something fit to be inscribed in gold' said the impressionable Schumann; and perhaps his friend's talk was, in a way, transmuted and put on permanent record. He revered Mendelssohn for his Shakespeare inspiration, his setting of themes from the Bible, and his current work on settings of Heine and Goethe (the *Westöstlicher Diwan*). Perhaps *great* poetry was the answer? Schumann's first song was a Shakespeare setting; it was followed by a setting of a theme from the Bible, versified by Heine, and then songs to words by Heine and Goethe (the *Westöstlicher Diwan*). The friends parted for a time on 31st January 1840; Schumann's first song as a mature composer is dated 1st February 1840. Even without the textual evidence of allusion in the music (see No. 1, note 2) it would be hard to resist the inference that Mendelssohn was the proximate cause of Schumann's sudden resumption of song-writing,[1] after ten years of piano works.

[1] For more details see *Musical Times*, February 1965.

2 · LEIPZIG 1840–41

1. (Op. 127, No. 5) Schlusslied des Narren (Feste's closing song from Twelfth Night)

Shakespeare (trans. Schlegel and Tieck) – February 1840

When that I was and a little tiny boy,
With hey, ho, the wind and the rain,
A foolish thing was but a toy,
For the rain it raineth every day.

But when I came alas! to wive,
With hey, ho, the wind and the rain,
By swaggering I could never thrive,
For the rain it raineth every day.

A great while ago the world begun,
With hey, ho, the wind and the rain,
But that's all one, our play is done,
And we'll strive to please you every day.

A clown's farewell seems an odd choice of serious début. This one though tentative is ingratiating. The opening figure presents Feste himself, mettlesome and coltish, yet wistful in A minor key and harmonies. There is resigned melancholy too in the dying fall at the end of each verse. But when Feste takes his bow with 'our play is done' the house lights go up in a bright A major.

NOTES. 1. Schumann omits the second and fourth verses, and repeats each 'hopheisa'. His text ended 'dass es euch künftig so gefallen mag'. 'Nun' for 'nur' in bar 7 may be a mistranscription of his manuscript (see also No. 53, note 1).

2. Can it be just coincidence that the opening figure and recurring melody echo Mendelssohn's *Midsummer Night's Dream Overture*, also about a Shakespeare clown, while the two composers had met the evening before this song was written? (See p. 32.)

3. The postlude sounds wrongly barred; it could have been brought in more effectively a half-bar earlier. The lesson was quickly learned (see No. 3, note 3).

4. The song was, no doubt rightly, withheld from publication by Schumann. Yet it is typically his; the motivic links with the words are in place from the very first. Thus, in the third verse the added bass notes (bars 21–22) must stand for the enduring earth (M 29), while the recurring motto-theme is laughter personified (M 14 and 15). This motivic sense as well as the piano part confirms that the higher octave in, e.g. bars 2 and 6, should be sung throughout.

2. (Op. 57) Belsatzar (Belshazzar)

Heine – February 1840

It was nearly midnight; Babylon lay dumb and silent. But high in the king's palace torches flare, the king's followers are shouting. Up there in the high throne-room Belshazzar the king was holding a royal feast. His vassals sat in shimmering rows, emptying beakers of sparkling wine. The beakers clashed, the vassals shouted and sang; the headstrong king revelled in the sound.

The king's cheeks glow; the wine has made him bold. And this boldness overmasters him and with wicked words he blasphemes the most high God. And he brags insolently and blasphemes wildly; his vassals roar and cheer him on.

Then with a proud look the king cried out. The servant runs out and returns, bearing on his head many a golden vessel plundered from out of the house of the temple of God. And with his sinful hands the king grasps a sacred vessel filled to the brim with wine. And he drains it at a gulp, and shouts aloud, through foaming lips 'Jehovah! I offer you scorn and defiance for ever – I am the king of Babylon!'

Hardly had these fearful words died away than the king felt secretly troubled in his heart. The shrill laughter was suddenly silent; it was as still as death in the hall. And lo and behold on the white wall there came forth fingers as of a man's hand, and wrote, and wrote on the white wall in letters of fire, and wrote and vanished.

The king sat there stunned, as pale as death, his knees knocking together. A cold shudder passed through the host of vassals; they sat quite still, making no sound. Then came in all the king's wise men, but they could not read the fiery writing on the wall.

In that same night was Belshazzar the king slain by his vassals.

'I am brimming with music, as always in February', wrote Schumann to Clara. But in the heat of this first song-writing inspiration it all boils over and goes to waste. The fine poem (cf. Daniel, 5) is perhaps the best in all Schumann's Heine settings; not so the song. The necessary objective treatment was not in Schumann's nature. His music expresses, instead of the drama, the changing moods of an imagined onlooker.

Thus, the poem begins with a contrast; all Babylon in a solemn stillness save where the king holds revel. But the piano offers one continuous mood of tense and mysterious excitement; not the scene but the watcher in the shadow. This mood changes with each couplet, first to a more deliberate figuration, for the shouting and stamping revellers, then to a frank military march for the serried lords. Then there is a new theme for the king's carousal, then a side-slipping sequence for the muzziness of the wine's first effect, then a jerking and angular sequence for the mounting quarrelsomeness of its second. Then follows another idea for the king's boasting and yet another for the roared applause of the retainers. The first theme is now recalled to make a brief interlude; after which the music is off again in a fresh series of convulsive reactions to the words. Delighted major harmonies greet the arrival of the golden vessels; new themes of eeriness, anxiety and impending doom dwindle into an awe-struck whisper of recitative.

NOTES. 1. The idea of responding to poetry in music was a new one to Schumann and inspired him to unprecedented invention. His setting is very respectful of the text, which was even printed separately in the first edition (1846). Heine has 'Knechte*n*schar' at bars 34 and 88.

2. The actual response however is mainly by proxy. Thus, the thunderous and doom-laden atmosphere of the poem puts Schumann in mind of middle-period Beethoven, just as Shakespeare made him think of Mendelssohn (song No. 1 above). The whole semiquaver impetus of this song is clearly indebted to the *Appassionata* (also an Op. 57), especially the last movement; the opening vocal melody is the motto-theme of the *Pathétique*; the ominous ascending semitones at 76 et seq. recall the first movement of Op. 31, No. 2. Then the thematic material of Beethoven is put through the ballad-writing techniques of Schubert (e.g. *Die Bürgschaft* and *Der Taucher*).

3. Schumann also has ideas of his own; and they are very revealing ones. The opening mood of tension and perplexity is created by figurations of the diminished seventh (M 41) associated with night-time as in *In der Nacht*, Op. 12, in

F minor (one published key of this song) and *Zwielicht* in E minor (its original key). Heine's 'Knechte' (vassals) seem to put Schumann in mind of soldiery; hence the typical march-theme in bars 15–18 (M 56). Very odd is the piano part's obvious pleasure at the gold vessels, which sounds almost covetous (M 1). As in *Lieb Liebchen*, the piano has syncopated heartbeats (M 61A), as 'heimlich in Busen bang'. Most intriguing of all is the use of Schumann's kingly motif (M 51) first broken up into arpeggios in bars 19–22 where the king is confused with his subjects; then harmonically distorted, at bar 33, etc., as if wine and blasphemy had knocked his crown awry; and ominously peaceful in the last bar.

4. Equally typically, the words as such are ignored, both as sound ('an' on a strong beat in a passage of recitative) and sense (e.g. the over-emphatic '*ich* bin der König', as if the Babylonic succession were in dispute).

Liederkreis von Heine (Cycle of Heine songs) Op. 24

'Dear Clara; I'm brimming over with music... you'll be amazed at what I've been writing – *not* piano pieces, but I shan't tell you what they are just yet.'

'Dear Clara; I'm still working hard at the piano – it is always there that you appear to me at your most beautiful.'

To his publisher Schumann wrote that he had worked at the songs 'long and lovingly' and that they 'formed a whole'; to Clara again that they were written 'solely in thoughts of her'.

The poems formed a complete set in Heine's *Buch der Lieder*, 1827. Schumann unifies them by a deliberate key-structure and the use of linking themes, e.g. motif 20. But we can hear that the texts are just pretexts for his love-music. The closest link is the Clara-theme Y, in the same B minor-major form as in the *Davidsbündler*, Op. 6, which were about 'wedding thoughts'. Perhaps some of the songs began as sketches for that work; their genesis as keyboard solos is often clear.

A new upsurge of inspiration; secrets under the surface of the music; the subjective approach; the cyclic form; the love-lyric; the piano song; here at last is Schumann's true song-writing vein.

3. (Op. 24, No. 1) Morgens steh' ich auf und frage

Heine – February 1840

Every morning I rise wondering: will my darling come today? Every evening I lie down grieving: another day without her. All night I lie awake, sleepless with sorrow; all day I wander about as if half asleep, in a dream.

Heine's verse is all despair and insomnia. But his last lines appeal to Schumann's own mood of amorous reverie. So the music walks in its daytime sleep. The piano prelude is brief but explicit; bright in D major with a stepwise movement in the single notes of the left hand, which alternate with lightly-touched chords in a mezzo-staccato trance. The pain of the poetry is anaesthetized. A muted questioning at the first 'heut' (today), a subdued pang at the second, resignation at 'in der Nacht', etc., are all that the music can feel of tragedy.

Once accept that limitation and this modest song has a beauty and a sincerity all its own. Music and words are together in spirit at 'träumend, wie im halben Schlummer' (dreaming as if half asleep). Here the piano part ceases to share in the melody, and is content to accompany and listen while for a brief but memorable moment the voice goes its own way. It twice lifts gently to the highest note of the song, turning down at the word 'Schlummer' and lingering there dreamily for a while before rejoining the piano's melody in the final vocal cadence. The postlude wanders off again abstractedly, pauses, and comes to rest in a sensuous musing.

NOTES. 1. Some further pointers to this interpretation:

(*a*) the stepwise melody in the left hand suggests walking (M 20). This as well as the walking movement of motif 18, is heard again in *Volksliedchen*, of which the opening words are 'When I walk in the garden'. The image is so central to Schumann's conception that he thrice repeats Heine's text in order to maintain it – 'auch heut' at bars 19–20, 'lieg ich' at bar 27, and 'träumend' at bar 33. The music thus smoothes over not only the impatience of the words but the uneven metre by which, *inter alia*, it is expressed;

(*b*) the dreamy effect of staccato is so characteristic (M 32) that it may be meant to continue, unobtrusively, throughout the piano part;

(*c*) the key-phase here at 'träumend', etc., in bars 29–32 re-appears at bar 13 of *Die Rose, die Lilie* at 'ich liebe alleine'. Compare also the bass line in the postlude to each, bars 17–18 there and bars 36–37 here.

2. Other thematic points are:
   (*a*) the rising horn passage at 'kommt Feinsliebchen' suggesting happiness (M 4);
   (*b*) the dominant at 'heut?', expressing the question (M 43).
   (*c*) the Clara-theme Y in thirds (M 57) in voice and piano at bars 13–15;
   (*d*) the decoration of the last treble note of the postlude is associated with the idea of beauty (M 65);
   (*e*) the last three bars allude to the last three bars of *Kreisleriana*, Op. 16, No. 2; their dominant chain is the love motif (M 64).
3. See No. 1, note 4. Bar 36 here telescopes the last bar of the voice's four bar phrases with the beginning of the postlude's.
4. Cf. Franz, Op. 25, No. 4; Liszt (two versions).

4. (Op. 24, No. 2) Es treibt mich hin

Heine – February 1840

I can't rest for knowing that in only a few more hours I shall see her again, the fairest of the fair. But why are you beating so hard, poor heart? The hours are a lazy lot; they dawdle along at a comfortable jog-trot, they creep along yawning; get a move on, you lazy lot!

I'm in a raging tearing hurry; but it's obvious that the Hours were never in love. Banded together in cruel secret league they mock the impatience of lovers.

Again the music contradicts the poem. In the previous song Schumann seemed more relaxed than Heine; here he seems more resigned. Clara was miles away in Berlin. 'Only a few more hours', says the poem; but the music knows better. For all its impatience of movement it has a B minor melancholy. In this way the prelude asks, by reference to the music of the previous song, 'will she come today?' thus anticipating the answer 'no'. Again, its chords are too full to be hurried along without a sense of strain. It is no surprise when at the mention of beauty, 'die schönste der schönen Jungfrauen', the music halts, hushed and reflective as if at the thought of the unattainable – not in the least as if her arrival were imminent, as the poem insists. True, the following syncopations anticipate the melody, urging it on, with the chordal accompaniment stripped down to octaves for brisker action. But again the music is pessimistic. Heine's words 'Aber wohl niemals liebten die Horen' (it's obvious that the Hours were never in love) are repeated and emphasized, expressing the composer's foreknowledge of disappointment. His own conclusion, first for voice and then for piano solo, is clear. The chords may expostulate, the syncopations exhort; but the postlude's melody still cries out 'auch heut, auch heut' from the first song – another day without her.

NOTES. 1. The text provides further evidence. 'Treues Herz' ('faithful heart'), says Heine, congratulating it. Schumann writes 'Armes Herz' ('poor heart'), commiserating with it. Again, 'was pochst du schwer!' is an exclamation in Heine, but in Schumann a question meaning 'what's the use?', with the imperfect cadence of motif 43. Then the main tune is the Clara-theme Y (harmonized with M 5). Nor would it be surprising if the use of D C♯ B (accents) A♯ B (bass notes) in the postlude were a deliberate allusion to her theme X.

2. Bar 17 shows Schumann's reaction to the idea of beauty (M 65); the word 'schön' occurs two bars earlier. The syncopation of the postlude is motif 60B.

3. Of the alternative vocal lines, the main notes are preferable.

4. Cf. Franz, Op. 34, No. 4.

5. (Op. 24, No. 3) Ich wandelte unter den Bäumen

Heine – February 1840

I was walking alone under the trees with my grief when the old longing returned and slipped back into my heart. Who taught you that word, you birds high in the skies? Be silent; it hurts my heart to hear it.

'A young girl came this way, and she sang it all day long; it was from her that we birds learned it, the pretty golden word.'

You should not have told me that, you scheming birds; you are trying to soothe away my sorrow, but I trust no one.

The postlude of the second song was a true prophet, it seems. The music is still walking, still dreaming, but slower now and more reconciled. The yearning prelude resolves into a modest Schubertian melody moving by step to a plain chordal accompaniment. The chords cease, the walking movement halts; the mood is relaxed and off-guard. Then the memory of love returns, unsought yet welcome as a friend, as the words 'und schlich mir ins Herz hinein' are eased over a wide span of melody in voice and piano, with a new and even more relaxed rhythm. The piano repeats this phrase till its overtones die away. After the second verse comes another magical change. A sadly flattened note (G in B major) becomes the new keynote in every sense. With the new key comes a slower tempo. The wholly relaxed rhythm of crotchet triplets now dominates the music. Above all the piano part is lifted into the higher octave with a disarmingly simple sweetness as the birds sing in the skies. But down to earth again the first strain seems less apt; the intense words chafe against the slow melody. This is resolved in a recitative passage, though the music still sounds puzzled, as if unsure of the poem's meaning. The postlude, on safer ground, remembers the yearning music of the prelude.

NOTES. 1. Schumann may not have known that Heine's original title was *Das Wörtlein Liebe* (The word 'love'). The text used has 'mehr' after 'nicht' in bar 31; the spare melody note suggests that the omission was unintentional. The last line is repeated in order to complete the melodic sequence; so the high alternative last note given is some editions should be avoided.

2. The opening vocal melody should be compared with that of the previous song. Both mean Clara, as does the left-hand memory that returns so aptly at the words 'kam das alte Träumen' (Clara-theme Q^2). The curious trick of an independent prelude and postlude suggests some secret meaning; perhaps cipher. Its dominant chain is the amorous motif 64; the prelude ends in motif 20 for 'ich wandelte'.

3. Mediant modulation for a change of mood or scene is Schubertian (e.g. in *Der Musensohn*, with the same keys as here). But its use for an interpolation, as the musical equivalent of brackets, is entirely novel (M 47).

4. The yearning acciaccature notes and chords of motif 16 are heard throughout. Some are evidential. Thus, the octave is spread in bar 35 at the word 'wollt' (try to) but not in the otherwise parallel passages at 9 and 18. Similarly there is no acciaccatura at the higher G♯ in 20, which suggests that its purpose in bar 11 is to express the word 'schlich' (crept).

5. The peacefully relaxed crotchet triplets are motif 36.

6. (Op. 24, No. 4) Lieb Liebchen, leg's Händchen

Heine – February 1840

Put your hand on my heart, my darling; do you hear a knocking noise inside that little room? A bad, wicked carpenter lives there; he's making me a coffin.

Knock, knock, it goes, day and night; I can't sleep for the noise. Come along, carpenter, hurry up, finish your work and let me rest in peace.

In Heine's cycle of poems, the first three have prepared the way for this, perhaps the most striking and effective of all his early lyrics of irony. The lost love of the previous poem, the pounding heartbeats of the second, the insomnia of the first, plus the deeply serious banter that Heine was to make his own, and Europe's, make an unaccustomed and delectable mixture. Schumann translates it into one of the most original songs ever written. Thoughts of death were never far from him; but these songs were written in a time of happiness. So his mood has something of Heine's ambiguity; and the result is, by coincidence, an intense fusion of music and meaning.

This is exemplified from the very first note. The voice begins the song alone; the sound comes hollow from inside the music, like the heart's own message from inside the oracle. The piano part too is deeply involved in the verbal meaning; its off-beats are heartbeats, the syncopations syncope. At 'Zimmermann' the trifling change of a few notes has, in Schumannian terms, grave implications: as if a shadow had suddenly fallen across the E minor harmony of the heart and darkened it to the E flat minor harmony of death. Then follows the most original touch of all, still unique in music. At 'zimmert mir einen' the piano goes fatalistically on its predetermined way. The voice stops dead, or nearly. 'He's making me a . . .' and then is cut off clean as a whistle, pounding heart in dry mouth, unable to pronounce the dread word that follows. But on hearing the piano's foregone conclusion the voice takes fresh heart and recovers sufficiently to provide the rueful echo 'Totensarg'.

All this time the piano part has been quietly insisting on its memory of the first song. This cadence recalls its words 'Abends sink ich hin und klage' (every evening I lie down grieving); but this time, the piano explains, it is into the grave. The ominous bass notes unobtrusively presage a deep dark burial as the voice resumes.

By the most fortunate of chances the text of Heine's second verse also is superbly apt to this music. The final 'schlafen kann' is just as daunting a phrase as 'Totensarg'. As the voice duly fails the piano ends, leaving the singer quite alone without any sound of comfort or support, looking down into the imminent and uninviting dark.

NOTES. 1. There seems to be some connexion in Schumann's mind between E minor and the heart, as well as twilight; certainly E flat minor is associated with the idea of death here and elsewhere. Perhaps both associations derive from Schubert's *Auf dem Flusse* (*Winterreise* No. 7) which has the same key, the same time, the same opening melody and the same modulation, and is also about the heart and silence. This shows too that there was no need to notate the harmonic change at bars 10–12 and at 30–32 in quite the way Schumann does; sharps would have done just as well. Indeed, the choice of C flat seems wilfully cryptic; perhaps the cipher is at work.

2. It is noteworthy that the idea of death underlying the music is entrusted to the left hand, perhaps as an expression of subconscious thoughts. Thus its first nine bars are one long rest: its first observation is that daunting C flat: and its second, after a brief reinforcement of the right hand, is the ominously descending bass of bars 21–23 (M 28).

3. The minor horn passages are motifs 5 and 6. Perhaps the I–IV–I at 'Herze mein', etc., foreshadows the nobility of motif 51. The off-beat quavers are motif 61A.

4. Cf. Franz, Op. 17, No. 3.

7. (Op. 24, No. 5) Schöne Wiege meiner Leiden

Heine – February 1840

Lovely cradle of my sorrows, lovely tomb of my peace of mind, lovely city, we must part. Farewell, I cry. Farewell, hallowed threshold where my dear love dwells; farewell, hallowed place where I first beheld her.

If only I had never seen you, fair queen of my heart, then I would never have been so wretched as now I am.

I never sought to soften your heart, I never sued for love; my only wish was to live at peace breathing the same air that you breathe.

Yet you drive me away, you speak harsh words; my mind reels in madness, my heart is sick and sore. So I must go, a poor pilgrim, dragging my numb weary limbs along until I lay down my tired head in a cold grave far away.

[*Lovely cradle of my sorrow, lovely tomb of my peace of mind, lovely city, we must part; farewell, farewell.*]

The poem's opening images finely express a lifetime of joys and sorrows, from cradle to grave. Schumann's response to language is sensuous and immediate, not reflective; and the idea of cradle and tomb present themselves to him as it were literally. So the prelude has a rocking and lulling alternation of the two hands, and this is combined with the gravely monumental solemnity of sustained bass notes. The direction 'bewegt' (quite quick) is hard to reconcile with this beautiful music, although the poem is all hectic harangue; a cry of farewell to the town of Hamburg, a cry of rebuke to lost love.

At 'hätt ich dich doch nie gesehn' (if only I had never seen you) the song resumes contact with the poem, with a brusque change to a minor tonality, a faster tempo, and a sudden doubling of the word-setting pace, cramming one line of the verses into two bars instead of four: each suggests a conscious attempt to translate the words. This impression recurs in the following hectic passage where new thematic material, already threadbare in broken-octave scales and arpeggios, is stretched to breaking-point to express both raging madness and dragging footsteps.

The tender opening strain is used to make a peroration and continued with a rhetorical piano coda unrelated either to the previous music or to the words – a postscript rather than a postlude.

NOTES. 1. Heine's poem can be restored by deleting the repetitions at bars 18–20, 37–39, 45, 68–70 and 94–end. The remaining text may explain Schumann's odd reaction. Even his melancholia had its limits; and in his wedding year he had no proposal to leave the loved one and find a cold grave far away. Again, his idea of repeating Heine's first verse at the end, and then replacing its amputated last line by a couple of artificial 'Lebewohls' could hardly have occurred to anyone setting the poem for its own sake.

2. We may guess what happened. The poem has to be set as part of the planned Heine group. A first reading provides a point of entry. 'Wiege' suggests motif 35A, 'Grabmal' suggests the bass notes of motif 29. The heartfelt melody (cf. M 63 and Ex. G on p. 2) occurs in *Ich wandelte*, *Widmung* and *Die Löwenbraut* as the image of requited love; it continues here as the Clara theme P^1 (bars 12–14, etc.). The thrice-repeated 'schön' evokes motif 65 at bar 17, etc. This music fits the second verse but not the third; so Schumann now lets the words impose their own rhythm, with unintentionally startling contrast. The fourth verse is more amenable to his love-song melody, which duly recurs. Now the words speak of quarrel and parting, madness and death. As we shall see in *Dichterliebe*, all this had a very special personal meaning for Schumann, remembering his estrangement from Clara and its effect on him. So he writes as it were the music of this idea, in Clara themes; first Q^2 repeated (bars 71–72, 73–74), then P^1 in the voice (most clearly at 'krank und wund', 79–80) with X thrice in the piano part (bars 75–76, 77–78, 79–80), while the dragging music of bars 80–91 ends in theme Y in the voice part at 'ferne in ein kühles Grab'. On this interpretation the postlude would be Schumannese for reconciliation with Clara; it seems hard to reconcile with Heine. Its theme, B♯ C♯ D♮ E♯ F♯, differs only in inflection from that of the wedding song *Mondnacht*; and to confirm that relationship the rest of the postlude here reappears as the prelude to that song.

3. The octave leaps at 'Wahnsinn' (73–80) express yearning elsewhere in Schumann (M 16); see for example the strikingly parallel passage in the aptly-named *Sehnsucht*. This and other atypical uses of motivic language (e.g. the disjunct diminished sevenths used rhetorically in the sense of 'alas' or 'woe is me' at bars 91–93) are further evidence of contrivance.

4. Finally, the impression of disorganization is confirmed by the actual text of the music from the first edition onwards. Thus the chord at bar 15 should surely be staccato as in bar 34. The clash B♯/B does not occur at the expressive word 'scheiden' where it would make some sense, but occurs instead at bars 33 and 64, where it makes very little. It is not clear why the D♯ should be introduced a beat earlier in bar 62 than in bar 31 or 12; nor why 'Grabmal' should have a grace note in bar 8 but not in 99; and so on.

8. (Op. 24, No. 6) Warte, warte, wilder Schiffmann

Heine – February 1840

Wait, wait, wild seaman; I shall be following you down to the harbour very soon. But first I must say farewell to my two loves; to Europe, and to her.

Let a stream of blood trickle from my eyes, gush from my wounded body; then I can write down my sorrows in hot blood.

But why, my love, should you shudder at the sight of my blood today?

You have seen me, pale with the loss of my heart's blood, confronting you these many years.

Do you recall the old tale of the serpent in the Garden of Eden, which plunged our ancestor into misery through the treacherous gift of an apple?

Apples have always brought ruin; with them Eve brought death, Eris brought the flames of Troy, and to me you have brought both – fire, and death.

Another wildly passionate and rather obscure harangue from the young Heine. Eris is the goddess of discord; the fierce boatman may be imagined as Charon. The verse has mock-heroic and ironic overtones. Schumann, who had little irony, treats the poem with peculiar earnestness. On the first page he repeats the word 'gleich' (immediately) to illustrate the urgency of the proceedings; and then suddenly slows down the tempo to underline the reluctance of the departure. On the second page he goes so far as to insert a deep tragic groan ('Oh') of his own devising.

Despite this apparent congruence with the words one suspects that the song is an artificial construction, based on a piano solo. The result can certainly sound enjoyable, even impressive, as a bravura piece.

NOTES. 1. To find Heine's text, delete 'gleich' at bars 10–12, 'oh' at bars 53–54, and 'du' at bars 91–92, and correct 'schaudert dich' to 'schauderst du'.

2. Top A is right, if practicable, at the last sung note. The alternative notes should be avoided in bars 45–52 (where the syncopation in the voice is the dragging of motif 60A for 'lange Jahre').

3. The beginning of the song looks remarkably like the superimposition of words on piano-music, and the expressive writing sounds oddly irrelevant to the text; only the falling minor second on 'Oh!' at bars 53–54 sounds at all convincing (M 8), but here the word as well as the music is Schumann's own invention.

4. Piano-music or not, this has clear links with the first song of the cycle, e.g. the same harmonic pattern of tonic, mediant and supertonic. Each has the Clara theme Y; here in a linked chain of two in the opening bars and *six* in bars 99–105.

5. Note the aptly mysterious effect of motif 40 in the unrelated dominants juxtaposed at bars 37–40 and 45–48.

9. (Op. 24, No. 7) Berg' und Burgen

Heine – February 1840

Mountains and castles look down at the mirror-bright Rhine. My boat sails gaily along with sunshine sparkling all around it.

Quietly I watch the play of golden waves curling; silently the feelings I once cherished in my heart reawaken.

The river's beauty is welcoming and friendly; but I know that under its calm gliding surface lurk night and death.

Fair to behold, treacherous at heart; river, you are the image of my loved one! She too has a friendly wave, a soft bright smile.

Heine's first two verses are dissolved into piano-music reflecting the lapping of sunlit waves, with a memorable vocal melody floating blissfully among them. But the damaging comparison in the last few lines is insoluble in Schumann's terms, though it is the whole point of the poem. Deceit and treachery, like dying for love in the previous song, were very far from his mind at the time.

NOTES. 1. Among the evidence that Schumann was using Heine's first edition of 1827 is the use of 'bringt' in the third verse (bar 17), which was corrected to 'birgt' in later editions of the poems and of the songs (see also No. 11, note 1).

2. Schumann is always aware of the pretty colours of a Heine lyric rather than of the sting in the tail. Yet there is after all a point here; hidden under the surface of the music is the Clara-theme Y (second notes of bars 12–16), with Q^2 in the first bass notes of bars 13–16.

3. The accompaniment is seasonably bright in A major. The wave movement (M 21) is explicit in the postlude; the main accompaniment figure has the idea of rhythmic movement (M 17) whether of waves, as here, or dancing as in *Der arme Peter*. In the interludes the feeling of drifting summer idleness holds the melody back (M 60A).

4. This song is no doubt among the sources of Brahms' *Bei dir sind meine Gedanken*, Op. 95, No. 2.

10. (Op. 24, No. 8) Anfangs wollt' ich fast verzagen

Heine – February 1840

At first I was almost in despair, and I thought I should never be able to bear it. In the end, I have borne it; but never ask me how.

After the previous fires this is refreshingly cool. Heine's last phrase may even be ironic, suggesting that the remedy was more dubious than difficult. Schumann again says, with evident strength and sincerity, something quite different. His brief music is all humility and self-denial, a Bach chorale; yet coloured with frank regret and nostalgia, a Chopin prelude.

NOTES. 1. The opening melody quotes the chorale tune 'Wer nur den lieben Gott lässt walten', used by Bach in six cantatas. This reference may well be deliberate, whether to the words (meaning a happy ending after great tribulation) or to the music (because of its Clara content, theme X). The affinity with the Chopin prelude, Op. 28, No. 20, then just published in Leipzig, may not be unintentional.

2. Heine's last phrase is plainly not a real question. Yet Schumann awards it a question mark in his music as in the poetry (M 43). This dominant also makes a pivot for a return to D major, the home key of the cycle, in the final song.

3. This is perhaps the world's shortest Lied in space (half a page) as No. 64 below is in time (half a minute).

4. Cf. Liszt.

11. (Op. 24, No. 9) Mit Myrthen und Rosen

Heine – February 1840

With myrtles and roses bright and fair, fragrant cypresses and rich gilt, I would adorn this book like a shrine wherein to bury my songs. If only my love for her could be buried with them. On the grave of love grows the flower of peace; it blooms there, it is plucked by others, but for me it will bloom only when I too am in my grave.

Here are the songs that once ran as fierce as lava from Mount Etna, boiling up from the depths of my passions and flaring in fire all abroad. Now they lie silent and as if dead, now they are transfixed and numb, pale as mist; yet once again their former fires will burn when love's spirit hovers over them.

And loud in my heart I feel a foreboding that one day the spirit of love will indeed revive them – when this book comes into your hands, my sweet love far away. Then the magic spell that now binds them will break; the pale letters will look up imploring into your beautiful eyes and whisper to you in sad love-longing.

Heine is in a vein of pure sentimentality, unrelieved by irony. Schumann responds by writing a Novellette; the music tells a love-story, it transports of alternating delight and dismay.

The prelude, repeated as the voice enters, is an elaborated gesture of bestowal, an offered tribute. But then doubt and hesitancy ensue; the harmonies are uncertain, the melodies wonder which way to turn. The presentation themes resume with added warmth and fire as a modest match for Heine's volcanic outburst. Then the song wanders off again into a new and seemingly endless reverie of melody, accompanied by lightly-alternating chords, so that the cycle ends as it began in a waking dream of waiting for the loved one.

Finally, the doubts recur and continue in the postlude, which is heard musing its delight and uncertainty together; 'how beautiful she is – but what will her answer be?' is the sense of the music.

NOTES. 1. As in No. 9, note 1, the text helps to show that the first (1827) edition of the *Buch der Lieder* was Schumann's Heine source; later editions deprive the cypress of its fragrance, and prune the myrtles altogether.

2. Here is a paradigm of Schumann song. Read the words; note the ideas. First there is past sorrow, present separation, future bliss; his own story. Next there are 'my songs' – love-songs to be sent to a distant beloved; his first songs for Clara, then in Berlin. Then there are letters of the alphabet looking up and whispering; with a special message for the greatest of musical cryptographers. Finally there is the presentation of a love-song-book embossed with myrtles; hence Op. 25, *Myrthen* in a de luxe edition which was to be Clara's wedding-present. This is Schumann's response to poetry in the 1840 songs; subjective, oblique, symbolic and passionate.

3. Next, the musical result. Heine's 'sweet love far away' would be as irresistible as Beethoven's song-cycle *To the distant beloved* has been four years earlier, when Schumann had lovingly woven its themes all through the texture of his *Fantaisie* (Op. 17). Clara herself now evokes her theme X, in B minor.

The experiment of playing those notes while speaking Heine's first line gives two or three syllables per note as the only rational possibility, thus:

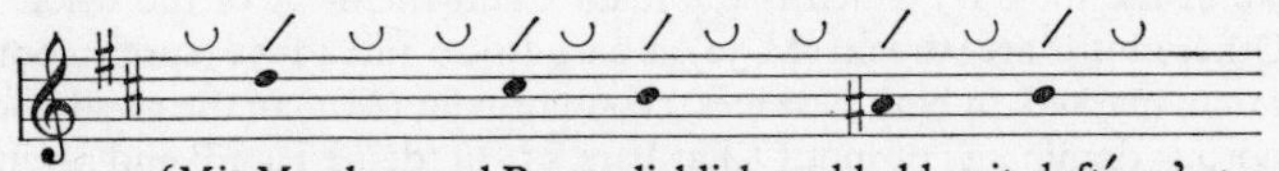

'Mit Myrthen und Rosen, lieblich und hold, mit duftgen,' etc.

This will hardly do as a joyous melody; but it would make an excellent bass. Over it, in ordinary two-part harmony, there is only one such melody to write, and it does not take a Schumann to find it.

As we have seen, that melodic shape had special significance for Schumann, the outgoing joy of motif 23; and when enhanced with the added zest of the rising motif 3 it is the very music of his mood.

3
Mit Myrthen und Ro-sen, lieblich und hold, mit duft': etc.
C
L
A
R
A

Not surprisingly it takes much the same shape (rhythm, time, tempo, melody, texture, final chords) as the *Novellette* in F major, Op. 21, No. 1, also addressed to Clara; and wears the same expression of chivalric ardour.

4. The process may seem contrived; but it is clear from the rest of the song that it was the main inspiration. Thematic insistence on B and A sharp pulls the tonality towards the minor, although the mood is one of elation. When the basic idea ends, Schumann is momentarily at a loss (bars 13–14). Words about the spirit of love are repeated in bars 44–47, with the Clara theme Q^2 thrice in the bass. Finally, the phrase 'du süsses Lieb' is very obviously repeated solely for the sake of the melody, which is the main Clara-theme X of the whole song.

5. Other motifs are: dream (M 32) at bars 19–20 and 49–54 (surely continuing longer than marked, in both passages); contentment (M 1) in the vocal line at 44; the amorous dominants of motif 64 at bars 55–58 'deine Hand' and again at bar 68 'schöne Aug'; the companionable tenths (M 57) side by side with Clara's theme X at bars 59–61; the yearning of motif 16 at 'flehend', bar 67. The most overtly expressive use is in the postlude: 'beautiful', muses the left hand at bars 71 and 73 (M 65); 'but what will her answer be?' wonder the diminished sevenths (M 41), bars 72 and 73–74; and the sad B flats in those bars are pessimistic for a moment (M 8) until the comforting final chords.

6. In the rather surprising progression at bars 40–42, the harmonies and register of the chords seem to express the idea of 'warmth', for 'die alte Glut'. But this has no parallel elsewhere in Schumann.

Myrthen, Liederkreis
(Myrtles, a song-cycle) Op. 25

Leipzig, February 1840: 'Dear Clara; since early yesterday morning I have written nearly 27 pages of music (something new!) about which all I can tell you is that as I wrote it I laughed and wept for joy.'

Hamburg, February: 'Dear Robert; if only I could see you again ... I love you so much it hurts my heart ... Tell me what you're writing – I would so love to know; oh, please, please. A quartet, an overture – even perhaps a symphony? Just tell me the first letter. Might it by any chance be – a wedding present?'

Indeed it might; perhaps Schumann had already thought of the idea himself (see No. 11, Note 2).

Later, he wrote to his publisher ... 'For some time now I've had a special thought in mind, which perhaps you might feel able to help me with. (Op. 25) is to be a *wedding present*! So that calls for an ornamental binding, as carefully and as tastefully designed as ever you can manage.'

Myrthen, like its predecessor, is composed of memories of past joys and sorrows, as Schumann himself explains. And he adds, 'These songs, unless I am much mistaken, will soon catch on and be sung a great deal; everyone who has heard them tells me that, and besides a composer always knows himself what has come from the heart and what must have its effect. ... But be sure not to tell anyone. ...'

Here are the same passions as before; for Clara, for mystery, for order. Is it likely to be just coincidence that this cycle has as many songs as there are letters in the alphabet? Thus Nos. 5 and 6 are Eusebius and Florestan to the life (just as those numbers are in *Carnaval*, which was also planned to have twenty-six pieces); and there is no doubt at all that No. 3, or C, is meant very specially for Clara. Nor will it just be coincidence that so many adjacent songs are in related keys; nor that the music offers so many Clara-themes in various guises and disguises. No doubt all this was what Schumann meant by saying that this Opus 'certainly affords a closer insight into the inner workings of my music'. But there was another factor of which he was perhaps less consciously aware.

As we have seen, he adapted his choice of poem to his own need for self-expression. It follows that there will always be a unifying theme underlying his song-cycles, namely the composer himself. These bridal songs, for whatever reason, are all about ideas of the nature of man and woman and their relation; an innocent reflection of his own innermost thoughts.

If one ventured, for the purpose of illustrating this thesis, to give verbal expression to the subconcious impulses that may have guided the choice of poems and their setting, the result might be something like this . . .

Dear Clara, I confess I have my faults. I may have been something of an adventurer (the two Venetian songs). Both Eusebius and Florestan like a drink, too (the two drinking songs from the *Westöstlicher Diwan* – and in this there is a certain irony, since it will be old Wieck's accusation of drunkenness that will delay the wedding). But I have more positive qualities; a trust in my fate and my star (the other mood of the Goethe songs, in *Freisinn* and *Talismane*), a sturdy independence (*Niemand*) and a sense of fun (*Rätsel*). It's true that I tend to get depressed and lachrymose (*Mein Herz ist schwer, Was will die einsame Träne*) but is that any wonder when we are apart (*Jemand*) and the strain of separation (*Hochländers Abschied*, *Ich sende einen Gruss*) is so grievous for me, as well as, I believe, for you (the women's songs of separation – *Lied der Suleika*; *Weit, weit*; *Im Westen*). It may be that I have nothing more to offer you than a woman's ordinary lot in life; as a girl waking to love (*Der Nussbaum*), as a fiancée (*Lieder der Braut*), as a wife grappling with life's problems (*Hauptmanns Weib*), as a mother (*Hochländisches Wiegenleid*), and even, it may be, as a widow, in poverty and grief (*Die Hochländer-Witwe*). But, my dear Clara, I do love you so very much, near worship (*Die Lotosblume*, *Du bist wie eine Blume*); and I hereby offer you my entire and dedicated devotion (*Widmung*, the first song in the cycle) and with it perhaps a share of immortality (*Zum Schluss*, the last); alpha and omega in twenty-six songs.

We may smile as we imagine Clara having the ciphers and key-schemes and hidden messages explained to her in great detail when the book was presented; young love bound in calf. But any smiles will take account also of the enduring sweetness and greatness of much of this music; and what bride ever had a finer wedding-gift?

12. (Op. 25, No. 1) Widmung (Dedication)

Rückert – *c.* March 1840

You are my heart and soul, my bliss and pain; you are the world I live in, the heaven I aspire to, the tomb where I have laid my sorrow to rest for ever.

You are repose and peace, and my share of heaven; your love justifies me, your gaze transfigures me, lovingly you raise me to new heights, my good angel, my better self.

[*You are my heart and soul, my bliss and pain; world I live in, heaven I aspire to, my good angel, my better self.*]

Divine love is traditionally presented in human imagery, to make it more understandable. Here, at the start of the humanist era, is the predictable converse; human love is decked out in pseudo-Christian imagery, to make it more impressive. Nowadays this coinage seems base metal all through. But it once passed current; and in this song, because of Schumann's genius, it rings true. Here are both aspects of his creative personality at their most engaging; the tender grace of Eusebius alternates yet blends with the vigorous ardour of Florestan.

The piano begins with elated arpeggios. For a moment it is content to provide an accompaniment. But soon it is joining in and leading the singing, paying its respects to the words in sadly flattened harmonies at 'Schmerz' (sorrow) and 'Grab' (grave). Under the surface of this music another more soulful strain has been continuing as a hidden undersong in the bass semibreves and minims. And in the slow middle section it is this sweet voice that speaks until the elated arpeggios resume, and a postlude uniting both voices rounds off the song.

Even without its title the passionate conviction of this song would show its dedication, not only of Op. 25 but of all Schumann's music, all his life, to his Clara.

NOTES. 1. The title is Schumann's own. So is the idea of repeating the first four lines followed by the last line to make A B A climax plus coda. Rückert has '*der*' not '*vom* Himmel' in bar 18.

2. The prelude combines the virile dotted rhythm of motif 56 with the joyous arpeggio of motif 23 and the long bass notes of motif 29, making a pattern of earnest elation. The opening vocal melody (Ex. G, p. 2) recalls that of *Schöne Wiege,* perhaps because of a similarity in the imagery and recurs as an

image of requited love in *Die Löwenbraut*. There is the contented motif 2 at 'lebe' and 'schwebe', countered by the sad semitone of motif 8 at 'Schmerz' and 'Grab'. This flattened sixth persists in the postlude, perhaps suggesting the idea of doubt or unworthiness.

3. The flattened seventh of motif 50 falls aptly from 'Himmel' at bars 18–19. Indeed the whole song is this motif writ large; whether in A flat major or E major the music clings round subdominant and tonic like a long Amen.

4. Clara-themes abound; notably Q³ as A♮ B♭ D♭ E♭. In the deliberately-added last line this is harmonized much as in *Dichterliche* (see No. 77, note 5) and repeated almost note for note in the climax of *Du bist wie eine Blume* (see Nos. 35 and 37, note 2).

5. There is yet another tribute to Clara. The melody at 'mir beschieden', bars 20–21, (Ex. D, p. 2) is already well known from, e.g., the *Novellette*, Op. 21 No. 1 (middle section), the *Arabeske*, Op. 18 (postlude), *Der Dichter spricht*, Op. 15, No. 13 (bars 3–4) and elsewhere. It may well be an allusion to the Schubert song *Das Rosenband*, at the words 'ihr Leben hing mit diesem Blick an meinem Leben' (at that look her life entwined with mine).

Schumann was certainly thinking of Schubert; no composer could have set Rückert's words 'Du bist die Ruh' without recalling with veneration Schubert's wonderful Rückert song of that title (cf. No. 51, note 4).

6. In some Peters editions the first left-hand minim of bar 40 is misprinted as G instead of F.

13. (Op. 25, No. 2) Freisinn (Independence)

Goethe – February 1840

Let me count for nothing save in the saddle. Stay in your huts and tents, while I ride out free and gay into the wide world, with nothing for me to raise my cap to but the stars.

God has set the stars in their courses as your guides by land and sea, for your wonder and delight as you look up for ever at them.

[*But let me count for nothing save in the saddle. Stay in your huts and tents, while I ride out free and gay into the wide world, with nothing for me to raise my cap to but the stars.*]

Under the rubric *Freisinn*, which suggests both free thought and liberal outlook, Goethe groups two separate quatrains with strongly Kantian overtones; obedience to the moral law within and contemplation of the starry heavens without. Schumann reduces the categorical imperatives into first a simple guide to horse-riding, and then a simple observation about star-gazing. Even at this literal level the music seems inadequate as a setting of words. While the words announce their intention of riding out to bold adventure, the music is privately resolving not to stir a step further than the drawing-room. But judged on its own modest terms the song is an enduring delight, a little masterpiece of boyish innocent eagerness to achieve great things. While remaining in the salon it really has gone out and conquered the world.

NOTES. 1. Goethe's text is unaltered; but its plain sense is violated in many ways (e.g. the lack of emphasis on 'Sattel' in bar 3 and 'ich' in bar 8). The impression once again is that of piano music with words added.

2. Even the harmony speaks of simple direct statement; the song consists almost entirely of tonic and dominant in major and relative minor.

3. The outdoor idea sends the music B flat-wards at bars 5–6, etc., in a style later remembered in *Der frohe Wandersmann* at bars 11–12. Here it is indebted to Beethoven's Goethe setting *Mailied* (Op. 52, No. 4) with Schumann's own typical ideas of virility (M 56) and happiness (the shape of motif 1 at bars 5–6).

4. Perhaps the most interesting response to Goethe's language is the flattened seventh (M 50) introducing the mention of the starry heavens (bars 11–12, etc). This makes the end of the song sound oddly irresolute.

14. (Op. 25, No. 3) Der Nussbaum (The walnut tree)

Mosen – February 1840

A walnut tree in the garden airily spreads its leafy boughs covered with paired fragrant blossoms that nod and whisper at the kiss of the wind. They whisper of a girl who dreamed night long and day long and herself knew not why. They whisper – but who could understand so soft a song? – of a bridegroom and the coming year. And at the sound and sway of the leaves she smiles and drifts into sleep and dream.

Perhaps only Schumann among the great song-writers would have countenanced so inept a lyric as the German text of this song. Then having chosen it, only Schumann would have so chopped and changed at its rhyme scheme as to prune away such small interest and merit as it had. But then only Schumann could have persuaded this cutting to flower into a unique masterpiece of charm and tenderness, which has entranced the whole world ever since.

It is in every sense ideal music, a springtime tree of sound, growing from the musical images of sleeping girl and wind-kissed foliage, each moved and stirred in dream. The piano sets the scene with its soft-spoken leaf-music, which also expresses the poem's secondary symbolism of sharing and pairing. The arpeggios are shared between the hands, the melody between voice and piano; all is wistful duality, sigh and echo, murmur and response.

In the final bars the small secret is unfolded. The voice lingers in its lower register, the piano part goes down to deeper subconscious levels, finally becoming music inside a dreaming head, music that smiles in its own sleep.

NOTES. 1. The original verse-form is obscured by the word-setting. Here, for example, is verse five:

> 'Sie flüstern, – wer mag verstehn so gar
> Leise
> Weise?
> Flüstern von Bräut'gam und nächstem Jahr.'

Similarly there is no 'die' or 'und' in bars 35–36. Schumann wrote 'Blätter' (leaves) for 'Äste' (boughs) in bar 9, perhaps because of an intuition that his music was expressing the movement of leaves (M 21).

2. The main melodic idea

mingles the contentment of motif 1 with the silence of motif 26; 'lulled by leaves' is the sense of the song.

3. At bars 31–40, the supertonic tonality wonders whether to establish a new key, corresponding to the sweet kernel of longing without knowing why. But the piano knows why; in bars 41–42 the motto theme, for the first and only time in the song, is harmonized with successive dominant sevenths, the love-motif 64.

4. The later passage at 'flüstern von Bräut'gam', etc. is chromatically unquiet; but there is no question of modulation because there is no surprise. On the contrary, there is serene assurance in the tonic pedal (M 29[C]).

5. Vaguer harmonic points are the possible effect of hidden Clara-themes, perhaps used subconsciously if at all, e.g. in the use of A♯/B in bars 49, 58, etc., and the implied inner voices in the crucial passages at bars 31–40 and 51–64 (the latter in particular may be compared with the Clara music of *Dichterliebe*).

6. The fair copy of this song is dated May in Schumann's manuscript. But his letters to Clara show that it was in existence by February; no doubt he sent it to her and did not have it back until her return. It was, perhaps, as her biographer Litzmann supposes, the song that was sent with the well-known 'scherzino' letter of 16th February. But there is another, and better, claimant (see No. 43, notes 1 and 2).

15. (Op. 25, No. 4) Jemand (For the sake of somebody)

Burns (trans. Gerhard) – February 1840

My heart is sair, I dare na tell,
My heart is sair for somebody;
I could wake a winter night
For the sake o' somebody.
Oh-hon! for somebody!
Oh-hey! for somebody!
I could range the world around
For the sake o' somebody.

Ye Powers, that smile on virtuous love,
O, sweetly smile on somebody!
Frae ilka danger keep him free,
And send me safe my somebody.
Oh-hon! for somebody!
Oh-hey! for somebody!
I wad do – what wad I not,
For the sake o' somebody?

The separation of lovers was much in Schumann's mind at this time. So instead of the expected setting in separate strophes the music clings to the verses with more than usual tenderness. The prelude announces its sad little tune of separation. Then gradually, as the thought of the loved one grows, the music becomes mollified, reconciled. In the second verse its expression changes from minor frown to major smile, and finally to vivid remembrance and delight, as the last phrase is echoed by the postlude.

NOTES. 1. By applying Schumann's own Procrustean techniques Burns' original words could be made to fit.

2. The descending minor theme of the prelude (M 6) is given the typical staccato of dream (M 32), (no doubt because of 'träumen' in bar 16). There are the affectionate dominants (M 64) at bars 31–32, etc., and impatient syncopations (M 60B) in the postlude.

3. Vaguer associations are that of E minor with the word 'Herz', and the affinity of the opening theme with that of the variations in the *Sonate*, Op. 118, No. 1 (surely an early work?)

5. Cf. also Franz, Op. 1, No. 8 (in a different translation).

16. (Op. 25, No. 5) Sitz' ich allein

Goethe – February 1840

Sitting alone, drinking my wine all by myself; where could I be happier?

With no one to hamper me, free to have my own thoughts; where could I be happier than sitting alone?

A charming miniature. It is piquant to recall here and in the next song that Schumann was at the time preparing a written defence to a charge of drunkenness brought by his prospective father-in-law Wieck, who hoped by this means to stop the wedding.

The poem, for whatever reason, seems to be construed as a good-humoured address to a friendly company which the speaker is on the point of leaving. In the one-bar prelude the separating octaves get up and move apart; the tiny cadence adds a smile. 'Sitting alone' the voice sings; what could be better? And the piano quite agrees, repeating the prelude. 'Drinking wine' the voice pursues. And this idea strikes a new chord and a new key, in which the piano's wish for solitude becomes even more insistent, while the voice is more meditative; the notion of being at ease and alone is sipped and savoured like wine. The return of the first strain, and a lilting postlude, round off the song.

NOTES. 1. The repeats (including a Da Capo ad lib.) are Schumann's.

2. Op. 25 suggests some alphabetical symbolism (see p. 49). This fifth piece (E) suggests Eusebius, and has the characteristic mediants (M 63), as strongly as the sixth (F) does Florestan.

3. The octaves in contrary motion are eloquent of the wish for freedom from constraint (M 16B); the semiquaver rise to the tonic has the gaiety of motif 3. These ideas reappear in *Verratene Liebe*, also about release. The interpolated reverie is hived off in the mediant key-change of motif 47.

4. The ruefully flattened sixth at bar 19 is motif 8; perhaps being alone had its drawbacks.

17. (Op. 25, No. 6) Setze mir nicht

Goethe – February 1840

Don't smack the jug down under my nose like that, you oaf; look cheerful, or you'll turn the wine sour.

But you, my graceful boy, don't just stand there by the door; come in! You shall pour my wines from now on; that will give them savour and brightness.

The poem is gay and zestful, and Florestan responds to it admirably.

The piano's minor key and crass thumping octaves display petulance at oafish clumsiness, a sour wine spilling; then the smooth major melodies express delight at boyish grace, a sweet wine flowing; and all this blends naturally into the mellow, slightly tipsy, elation of the postlude.

NOTES. 1. Goethe's quatrains (addressed to waiter and cupbearer respectively) have 'zierlicher' not 'lieblicher' in bar 12.

2. The companionable tenths of motif 57 are particularly pleasing here. The attractive postlude is a blend of two ideas – freedom from inhibition as promised by *Sitz' ich allein* (the upward octave of motif 16B), together with the suggestion of dancing in the dual rising movement (M 17). An elated capering is the sense of the music.

18. (Op. 25, No. 7) Die Lotosblume (The lotus flower)

Heine – February 1840

The lotus flower is fearful of the sun's splendour, and with bowed head dreaming she awaits the night.

The moon is her lover; he wakes her with his light and to him she joyously unveils her devoted flower-face.

She blooms and glows and shines and looks up speechless at the sky, trembling for love and the pain of love.

For Schumann, the sun is already down, the moon about to rise; all is hushed ecstatic dreaming and waiting. There are repeated hypnotic chords in the right hand, together with the profound calm of long low bass octaves. At 'mit gesenktem Haupte' (with bowed head) the melody withdraws into the accompanying chords, and stays there, waiting, as the scene changes. This sense of expectancy is heightened by a halt on the dominant of the main key of F major. Then the tension resolves on the mellowness of A flat major, a moonrise in music. Now the humility of the repeated chords has an added sense of elation. For the last verse, at 'Sie blüht' (she blooms), etc., the vocal melody resumes its rightful place at the centre of interest of the piano part also; the pulse of the music quickens, more awake and aware. The absence of a postlude enhances the effect of unstilled longing with which the song ends.

NOTES. 1. Heine has 'das' not 'der' in bar 10.

2. The sheer depths of devotion revealed in this song are almost frightening. The idea of the unveiled bride is the secret source of the music. The first notes display Clara en clair, theme X, (and in doing so help to reveal Schumann's cipher-systems*). Note how this expressive melody is deliberately forced on to

*See p. xi.

the words, driving a wedge of three slow crotchets' silence into the reflexive verb at 'ängstigt . . . sich'.

3. 'Mit gesenktem Haupte' yields the humility of motif 38; 'träumend' motif 32 (the staccato should be heard throughout despite the fact that only the opening chords are so marked); 'die Nacht' the calm of motif 35.

4. The augmented sweetness of motif 12 presages the fragrance of 'duftet', in bar 21. There is the expectant dominant at 'die Nacht' (M 43) and the typical A flat major at 'Der Mond'.

5. This intense focus on night and dream leaves other areas blurred. By Heine's last verse the moonrise has lightened the dark night, the waiting is over, the flower face unveiled and lifted, the calm replaced by excitement, the dream changed to waking. As a result the relevance has faded from Schumann's inspiration; all that is left is the idea of humility in repeated chords (M 38).

6. But in the first page the music is the clearest of mirrors for the composer's excited imagination. Perhaps he was so inspired by Heine's poem that he had enough left for a new work. There is a curious family resemblance with the contemporary duet *Familien gëmalde*, Op. 34, No. 4, which is in F major, begins on six-four chords, modulates to A flat major and uses augmented chords in a very similar way.

7. Cf. Franz, Op. 25, No. 1, and Schumann's own part-song, Op. 33, No. 3.

19. (Op. 25, No. 8) Talismane (Talismans)

Goethe – *c.* February 1840

God's is the east, God's the west; lands to north and south are all at rest in the peace of his hands. He, the sole source of all justice, shows the right path to all men; of his hundred names let this name be praised with great praise. Amen.

[*God's is the east, God's the west.*]

Error may lead me astray, yet thou canst show me my path plain; in all my deeds and works guide thou me aright.

[*God's is the east, God's the west; lands to north and south are all at rest in the peace of his hands. Amen, amen.*]

The humanistic piety of the words elicits a small-scale secular oratorio. The song begins as recitative, as the declaimed opening phrases are punctuated with sharp chordal interventions from the piano; then turns to aria for the more reflective second quatrain; then sketches a contrapuntal chorus in three and four parts as the melodic lines disperse at the mention of going astray; and culminates in a repeated declamation and a fine flourish of Amens.

NOTES. 1. Goethe has five short separate poems under the rubric *Talismane.* Schumann uses the first three only, setting the first two entire, then the opening couplet of the first again, then the third, then the first repeated, and then the

'Amen' from the second repeated. The fair copy of this and No. 20 is undated; but each is probably February like the others (16, 17) from the *Westöstlicher Diwan*.

2. At 'will für Jedermann das Rechte' the composer harks back to 'Freisinn' (No. 13) (compare bars 4 and 14 in that song with 11–13 in this) as if thinking to himself that the right thing for him personally would be unfettered freedom. A possible pointer to this personal involvement is motif 23.

3. At 'mich verwirren . . .', etc., the music is strongly reminiscent of 'All we like sheep' in *Messiah*, where also the music goes astray (M 58). For another parallel see No. 46, note 3.

4. There cannot be many examples of the word 'Amen' thrice set to non-plagal cadences, as here at bars 16 and 39–42, or of an address to Deity being relegated to the final quaver of a bar (24, 28).

20. (Op. 25, No. 9) Lied der Suleika (Suleika's song)

Marianne von Willemer – *c.* February 1840

With what heartfelt joy, song, I grasp your meaning.

Lovingly you seem to say that I am at his side; that he ever thinks of me alone, and ever bestows the bliss of his love on me far away who dedicate my life to him.

For my heart, dear friend, is the mirror wherein you have seen yourself, this breast where your seal is imprinted kiss on kiss.

Your sweet art, its whole truth, chains me in sympathy; pure embodied radiance of love wearing the robe of poetry.

[*With what heartfelt joy, song, I grasp your meaning.*
Lovingly you seem to say that I am at his side.]

Here is Schumann's personal voice sounding at its clearest and sweetest. If song can be instrumental music, with the voice hardly more than a means of stressing the piano's melody, then the literature has few finer examples than this modest and beautiful work. And its connexion with the poem though tenuous is real. Thus the joyous opening melody varied with more reflective repeated chords is in its own way a perfect expression of the sententious pleasure in the verse; and in the post-lude the melodic lines intertwine with equal felicity as music and as metaphor.

NOTES. 1. The poem is Marianne von Willemer's reply to Goethe's *Abglanz*, which is the 'song' of the first line. The repeats are Schumann's. For the date see No. 19, note 1.

2. There is the same joyous arpeggio (M 23) in the opening piano phrases as in *Widmung* (No. 12); there is the same contrast of devoted humility (M 38) here at bars 11–15 etc.; each song is about dedication.

3. The postlude with its motif 10 reminds us of *Intermezzo*; each poem has a vision of the loved one far away.

4. The beginning of this song has the identifying B minor Clara-theme Q^2 – at the words 'Lied, empfind ich deinen Sinn'; the penultimate bar has Q^1.

21. (Op. 25, No. 10) Die Hochländer-Witwe (The highland widow)

Burns – February 1840

Oh, I am come to the low countrie,
Och-on, och-on, och-rie!
Without a penny in my purse
To buy a meal to me.

It was na sae in the Highland hills,
Och-on, och-on, och-rie!
Nae woman in the country wide
Sae happy was as me.

For then I had a score o' kye,
Och-on, och-on, och-rie!
Feeding on yon hills so high,
And giving milk to me.

And there I had threescore o' yowes,
Och-on, och-on, och-rie'.
Skipping on yon bonnie knowes –
And casting woo' to me.

I was the happiest of a' the clan –
Sair, sair may I repine;
For Donald was the brawest man,
And Donald he was mine.

Till Charlie Stuart cam' at last,
Sae far to set us free;
My Donald's arm was wanted then
For Scotland and for me.

Their waefu' fate what need I tell?
Right to the wrang did yield;
My Donald and his country fell
Upon Culloden-field.

Och-on, Donald, O!
Och-on, och-on, och-rie!
Nae woman in the warld wide
Sae wretched now as me.

The translation preserves some of the rhythmic drive and vigour of Burns' original. Schumann's music restores any missing lamentation. The hammered chords in each hand, gestures of despair, continue throughout the song. The vocal melody is first all minor melancholy and resentment, then more relaxed in the major to tell the story. But all the while it maintains its constrained stepwise movement except for two bright dominant arpeggios, each coinciding with the lively memory of past joy; at 'ein hochbeglückter Weib' (nae woman . . . sae happy) and 'Donald war der schönste Mann' (Donald was the brawest man). Then, at exactly the right moment, in the very tonal centre of the song, Bonnie Prince Charlie is remembered, in the uncomplaining gentleness of an unexpected major modulation; his cause, the music tells us, is still just. In the last verse, as the voice ends its story the piano resumes its lament; then the vocal melody keens on its highest note, falling ruefully down and away into the postlude, where the gestures of despair are checked and relieved in grief.

NOTES. 1. The expressive content of this song is stated in terms so modest that there is a real danger of its being missed or misunderstood. Musical pointers are:

(*a*) the two opening chords, a signpost to melancholy here as in e.g. *Der arme Peter* (M 7);
(*b*) the ubiquitous sorrow of motif 8, e.g. in the opening vocal melody, and the piano postlude;
(*c*) the resentment or indignation of the rising minor scale with horn passage accompaniment (M 5).

These features confirm what the translation may have obscured, namely that there is absolutely no question here of humour or even irony.

2. The key-change is tonally so significant that it seems permissible to pause on the introductory chord at 'blieb's', which Schumann has also stressed by repetition.

3. The joy of motif 23 is briefly evident at bars 15 and 39 in the voice.

22, 23. (Op. 25, Nos 11, 12) Lieder der Braut (Songs of a bride-to-be)

Rückert – February 1840

22.

Mother, never believe, because I love him so, that I love you any less than before.

No, mother, it is only since I fell in love that I have truly loved you; let me hold you and kiss you, as he kisses me.

Mother, it is only since I fell in love that I have truly loved you, for giving me the life that now glows in such radiance.

23.

Let me embrace him, mother. Be not afraid; do not ask what will come of it, how it will end. End? It never will. Change? It cannot. [*Let me embrace him; let me!*]

Two fascinating failures. The words move Schumann deeply; but this very involvement vitiates the music. However, the intention is there; and the melodic charm is such that it would be a pity to miss these songs, which are at least a study for *Frauenliebe und-leben*.

NOTES TO 22. 1. Revealingly, Schumann wrote, at bar 34, 'sehr' (very) instead of 'ganz' (quite); and chose to repeat, of all phrases, 'wie mich er' (as *he* kisses *me*). Here (bar 25) the music piles up a huge unresolved dominant seventh clamouring for resolution (M 44); mother may well have been more disconcerted than reassured.

2. Bars 47–49 (which the manuscript shows to have been an afterthought) may be a deliberate reference to the postlude of *Du bist wie eine Blume*.

3. A letter to Clara of 24th February 1840 says 'I am sending you this little song to comfort you; sing it to yourself quietly and simply, just as you are . . .' Again on 2nd March, apparently in reference to the same song, Schumann writes: '. . . a text like this can move me to tears, and is so very profound for all its simplicity.' This song has never been identified. But on the reasonable assumption that Schumann really meant that the song was to convey an actual reassurance on an actual point on which Clara had had misgivings, this is the only likely candidate. The Clara theme X, C B A G♯ A, is clear enough in the piano at 'ihn liebe also sehr'.

NOTES TO 23. 1. The final repetition is Schumann's.

2. Again the music seems to offer a revealing insight into the composer's personality. 'End?' says the poem, defiantly, almost derisively; 'of course it cannot; it never will'. The music matches the rhetorical question with the diminished seventh chord of motif 42. We now await the contrasting music of strong affirmation and undying love. Instead we have first the melody of

Schubert's *Die Rose*, where the rose is about to fade, and then a trite sequence of listless chords. For once the music is far from espousing the faith expressed in the words.

24. (Op. 25, No. 13) Hochländers Abschied (My heart's in the Highlands)

Burns (trans. Gerhard) – February 1840

My heart's in the Highlands, my heart is not here;
My heart's in the Highlands, a-chasing the deer;
Chasing the wild deer, and following the roe –
My heart's in the Highlands wherever I go.
Farewell to the Highlands, farewell to the North!
The birthplace of valour, the country of worth;
Wherever I wander, wherever I rove,
The hills of the Highlands for ever I love.

Farewell to the mountains high covered with snow!
Farewell to the straths and green valleys below!
Farewell to the forests and wild-hanging woods!
Farewell to the torrents and loud-pouring floods!
My heart's in the Highlands, my heart is not here,
My heart's in the Highlands, a-chasing the deer;
Chasing the wild deer, and following the roe –
My heart's in the Highlands wherever I go.

There is a sturdy vigour in the prelude and a fine swing to the opening melody; strong driving octaves accompany the hunting. The repetition of the second verse to the same material is less apt to scansion or meaning. When the patriotism relaxes in a broader view of snow-capped peaks and valleys filled with flowers and clover (a detail for which we have to thank the translator) Schumann's response is correspondingly more tender. The music changes from minor to major in a smile of welcome; the piano part is tremulous in broken chords. The return to the first verse is pleasantly varied as the voice comes in, impatient in its devotion, before the prelude has ended.

NOTES. 1. The last quatrain runs 'mein Herz, liebe Heimat, ist immer bei dir. Es jaget . . .' etc.; Schumann repeats the first verse instead. The title is also his.

2. The octaves in each verse, despite the hunting in the first, seem insufficiently motivated. Perhaps the words 'ihr Wälder, bemoostes Gestein' remind

Schumann unconsciously of 'Gräber und morsches Gebein' and their treatment in octaves in Schubert's *Geistertanz*.

3. Cf. Franz, Op. 31, No. 6.

25. (Op. 26, No. 14) Hochländisches Wiegenlied (Hee balou)

Burns – *c.* February 1840

Hee balou! my sweet wee Donald,
Picture o' the great Clanronald:
Brawlie kens our wanton chief
Wha got my young Highland thief.

Leeze me on thy bonnie craigie!
An' thou live, thou'll steal a naigie;
Travel the country through and through,
And bring hame a Carlisle cow.

Through the Lawlands, o'er the border,
Weel, my babie, may thou furder!
Herry the louns o' the laigh countrie,
Syne to the Highlands hame to me.

The relationship of Burns' open-hearted poem to its stilted translation is neatly epitomized by the title of each. But something of the original's homely tenderness has got into the German text and thence into the music, making this a worthy successor of Schubert's cradle-song, and a worthy forerunner of Brahms'. Indeed, in one respect it surpasses theirs, for all their beauty. Schumann has fashioned his rhythm from the rock and return of a rough cradle; and inside his music (as in Wolf's *Wiegenlied im Sommer*) lies the idea of a sleeping child.

NOTES. 1. There is no dated manuscript; but the song belongs with other Burns songs of *Myrthen*. The German text either mistranslates or bowdlerizes the original, which might be sung instead.

2. Naturally enough the music recalls *Schöne Wiege*, to the extent of beginning with the same lulling motif 35A. There is the quietness of motif 26 in the vocal and piano melody at e.g. bars 7–10. The song is typically Eusebian in its opening mediants (M 63) and similarly in its ending on that note conveying the 'music dying' idea of motif 46.

26. (Op. 25, No. 15) Aus den 'Hebraischen Gesängen' (from 'Hebrew Melodies')

Byron (trans. Körner) – February 1840

My soul is dark – Oh! quickly string
The harp I yet can brook to hear;
And let thy gentle fingers fling
Its melting murmurs o'er mine ear.
If in this heart a hope be dear,
That sound shall charm it forth again;
If in these eyes there lurk a tear,
'T will flow, and cease to burn my brain.

But bid the strain be wild and deep,
Nor let thy notes of joy be first:
I tell thee, minstrel, I must weep,
Or else this heavy heart will burst;
For it hath been by sorrow nursed,
And ach'd in sleepless silence long;
And now tis doom'd to know the worst,
And break at once – or yield to song.

The poem suggests Saul's being healed of an evil spirit by David's harp. Much of its meaning is lost in the translation. Schumann is expressing, not the plea of a distraught and grief-stricken man for matching music, but a mood of his own, compounded of twilit reverie and romantic musing against a vague background of plucked strings.

The prelude suggests the sound of the translator's 'lute', with falling phrases merging into a soothing chain of dominants as the voice enters. Now the piano has soft cascades of minor arpeggios that flow blissfully into the major mode at the least hint of hope in the words. The memorable melody of this section yields to an aptly wide-ranging vocal line at 'wild and deep' until the minor arpeggios of the first strain resume. At the end hope prevails. 'My heart will either break or be healed by the song' says the translator. The musing postlude pursues the question. Which will it do? the music wonders, until in the assurance of the tonic major the answer comes in three closing chords; it will heal, not break.

NOTES. 1. The indifferent translation had been published by Schumann's father in Zwickau in 1821. The text is much altered, as in the later Byron songs from the same source (Nos. 184–6). The main variants are:

bars 11–12 'sie nur mag ich noch hören'
bars 15–16 'den Schmerz' not 'das Herz'
bar 54 'weil' not 'dass'
bars 69–71 'jetzt ward's' not 'und jetzt' repeated
bars 75–77 'bricht's, wo nicht, heilt's im Gesang.'

2. The E minor twilight anticipates *Zwielicht*. Rhythm (M 33), key and actual notes (see e.g. bars 7 here and 13 there) show that the two works have an expressive idea in common.

3. There is the sorrow of M 8 passim, and the diminished seventh of rhetorical questioning (M 42) in the penultimate bar. The dominants of the prelude, while not quite typical of motif 64, may suggest that this was in some sense a love-song.

27. (Op. 25, No. 16) Rätsel (A riddle on the letter H)

Attrib. Byron (in fact Catherine Fanshawe) (trans. Kannegiesser) – February 1840

'Twas in heaven pronounced – 'twas muttered in hell,
And echo caught faintly the sound as it fell;
On the confines of earth 'twas permitted to rest,
And the depths of the ocean its presence confessed.
'Twill be found in the sphere, when 'tis riven asunder,
Be seen in the lightning, and heard in the thunder;
'Twas allotted to man with his earliest breath,
Attends at his birth and awaits him in death:
Presides o'er his happiness, honour and health,
Is the prop of his house and the end of his wealth.
In the heaps of the miser 'tis hoarded with care,
But is sure to be lost on his prodigal heir.
It begins every hope, every wish it must bound,
With the husbandman toils and with monarchs is crowned.
Without it the soldier, the seaman may roam,
But woe to the wretch who expels it from home.
In the whispers of conscience its voice will be found,
Nor e'en in the whirlwind of passion is drown'd.
'Twill not soften the heart, and though deaf be the ear
It will make it acutely and instantly hear.
Yet in shade let it rest like a delicate flower,
Ah, breathe on it softly – it dies in an hour.

The composer is so excited by the idea of musical cipher that there is no question of keeping the secret; the opening piano octaves blurt out the answer before the riddle is even asked. At the mention of battles and heroes a new tune comes striding in wearing octaves like thigh-boots; and the melody turns aside with an engagingly absurd tenderness to contemplate the flower at the end of the song.

NOTES. 1. The text above was published in *Lyra Elegantiarum* (London 1867) with a note on its mistaken attribution to Byron. The German version (published by Schumann's father in Zwickau, like No. 26) has only nine couplets, and lacks the elegance of the original. The repetition at bars 16–17 and 'was ist's' at the end – to stress the joke yet again – are Schumann's.

2. The Peters Edition has Schumann's own gleeful gloss 'the composer believes that his omission of the final syllable is self-explanatory'. English readers (especially of the transposed editions) need to know that the omitted word is 'Hauch', i.e. a breath or, as here, an aspirate; and that its note, B, is 'H' in German. The original intention was to end the song with a four-part chorus singing 'Hauch' on H(B) in unison. These notes of emphatic and eccentric enigma are typically Schumannian.

3. The manly motif 56 stands for battles at bars 10–11 and (in the bass) for heroes at bars 29–30 (where it is fascinatingly akin to Schubert's 'So lebt denn wohl Heroen' in *An die Leier*). The dallying on 'Blümchen' has the joy of motif 2 and perhaps beauty as in motif 65. The pause and diminished seventh of motif 42 at 'was ist's' convey Schumann's reaction to this inexhaustible drollery; was ever a question more rhetorical? And at last the note H itself is given the breathlessly excited syncopations of motif 61 in the penultimate bar.

28. (Op. 25, No. 17) Venezianisches Lied I (Venetian air I)

Moore (trans. Freiligrath) – March 1840

Row gently here, my gondolier; so softly wake the tide,
That not an ear on earth may hear but hers to whom we glide,
Had Heaven but tongues to speak as well as starry eyes to see,
Oh! think what tales 'twould have to tell of wandering youths like me.

Now rest thee here, my gondolier; hush, hush, for up I go,
To climb yon light balcony's height, while thou keep'st watch below.
Ah! did we take for Heaven above but half such pains as we
Take day and night for woman's love, what angels we should be.

In translation Moore's internal rhyming is obscured and the rhythm of the verse is slowed down. The form of Schumann's setting destroys most of what is left of the rhymes; performances tend to destroy all that is left of the rhythm. But with only a modicum of Moore's light laughter as a leaven this song will rise as appetizing as any ever written in this genre.

NOTES. 1. Schumann repeats 'leis' in bars 10–11 and 29–32, and 'sacht' in bars 48 and 61–64. His treatment also conceals the rhyme of 'sprühn' in bar 14 with 'ziehn' in bar 20. As in the Burns songs, singers might find it worth while to make their own reconstruction of the original text as a help to the necessary lightness of thought and tempo.

2. The piano prelude has been likened to the rowing action of a gondolier (M 16A); but it can hardly have been consciously so used, as this makes nonsense of the second verse. Such music might also, because of its close association with motif 17, convey the idea of the douce lapping of water in a quiet lagoon – as in *Berg und Burgen*, where rising intervals express a wave motion.

3. However this may be, there is some musical evidence that Schumann had the figure of an oarsman in mind. The whole first page of the song sounds like a subconscious adaptation of the music of *Warte, warte*, still fresh in Schumann's mind as an address to a boatman. A comparison of vocal line and harmony at bars 12–16 in the earlier song with bars 12–20 here will make the point clear.

4. Again a reference to Heaven is accompanied by a flattened seventh, at bars 21–23 (M 50).

29. (Op. 25, No. 18) Venezianisches Lied II (Venetian air II)

Moore (trans. Freiligrath) – March 1840

When through the Piazzetta
Night breathes her cool air
Then, dearest Ninetta,
I'll come to thee there.
Beneath thy mask shrouded
I'll know thee afar,
As Love knows, though clouded,
His own Evening Star.

In garb then resembling
Some gay gondolier,
I'll whisper thee, trembling,
'Our bark, love, is near:
Now, now, while there hover
Those clouds o'er the moon,
'Twill waft thee safe over
Yon silent lagoon.'

This time Freiligrath's version has more of the spirit of the original.

Schumann responds to the charm of rhyme and metre with the most obviously appealing and tuneful of all his piano preludes.

After eight bars this unobtrusively divides and becomes a song by simple fission; its left-hand harmony is shared between the two hands, its right-hand melody is allotted to the voice. The ideas of the music are simplified; it is as if the prelude imagines a gay disguise and then doffs its fancy-dress trifling to speak its heart in homespun. But the masquerade is too attractive; in the postlude heard after each verse the prelude returns, all silk and flourish, to take its bow.

NOTES. 1. Freiligrath has 'O komm! jetzt, wo Lune'n' in bar 18.

2. Zest and gaiety in prelude and postlude are manifest in motifs 2 and 3. Even in this mood Schumann is earnest rather than flamboyant, and the temptation to play this music flippantly must be resisted.

3. The costume is as new, while the homespun has worn thin. In particular the B minor section sounds contrived. But Schumann could hardly be expected to resist recognizing the loved one despite mask and veil; and his veiled allusion to Clara forces the melody of her theme X, in its B minor guise, on to the last words.

4. Cf. Mendelssohn, Op. 57, No. 5 (with an altered text), which was perhaps Schumann's introduction to Freiligrath's poems.

30. (Op. 25, No. 19) Hauptmanns Weib (The Captain's lady)

Burns (trans. Gerhard) – February 1840

O, mount and go,
Mount and make you ready;
O, mount and go,
And be the Captain's lady.

When the drums do beat,
And the cannons rattle,
Thou shalt sit in state,
And see thy love in battle.

When the vanquished foe
Sues for peace and quiet,
To the shades we'll go,
And in love enjoy it.
O, mount and go,
Mount and make you ready;
O, mount and go,
And be the Captain's lady.

Schumann wrote to Clara that he thought this song 'really original, and romantic too'. So it is still.

We may owe this admirable music to a mistranslation. There is no suggestion in Burns that the lady is any kind of Amazon. But the German text has her armed, armoured and helmeted like a Valkyrie. Schumann seems to find this charming rather than awe-inspiring.

The opening E minor chords in voice and piano express a heroine all the more mettlesome for having had to overcome a certain reluctance. At the mention of battle the music is duly issued with the prescribed drums and cannon. But the brisk march theme which then intervenes is given a more reflective and tender turn with major harmonies for the peaceful reunion promised by victory after 'Schlagen wir den Feind' (When the vanquished foe). The return of the first theme stands out bright and eager in G major. Here a variation of verbal stress makes, wittingly or not, a telling point. '*Suit* a captain's lady', said the first verse. 'Suit a *captain's* lady', says the final repetition, with a new pride in the voice. The postlude rides off to adventure, a little jerkily but with head held high.

NOTES. 1. In the martial canon of the first eight bars the piano exhorts the voice part to follow, in the spirit of the verses (M 59[B]).

2. The first bar's E minor melancholy (M 7) blends with the nobility of motif 51, the aural image of a diffident but queenly figure on horseback (cf. *Der Gärtner*). There is also the discontent of the rising minor horn-passages (M 5) at bars 3, etc. But the main vision is of Clara, with theme X in voice and piano, charmingly, at 'Küssest du den Gatten' (you'll kiss your husband) and again at the last words.

3. See No. 31, note 4.

31. (Op. 25, No. 20) Weit, weit (The bonnie lad that's far awa')

Burns (trans. Gerhard) – *c.* February 1840

O how can I be blithe and glad,
Or how can I gang brisk and braw,
When the bonnie lad that I lo'e best
Is o'er the hills and far awa'?
When the bonnie lad that I lo'e best
Is o'er the hills and far awa'?

It's no the frosty winter wind,
It's no the driving drift and snaw;

But aye the tear comes in my e'e
To think on him that's far awa';
But aye the tear comes in my e'e
To think on him that's far awa'.

A pair of gloves he bought for me,
And silken snoods he ga'e me twa;
And I will wear them for his sake,
The bonnie lad that's far awa';
And I will wear them for his sake,
The bonnie lad that's far awa'.

A sweet but rather tame little song, relying overmuch on its modest melody. But the postlude, with a delightful sureness of touch, expresses an involuntary gesture towards the high hills, outstretched arms falling in sad resignation.

NOTES. 1. Revealingly, Schumann wrote 'der mich liebt' (who loves me) instead of 'den ich lieb' (whom I love) in the first verse.

2. Burns' fifth verse, about the child soon to be born, was omitted by the translator. The third verse, about being hounded from home in disgrace, is omitted by Schumann – understandably enough in view of his intention to use these songs as a wedding gift, and the identifying Clara-theme X (C B A G♯ A) in the piano at bars 14–15.

3. The dominant question (M 43) is apt at bar 8, for the first two verses at least.

4. This song like No. 30 supra was published as a supplement to the *Neue Zeitschrift für Musik* in March 1840.

32. (Op. 25, No. 21) Was will die einsame Träne?

Heine – February 1840

Why has this solitary tear remained from former days to trouble my sight? It had many shining sisters who have all vanished, gone with my joys and sorrows in the night and the wind.

And those twin blue stars that smiled those joys and sorrows into my heart, they too have vanished like mists. Ah, my love itself has vanished like a vain sigh! Old solitary tear, now you in turn must vanish.

NOTES. 1. Perhaps the vapid poem had a special appeal to Schumann: not a word is changed or repeated. The unusual A B B A musical form is also derived from the sense of the verses.

2. This basic pattern has interesting variants. Thus the high note at 'Hauch' in bar 29 (E as compared with C♯ in bar 5) has clearly been held in reserve for

a climactic moment. The arpeggio in the left hand at bar 18 but not bar 10 may express the new idea of melting away like mist, while the difference between the first chords of bars 15 and 23 suggests the contrast between 'Freuden' and 'Qual' (M 13).

3. This latter expression is cognate with the basic musical idea of the song, namely a diminished seventh chord resolving on to the supertonic, as in bars 1–2, 5–6, 15–16, 25–26, and 29–30. Here is the form taken by the last of these examples compared with music written by Schumann at seventeen in the Byron setting *Die Weinende* at the words 'Ich sah dich weinen' (I saw thee weep)

This is an expression meaning 'tears' (M 9) that has remained from former days like the tear in the poem.

4. The 'going away' idea of motif 45 is strikingly apt at 'zerflossen in Nacht und Wind', bars 16–17.

5. Cf. Franz, Op. 34, No. 1: Cornelius.

33. (Op. 25, No. 22) Niemand (Naebody)

Burns (trans. Gerhard) – *c.* February 1840

I ha'e a wife o' my ain –
I'll partake wi' naebody;
I'll tak' cuckold frae nane,
I'll gi'e cuckold to naebody.
I ha'e a penny to spend,
There – thanks to naebody;
I ha'e naething to lend –
I'll borrow frae naebody.

I am naebody's lord –
I'll be slave to naebody;
I ha'e a guid braid sword,
I'll tak' dunts frae naebody;
I'll be merry and free,
I'll be sad for naebody;
If naebody care for me,
I'll care for naebody.

A wholly delightful song, sprightly and forthright as Burns himself. The melody springs straight from the rhythm of the German text; no doubt in Schumann's embattled personal circumstances at the time the words had some special appeal for him. Especially enjoyable is the grace with which the melody unwinds on to a falling phrase and cadence at the word 'Niemand' each time it occurs. These are then carried over into the elated music of the interlude and postlude as if it were hugging this thought to itself and dancing for joy.

NOTES. 1. The close connexion between German words and melody has the disadvantage of making the original text rather difficult to adapt.

2. In the postlude the joyous resolution of motifs 2 and 3 is given the typical one-two movement of Schumann's idea of dancing (M 17) (the postludes to *Verratene Liebe* and *Setze mir nicht* have much the same idea).

3. Perhaps the tenths in the opening bars have the idea of togetherness of motif 57; and in a song about 'my wife and I' the Clara-theme Q^2 in the same bars will not be accidental.

4. There is no dated m/s; but poet and style alike speak for February 1840.

34. (Op. 25, No. 23) Im Westen (In the west)

Burns (trans. Gerhard) – February 1840

Out over the Forth I look to the north,
But what is the north and its Highlands to me?
The south nor the east gi'e ease to my breast
The far foreign land, or the wild-rolling sea.

But I look to the west, when I gae to rest
That happy my dreams and my slumbers may be;
For far in the west lives he I lo'e best,
The lad that is dear to my baby and me.

The first four lines of German text and music are rather square and unresponsive. However, this arguably corresponds to the sense of the verses; and certainly the following contrast, as the vocal melody and piano arpeggios begin to flow out free and tender towards the west, is finely effective and moving.

NOTES. 1. Perhaps the arpeggios imagine the rolling sea, motif 21A. The lullaby melody has the quietude of motif 26. Motif 16A is eloquent at 'Kindlein' in bar 15.

2. The C B A G♯ A pattern hidden in bar 5 is an interesting example of how the Clara theme X deflects the tonality – here towards the mediant minor.

35. (Op. 25, No. 24) Du bist wie eine Blume

Heine – *c.* March 1840

You are like a flower, sweet and pure and beautiful. I look at you, and sorrow steals into my heart.

I feel as if I should lay my hands on your head and pray God to keep you so pure and beautiful and sweet.

Heine's poem is perhaps the most immediately appealing ever written. The German text has a simple and direct artlessness which makes it all but impossible to appreciate as art. Some critics detect pomposity, others a self-deprecatory irony. But it seems that Heine's look is level, his appeal clear. His poem is said to have been set to music more times than any other; and of all these settings Schumann's is surely supreme. His genius matches Heine's for intimacy and fervour; and here its whole force concentrates on his love for Clara Wieck, making his music so sumptuously sensuous and ceremonial that the laying on of hands is made to seem a ritual gesture of consecration.

The hushed opening chords are a meditation unbroken by the quiet entry of the vocal melody; the words and strong bass octaves sound the depths of devotion. The music quickens for the gesture, speaks for the prayer, and intones fervently in the postlude. If we now find the harmonies too rich, even cloying, it is right to remember a time when they were the very ceremony of innocence.

NOTES. 1. It seems incredible that not only the (undated) manuscript but the first and many subsequent editions have the misreading of 'so schön und rein und hold' for the second line as well as the last. But Schumann as ever is concerned with his own feelings, not the words as such. This is obvious from the opening melody (to which the words are fitted, not vice versa).

2. This song was one of Clara's own special favourites; and one can hear why. First her theme Q^1 steals in at bars 5–7 in the top notes of the left hand. Then bar 16 is a whole history of meaningful allusion. It is quoted from *Widmung*, at the words 'mein guter Geist, mein bess'res Ich'; bars 6–8 of *Zum Schluss* have a similar progression; thus the cycle begins and ends with the idea of Clara. Each time it is in A flat. So is the beautiful Schubert song *Fülle der Liebe*, where the same progression in the same key recurs so expressively (e.g. at 'das tiefe Leiden der Liebeslust') that any composer might be moved by it to his own love-songs. The melodic movement A B♭ D♭ E♭ in these meaningful contexts leaves no doubt that here once again is the meaning of the postlude to *Dichterliebe*, where love for Clara is proclaimed and declaimed at its clearest; her theme Q^3.

3. The initial mood has the mezzo-staccato reverie of motif 32, which should surely continue throughout. The bass notes have the assurance of motif 29^C.

The humility of motif 38 is just right for the blessing of bars 10–13, and the modified recitative chords of motif 48 for the solemn speech of bars 14–16. The canon in voice and piano at 14–15 is processional in effect (M 59) as if the whole scene were imagined in church, with Schumann's religious key of A flat major. The word 'Gott' leads predictably to the song's only flattened seventh (M 50) at bar 15. The yearning motif 16 in bar 13 and the postlude is evident enough; its meaning is confirmed by the 'beauty' motif 65 in the decorated final note.

4. Cf. Liszt; there is also an early setting by Hugo Wolf.

36. (Op. 25, No. 25) Aus den 'Östlichen Rosen' (From 'Eastern Roses')

Rückert – April 1840

I am sending a greeting like the scent of roses; I am sending it to a face like a rose.

I am sending a greeting like love in springtime; I am sending it to eyes full of the light of spring.

And from the storms of sorrow that rage in my heart I send a breath – may it not touch you ungently.

When you think of me in my sadness the dark sky of my nights becomes bright.

Fresh fragrance blown by on a breeze is a favourite image of Rückert's, which inspired Schubert in *Dass sie hier gewesen.*

Here too the light verse is wholly outshone by an ecstatic Schumann. In the margin of the manuscript he wrote 'In Erwartung Claras' (awaiting Clara); the music is quick with a tender anticipation.

The prelude has the play of an April wind. The slight texture and the piano interludes let air and space into the music, which is all sweet innocent yearning. The major and minor seconds in voice and piano sigh and sing until song and longing alike are blown delicately away in the postlude.

NOTES. 1. *Östliche Rosen* (Eastern Roses) is the name of a group of poems. Schumann alters 'Auge frühlingslicht' (spring-bright eye) to the more conventional 'Aug' voll Frühlingslicht'. Some Peters Editions have A♭ on the second syllable of '-kosen' in bar 12; it should be C, as in bar 4.

2. There is impatience in the small urgings of the vocal melody in bars 2, 6, 7, etc. (M 61). The poetic image of wind-blown fragrance is enhanced by the musical image of waving arpeggii that begins and ends the song (M 21A) somewhat as in *Jasminenstrauch*. The word 'Himmel' is heard in association with the flattened seventh (M 50).

3. The descending melodic lines in the piano right hand in bars 32–33 and 36–37 and their ascending counterpart in the voice at bars 33–36 are the Clara-themes P^1 and Q^1. X appears in the left hand at bars 20–22, and Y at bars 28–30.

4. For other *Dichterliebe* anticipations compare bar 24 here with bar 16 of *Am leuchtenden Sommermorgen*, and the vocal melody at bars 19–20 here with that at bars 11–12 of *Hör' ich das Liedchen klingen.*

37. (Op. 25, No. 36) Zum Schluss (In conclusion)

Rückert – March 1840

Here in this vale of tears I have woven this imperfect wreath for you, my sister, my bride.

But one day on high, in the radiance of God's sun, love will bestow on us a perfect crown, my sister, my bride.

Schumann dearly loved a peroration. But it was his gift to be expressive rather than impressive, and his finales sometimes appear contrived. This trait and the portentous lyric defeat the music, for all its beauty and dignity.

NOTES. 1. Rückert has 'Aufgenomm'nen' (bar 10).

2. For No. 26 of his bridal bouquet of myrtles Schumann invents a title beginning with Z and picks a poem about completing a wreath to symbolize alpha and omega, love all-perfect. He weaves into his music his bride from the first song ('mein guter Geist'), herself a fairer flower ('so rein und schön') in the 24th (see No. 35, note 2). Note also the melodic correspondence between bars 3–4 here and the postlude to *Widmung*.

3. There is the sad motif 8, G♭ F, after 'Wehmut' (see No. 82, note 2(*g*)). It is fitting too that so resounding a conclusion should contain so explicit a statement of the finality motif 49 in bars 13–14 and the postlude.

* * *

By mid-February Clara had to be told the secret (see p. 49). Hints had already appeared in Schumann's editorial choice of quotation for each issue of the *Neue Zeitschrift*. On 11th February 1840, for example, this was:

'Essential song,
By which I mean its sound, its melody,
Is needful to us as our daily bread.' (Z. Werner)

Later in the month another ran:

'The art of song is ever young,
The heart will never die.' (Old song)

Then, just as Schumann was writing out *Du bist wie eine Blume* in fair copy, came a heartfelt appeal from Clara: 'What *is* it you are writing? Do tell me.'

On 16th February, he told her. 'I've written *six books* of songs and ballads, large and small, solo and four-part! I know some of them will delight you.'

In March, *Myrthen* was sent for publication. Some songs which were not available or not suitable for inclusion were published[1] later as part of Op. 27 and 51.

* * *

38. (Op. 27, No. 1) Sag' an, o lieber Vogel mein (Tell me, my dear bird)

Hebbel – *c.* 1840

Tell me, my dear bird, tell me where you are going? 'I can't say where; but instinct guides me, so my path must be the right one.'

Tell me, my dear bird, what does the future promise you? 'It promises me soft airs, sweet scents, and a new springtime.'

You have never seen the far distant southlands, and yet you believe in them? 'You ask many questions, and that is easy to do, but I find them very hard to answer.'

Then the bird in great faith flew away across the sea; and soft airs and sweet scents and a new springtime were really and truly its reward.

The lyric is typical of Hebbel in its combination of surface charm with a striving for deep allegorical significance. But the song offers no evidence that Schumann found either aspect very rewarding; the flights of naïveté are clumsy, the bird a clay pigeon. Indeed, as an equivalent for the ideas of instinctive faith and effortless soaring into a better life the music is so inadequate that one is tempted to suggest a much earlier date than the otherwise great song-year of 1840.

NOTES. 1. In fact there is no clear evidence of date, and Hebbel's *Gedichte* were not published until 1842. However, this lyric, from his Münich period in 1837, may have been published in a journal or communicated privately; he had a Münich friend named Schumann who may have been a kinsman.

2. At bars 3–4 the dominant question (M 43) can also serve as an early example of the going away motif 45 induced by the words 'wohin die Reise dein'. The manliness of motif 56 may similarly be a response to the idea of adventure

[1] Except the insignificant *Ein Gedanke* (Ferrand) for which see *Musical Quarterly*, January 1942.

at bars 5–6; and the horn passages in which it is set may also be expressive of the idea of wandering afar (M 4).

3. At the moment when the words describe an actual flight the music responds with a figuration associated with 'fluttering' in later songs (see No. 181, note 3). This like the motifs above is used in an unfledged form which suggests that this work is among Schumann's earlier attempts at expressive song-writing.

39. (Op. 27, No. 2) Dem roten Röslein gleicht mein Lieb (O, my luve's like a red, red rose)

Burns (trans. Gerhard) – *c.* March 1840

O, my luve's like a red, red rose,
That's newly sprung in June:
O, my luve's like the melodie
That's sweetly played in tune.

As fair art thou, my bonnie lass,
So deep in luve am I;
And I will luve thee still, my dear,
Till a' the seas gang dry.

Till a' the seas gang dry, my dear,
And the rocks melt wi' the sun,
I will luve thee still, my dear,
While the sands o' life shall run.

And fare thee weel, my only luve!
And fare thee weel a while!
And I will come again, my luve,
Though it were ten thousand mile.

Schumann's tune may not displace the melody to which these fine words are traditionally sung. But it nods and droops very winningly. And below the surface charm the left hand adds independent life to the music; first in contrary motion with the opening melody, then in octaves, with the added assurance of long bass notes. A sadly flattened sixth with uneasy syncopations expresses the sadness of heart at 'wird das Herz mir schwer'; firmly rooted progressions speak for firm resolve; and there are bass octaves to sound the depths of a devotion that will last 'lebenslang', lifelong.

NOTES. 1. This was probably written earlier than the date on the fair copy

15th May (perhaps it was sent to Clara) but too late for inclusion in *Myrthen*. The German text has 'Melod*ie*, vo*n* der' and 'und', not 'nun' in bar 24.

2. There is certainly a barrier between Schumann and popular style; this song and several others are much better known to different and often rather inferior tunes. He saw this as a flaw, as we know from a diary entry, and worked to eradicate it. But it is in the grain of his song-writing material; there is no folk piano-music.

3. Falling fifths for roses are motif 27. There is nobility (M 51) at bars 17–18, 19–20 – in a rather self-conscious form – and sweetness (M 12) in the chromatic passing notes in bar 27 (otherwise the same as bar 11). There is yearning (M 16) in the rising bass octaves at bars 9–10, etc.; sadness (M 8) in bar 11 'wie wird das Herz mir schwer' and calm stability (M 35) in the octaves added at bars 21–22.

4. The Clara-theme X in each verse was no doubt prompted by the words 'leb wohl du süsse Maid'. It recurs in its more favoured B minor guise in the Burns part song Op. 55, No. 5, attributed to 1846, at the last word of 'holde Maid vom Niederland'. The phrase 'die holländische Maid' (the Dutch maiden) is found in one of Schumann's early diaries, apparently in reference to Clara.

5. Cf. Franz, Op. 31, No. 3.

40. (Op. 27, No. 3) Was soll ich sagen (What can I say?)

Chamisso – February 1840

My eyes are dim, my lips sealed; you bid me speak and so I cannot.

Your eyes are bright, your lips red; and your wish is my command.

My hair is grey, my heart sad; you are so young and sweet. You bid me speak, and so I cannot; and as I look at you I tremble.

The poem for all its naïveté has great force of expression. It makes an interesting choice of text for the thirty-year-old Schumann in the year of his marriage to Clara Wieck, whom he had first met when she was a child of nine, twelve years earlier. The music is hesitant and perplexed, as if expressing unaccustomed responsibility.

The piano prelude is already in decline. But as the sturdy octaves go resignedly downhill and away, the right-hand octave turns and cranes up wistfully; a last look back. After an interlude of tender singing the last word, left to the piano postlude, sounds very like 'farewell'.

NOTES. 1. Schumann was already familiar with this poem in 1839, so the song may be earlier. The first 'ist ein Gebot' bars 11–12 is his addition. The typically personal interpretation is clear from the music. The first half of each verse, where the contrast of age is stressed, is responsive (bars 4–6, 8–10, 13–15, etc.), the second half more perfunctory (bars 6–8, 10–13, 15–17).

2. The text invites misunderstanding. The song is rarely heard; perhaps the hint of impotence inhibits performance. It is worth noting therefore that these verses were written by Chamisso at the age of thirty-eight, just before his own

marriage to a girl of eighteen whom he had known from her childhood. This is a true love-song, from both poet and composer; discrepancy, not inadequacy, is its theme. Even so it was obviously unsuitable for inclusion in *Myrthen.*

3. The declining theme of the prelude may be metaphorical. The yearning of motif 16 is evident at bars 2–3; the worried diminished sevenths are motif 41. Bars 13–15 seem to express numb sorrow (cf. *Mit Myrthen und Rosen* at 'nun liegen sie stumm und totenbleich'). The amorous dominants at bars 16–17 – for 'jung und gesund'? – are motif 64. The postlude has affinities with that of *Tragödie* I, where the meaning seems to be the sorrow of parting; in its use here is a suggestion of the nobility of motif 51, suitable for renunciation.

4. There are the usual editorial problems; thus, why should the last right-hand quaver octave of bar 3 become a semiquaver in bar 20?

41. (Op. 27, No. 4) Jasminenstrauch (The jasmine bush)

Rückert – March 1840

The jasmine bush was green when it went to sleep last night. But when breeze and sunlight woke it this morning it was snowy white.

'What has changed me overnight?'

This, you see, is what happens to trees that dream in springtime.

Schumann noted in the margin of his manuscript that the song was only an attempt at the all but impossible task of finding music for the secret stirrings of Nature. We know too from a letter to Clara that the poetic symbolism of human love had not escaped him. No wonder that his response is so eager and vivid.

Springtime itself may have suggested the key of A major. In that bright tonality the piano prelude has a brief lifting arpeggio; an elated stirring as of a bough of flowering jasmine frilled by the wind. The thought of this beauty is expressed in the decorations of the right hand. At 'eingeschlafen' (went to sleep) the arpeggio goes nodding down on to a staccato semiquaver, a light dream. And then, delightfully, the flower-image is only half there; it appears in the first part of the bar only. There it breathes in its sleep, as we hear in the crescendi and decrescendi. Then the downward arpeggio is transformed into a troubled reverie at the bewildered question 'Wie geschah mir in der Nacht?'

But Rückert had to have a sententious conclusion; so Schumann had to point the moral in the form of a peroration or coda. This, though still charming, mars the consistency of the music. But with the postlude the constraint again vanishes, and we hear Schumann's marvellously articulate imagination at its secret work. The arpeggio moves up in joy, staccato for a light dream, and is deliciously troubled, reassured, perplexed, resolved, and finally bright and reassured again, waving in spring sunlight; and all in four bars.

This essence of jasmine is also the essence of Schumann: domestic or salon music, yet expressing a moment of pure perception as real and as rare as anything in the greatest art.

NOTES. 1. The following are the motivic components of the interpretation offered:

(*a*) A major is a springtime key with Schumann as later with Wolf.

(*b*) The arpeggio of the prelude and postlude is motif 21A for the waving of foliage.

(*c*) The decorations are a variant of motif 65 for beauty.

(*d*) The descending diminished seventh arpeggio expressing bewilderment (M 41) ends very neatly on the staccato of motif 32 for the ensuing dream-state.

(*e*) 'Breathing' is clearly enough the idea of < > in bars 7 and 11. (Note 'Hauch' – breath – in the former.)

(*f*) The diminished seventh chords of the postlude are the rhetorical question of motif 42, blending into (*b*) above.

2. The tender allusions to B minor in A major suggest the concealed presence of Clara – her theme Q^2 in the bass line in bars 2–3.

3. For Op. 27, No. 5, see No. 111 below.

42. (Op. 51, No. 2) Volksliedchen (Folk-song)

Rückert – *c.* March 1840

When I go walking in the garden early, wearing my green hat, my first thoughts are always of my sweetheart and what he's doing.

I'd give my friend every star in the sky; I'd give him the very heart out of my breast, if I could.

[*Whenever I go walking in the garden early, wearing my green hat, I'm always thinking of him and what he's doing.*]

For the right hearer in the right mood this is a perfect little masterpiece, with a beauty and depth out of all proportion to its small scale and lack of pretension.

Voice and piano both speak of walking in the garden, the latter in delicate downward stepwise movement; both share a moment of simple pleasure at the thought of the new green bonnet. But as the walking resumes, the voice is hesitant with a new thought, high and bright over questioning dominant harmony 'Was nun mein Liebster tut?' Then the walking music, warmer and deeper than before, lingers in more wistful melodies, to which the piano contributes two unobtrusive gestures of affection. As the walking resumes yet again, the piano interlude is shortened, the music less leisurely. Endearingly, it is as if all this wondering about him has led to worrying about him. Then the harmony becomes chromatically disturbed, frankly uneasy; wondering not so much what he's doing as what he's up to. The words are slow and pensive; at 'mein' the voice breaks off, and a chord and a half-bar of silence wonder whether that is still true, whether he is still true. Then the doubt and the harmony are alike resolved in smiling reassurance as voice and piano end together.

There follows a further delightful surprise in the piano postlude. This is at first very tender; but then there is suddenly a hint of impatience, even petulance, as the contentment of 'I'm sure it's all right' changes to 'Then why isn't he here?' as the song ends.

Such invention and subtlety of expression had never been heard in the Lied on this miniature level before; and would not be again until Wolf, nearly fifty years later.

NOTES. 1. Schumann himself must have thought quite highly of this song, as his contribution to a commemorative Mozart album planned in 1839 (but not completed until 1843, when Mozart's statue was unveiled in Salzburg). There is no other indication of date, but the Rückert source (which has two verses only) and the style alike point to early 1840. It is noteworthy that the music for all its typically Schumannian inflexions is also an eloquent act of homage to Mozart.

2. The song is fashioned entire from motivic material. Thus the Eusebian vocal melody (M 63) marked 'Einfach', is akin to those of *Widmung* and *Schöne Wiege*. The dreamy walking theme (M 20 and M 32) is also that of *Morgens steh ich auf*. The smiling music at bar 3 looks forward to that of *Im Rhein* (at the words 'freundlich hineingestrahlt') and back to that of Schubert's *Die Rose*, which may have been in Schumann's mind at the time (see No. 23, note 1).

3. At bars 8–9 is the happiness of motif 1 combined with the dominant question of motif 43. The word 'Himmel' suddenly deflects the harmony toward the subdominant (M 50) at bar 13; in bars 14–16 are the characteristic yearning leaps of motif 16. 'Herz' is E minor. This passage is cousin to bars 21–28

of *Hauptmanns Weib.* The uneasy chromatics in three-part harmony at bars 28–31 are paralleled in other songs for a woman's voice (M 34); the worried diminished seventh dispelled duringt he crotchet rest in bar 31 is motif 42; the last few bars of piano postlude have the impatience of motif 61.

43. (Op. 51, No. 3) Ich wandre nicht (I shall not wander)

Christern – *c.* February 1840

Why should I wander afar as others do? Their ways are not mine, and my loved one is staying at home. They sing in a thousand songs of the mountains and their high peaks; but why should I travel when our homeland is so fair?

I'll believe all they say of what grows and blooms in foreign parts, and how the gold of the grapes flashes there like sparkling sunlight. But we have wine here too, and my dearest love to pour it for me; what more could I ask?

I'll never go into the hustle and bustle of the great wide world; my love's eyes are the clearest bluest skies of all. And her smile promises me more than the bliss of spring; no, I shall never leave home and my own dear sunshine.

The free engaging melody and directness of the accompaniment wear well; and they seem to confirm that not only the poet but the poem had some special appeal and significance for Schumann.

NOTES. 1. There is a fair copy dated 30th December 1841. But the first song-writing phase had ended long before then, and the style is clearly that of the earliest songs. It was in 1840 too that Schumann had a personal interest in the question of leaving his country. He and Clara had considered eloping to England in a desperate effort to foil her father's opposition to the marriage; but they had decided against this by mid-January 1840. It seems very probable that Christern, who was a contributor to the *Neue Zeitschrift fur Müsik,* wrote these verses in sympathy, and that Schumann set them in appreciation shortly afterwards.

2. A letter of 16th February 1840 begins; 'My dear Clara, I enclose a song I have just written. First read the poem carefully and then think of your Robert. As a matter of fact, it's the Scherzino in another form.' This has been generally supposed to be *Der Nussbaum.* Clara Schumann's biographer, Litzmann, thought that it probably was; and it would have been very pleasant and fitting if it had been. However, there is no need to assume that it was, still less to postulate a lost *Scherzino* (cf. *Grove* 1954) apparently on the ground that none of the published piano works sounds in the least like *Der Nussbaum.* In fact the song might have been any one of a great number. In particular it might well have been this one, because it is another formof the *Scherzo* of the*Klavierstücke,* Op. 32, No. 1 (1839), e.g.:

The opening melody of each is also analogous; the thematic material of each is the Clara-themes X and Y.

3. Schumann himself must have thought quite highly of this work; it was twice published separately, in 1843 and 1844, before being collected into Op. 51.

4. The key of B flat major is associated with outdoor music; there are resemblances to *Der Hidalgo* (opening accompaniment and vocal melody) and to *Wanderlied* (high A to similar harmony at the climax of the voice part).

* * *

By mid-March 1840 Schumann had been completing songs, many of them enduring masterpieces, at the rate of one a day. The letters are radiant with the joy of it. 'Oh, Clara, what bliss it is to write for voice! I have done without it for too long.'

But the strain was becoming unbearable; even the sheer manual labour of writing out the music, let alone the work of composition, would be daunting. He had to rest. A visit from Liszt at this time provided a much-needed diversion; they began a lasting friendship, amid prodigious music-making and amusement. Then Clara returned to Leipzig and joined them, until at the end of March Liszt gave his final concert there and left in triumph for Paris.

At the beginning of April Clara heard many of the songs for the first time. She was overwhelmed. The few she had seen had pleased her well. 'I was delighted to find you succeeding so finely in this new form', she had written. But now she confided to her diary, 'I had never really expected anything like this. Not only my love for him but my respect for him grows more and more. No other man living has such genius for music.'

No wonder that the song-writing resumed in April with the promise of a new and greater achievement than ever.

* * *

44. (Op. 53, No. 2) Loreley (The Lorelei)

Wilhelmine Lorenz – April 1840

The waves whisper and murmur over her silent house. In the quiet moonlight a voice calls 'Remember me'. And the murmuring waves flow over her silent house; 'Remember me, remember me!'

The poetess has with palpable effort contrived one dull image and one faded rhyme to trick it out with. Schumann matches this with borrowings and clichés of his own; even so, his music is a vivid evocation, as a hint of mystery is smoothed away into memory and silence.

NOTES. 1. This was an age of earnest literary endeavour. Wilhelmine Lorenz published a whole novel in Leipzig in 1845 at only a slightly more advanced level than these words. Only some domestic or family connexion could explain how the greatest living song-writer came to set such pitiful trash; even so, Schumann must have been a very modest man. No doubt the intermediary was Oswald Lorenz, Schumann's friend and collaborator on the *Neue Zeitschrift für Musik*, to whom *Frauenliebe und-leben* was dedicated.

2. For the Lorelei legend see No. 51 below. Here the Brentano poem is in mind.

3. Schumann is not to be outdone in pastiche. The song is conceived as piano-music: bars 7–8 are typical. Bars 1 and 11 pay affectionate tribute to Schubert's *Die Stadt*. The mysterious sighing of diminished sevenths is motif 41, as in *Jasminenstrauch*. The postlude's similar but simplified arpeggio for the movement of waves is motif 21A.

45. (Op. 53, No. 3) Der arme Peter (Poor Peter)

Heine – *c.* April 1840

I

Jack and Jill are dancing together, laughing for sheer joy. But poor Peter just stands there speechless, looking as white as chalk.

Jack and Jill are groom and bride, and gleaming in wedding finery. But poor Peter is gnawing his nails and wearing his working clothes.

And as he looks sadly at them together poor Peter says quietly to himself, 'It's a good thing I'm a sensible chap or I might easily do myself a mischief.'

II

The grief in my heart will burst my breast; it drives me onward wherever I go.

It drives me to be near her, as if she could ease my pain; but when I look into her eyes I have to hurry away again.

I climb up to the high hills; at least one can be alone there. And when I reach the top, there I stand all silent and alone; and weep.

III

Poor Peter totters slowly past, pale as death and fearful. People in the street almost stop in their tracks to look at him as he goes by.

The girls whisper to each other, 'Surely he must have just climbed out of his grave?'

'Oh no, my dear young ladies, quite the other way about; he's just off to lie down in it.'

For he has lost his sweetheart; and so the grave is the best place for him, where he can lie and sleep till doomsday.

Scene one is a rustic wedding. Two hurdy-gurdy chords, and the dance begins. The words tell us about poor Peter, the onlooker and outsider. There is no place for him in the music either. His grief is felt as an intrusion, an irrelevance. At the mention of bride and bridegroom, two melodic lines dance together and are one melody; poor Peter's non-existence is made audible. Each time his name or his grief is mentioned, the dance tune returns with a renewed swinging impetus, as if to brush him aside.

He appears for the first time in scene two, his soliloquy. The piano's loud introductory chord is now minor, a stage direction of melancholy. The idea of eagerness to be away is anticipated and expressed in the rest of the piano part. There follows a more tender reflection on the sense of assuagement her presence brings. Finally there is a declaimed outpouring of grief. The tempo throughout the song has steadily slackened. At the last words it is about to come to a standstill when the piano's quick impatience to be away suddenly tugs at the sleeve, until at the end of the postlude it too acquiesces in speechless grief.

Scene three; outside the village, perhaps on the way to the hills, as the opening phrase suggests by a vague reference to the idea just heard at 'Ich steig hinauf des Berges Höh'' (I climb up to the hill-top). Here Heine's irony is obvious enough except to Schumann's music. This is a cortège, tottering gravewards in an ominous jerking rhythm that finally relaxes on a last long restful major chord.

NOTES. 1. 'So' is added in bar 13 of I to help out the melody; in III Heine has 'wenn' in bar 5, 'der Strasse' in bar 7, and 'legt sich erst ins Grab hinein' in bar 15.

2. There is no precise indication of date; but musical style, and the place of the poem at the beginning of *Buch der Lieder*, speak for early 1840. If so, the 'unhappy wedding' theme anticipates the later and finer treatment in *Das ist ein Flöten und Geigen*. There are other harbingers of *Dichterliebe*; the bride in finery is in *Ich grolle nicht*, the ironic use of the third person is in *Ein Jüngling liebt ein Mädchen*, the escape to the brow of the hill is in *Hör ich das Liedchen klingen*.

3. Musically however the song has more affinity with Op. 24 than with Op. 48. Thus the idea of effortless dancing for joy is here expressed with the wave-motion already noted in the piano part of *Berg und Burgen* (M 17), and the melodic lines of each song are closely akin. Again, the minor triad at the beginning of II here is typical of the early 1840 songs (M 7).

4. There are other interesting affinities. There is *Winterreise* in the opening chords of I (cf. the hurdy-gurdy music of *Der Leiermann*) and in the vocal line of bars 19–32 of II. The idea of being crossed in love and taking to the hills would be enough to suggest Schubert to any mind, let alone one so suggestible as Schumann's. Perhaps too it is the notice of being thrall to a heartless charmer that makes III a source book for *Waldesgespräch* (see note 3 to that song, No. 51).

5. Other motifs: I has the canonic symbolism of motif 59; II has, at bars 11–18, the calm bass notes of motif 35, which calmly contradict the words; III has the dominant question (M 43) at its bar 12.

46. (Op. 45, No. 3) Abends am Strande (Evening by the sea)

Heine – *c.* April 1840

We sat by the fisherman's house and looked out to sea. The evening mists gathered and lifted into the sky. The lights were gradually lit in the lighthouse, and in the far distance there was just one ship still to be seen.

We talked of storms and shipwreck, of the sailor and his life between sea and sky, between fear and joy. We spoke of far lands south and north, and of the strange people and strange customs to be found there.

By the Ganges it is sunny and sweet-scented, and great trees blossom, and beautiful serene people kneel before the lotus flower. But in Lapland there are small dirty folk with flat heads and wide mouths who squat round fires and cook fish and croak and howl.

The girls listened attentively, and when at last silence fell the ship was no longer to be seen; it was far too dark.

Here is a perfect illustration of an aspect of Schumann's genius that has been unaccountably neglected; an inward music of fancy engendered in the mind's eye as well as the mind's ear.

The steady quavers of the prelude evoke a full moving tide. To this strain the voice enters; and as the mists rise in the evening air the piano part rises, though the low sonorous notes of the deep sea are always heard. The music strays around in momentary confusion until the lights have all come on in the lighthouse, and the gaze can return seaward.

Then follow new themes of power and effort as the sailor's life is described, always interspersed with the regular swing of the tide. And as the talk ranges still further the music goes out in imagination to dwell on the deep sea. Thence it rises in a piano interlude, bright in an unexpected E major and devout in repeated quaver chords for the worship of the lotus-flower. Still more new music presents a comic sketch of Laplanders, ending in a most melodious howl. The two contrasting pictures are presented vivid and complete, yet without incongruity. As the music returns seawards the main theme is heard once more and then yields to a new version of the opening melody. This is now given an effect of distance and reverie by its lightly alternating quaver accompaniment, as the scene fades and dissolves into darkness.

NOTES. 1. The port is Hamburg, the 'schöne Stadt' of No. 7. 'Und' is omitted after 'breitmäulig' in bar 53; otherwise Heine's text is intact, often a sign of special responsiveness on Schumann's part. No doubt the poem's content of social satire escaped his notice; but this setting does all that music could reasonably be expected to do, and more. Its mastery suggests April or May 1840.

2. The steady quavers of the prelude are akin to Schubert's water-music (e.g. *Danksagung an dem Bach*); their significance and that of the deep bass notes throughout (M 29A) is self-evident.

3. The similarity between bars 13–16 here and bars 21–26 in *Talismane*, where the parallel thirds are evidently illustrative (M 58), might suggest that Schumann in his mind's eye was watching the lights come on not purposefully in the lighthouse but at random in the houses throughout the port.

4. Other motivic bases for the interpretation offered:

(*a*) in bars 21–28 is the strength motif 53 – nowhere used more memorably than here and in No. 77, each time in connexion with the sea (which from this and other evidence must have played a profound part in Schumann's creative procedures);

(*b*) bars 41–50 have the devout motif 38; bars 47–48 in particular suggest a study for *Frauenliebe und-leben*;

(*c*) the lowly Lapps are interestingly evoked more vividly than the lofty Hindus for both Heine and Schumann – whose music recalls *Schlusslied des Narren*, perhaps because the verse suggests their clownish appearance;

(*d*) the last bars (67 on) may well suggest the reverie of motif 32 (if so they should be played mezzo-staccato);

(*e*) a comparison of the restatement at bars 63–66 with the original statements at bars 1–4, 5–8, and 17–20 illustrates the quality of Schumann's inventiveness in this song.

47. (Op. 49, No. 1) Die beiden Grenadiere (The two grenadiers)

Heine – May 1840

Two grenadiers were on their way back to France from Russia, where they had been taken prisoner. And when they reached Germany, they hung their heads.

For there they learned the sad tidings that France was lost, the brave Grande Armée beaten and shattered, and the Emperor, their Emperor, taken prisoner.

Then the grenadiers wept together at this pitiful news. The first said, 'What pain I feel; how my old wound burns!' The second said, 'It's all over. Would we could die together. But I have wife and child at home, and they would starve without me.'

'What do I care for wife and child, my aims are far higher; if they are hungry, let them beg – my Emperor, my Emperor a prisoner!

Grant me one last wish, brother, now my life is done; take my body to France, bury me in the soil of France. Lay on my breast the medal with the red ribbon, put my musket in my hand and gird my sword about me.

So I shall lie and listen silently in my grave, like a sentry, until I hear the roar of cannon and the trampling of neighing horses. That will be my Emperor riding over my grave. There'll be a clang and a flash of many swords; and then I'll stand up from my grave armed to defend the Emperor, my Emperor!'

Heine was in Düsseldorf in 1816 and may have seen French prisoners returning from Russia. In his great poem a brief glimpse becomes enduring reality. Schumann's lyricism here as elsewhere suffuses his music with personal feeling.

The opening and closing bars are as vivid an epitome as anything in music. A sad bugle, a dull drum, two paces apart; defeated soldiers. Yet the themes have spring and pride in the step; defeated but undaunted. Then, slow harmonic twist by twist, a latent energy is keyed up until the music is at last released as the *Marseillaise*, a steel spring of French patriotism and hero-worship strong enough to hurl a dead man bolt upright sheer out of his grave. And then it is as if all this frenzied fervour is fatal; in the postlude a soldier falls and dies.

NOTES. 1. Heine's title was *Die Grenadiere*. He has '*zer*schlagen' at bar 15.

2. Schumann's lyrical and subjective treatment of the text can be illustrated by a comparison with Wagner's setting (written in the winter of 1839–40 to a French translation). This also uses the *Marseillaise*, but with a real dramatic

point at the imagined resurrection. Schumann's outburst assorts oddly with the words 'so will ich liegen und horchen still'. (I shall lie and listen in silence.) Again, Wagner's piano postlude is rightly triumphant; Schumann's adagio chords are not the note on which the poem ends. Their simple pathos after the *Marseillaise* music creates – quite unintentionally – a striking effect of irony. In each instance the music's contrast with the words is more dynamic than its compatibility; so that it is as hard to forget Schumann's song as to remember Wagner's.

3. The harmonic technique is worth noting. The music wears the simplest of uniformity. Tonic and dominant chords in march time, to a minor memory of the *Marseillaise*, are the sole material (into which the text is bundled neck and crop, with odd results in the accentuation, e.g. the first line). The dominant chord is selected for repetition and emphasis, bars 5–6. Its resolution in bar 7 however is so modest that much unresolved tension remains. The strong dominants recur, bars 9–10, and this time are not resolved at all. Through the following recitative passage the minims mark time and charge the music with rhythmic tension. Rhythm and harmony together strive to discharge at bar 18, only to misfire in the weakest resolution so far. More powder-train is laid in the feebly-resolved dominants at bars 24–25, and 33–38 and 39–41, and 43–45 and the frustrations of the march rhythm held back at bars 45–52. At last the dominants hammered with both hands at bars 53–60 finally fire off a stupefying detonation of G major as the *Marseillaise* makes its triumphant entry. Really it is not surprising that this tune bursts out uncontrollably before the sense of the verse is ready to receive it; the marvel is rather that it was held back so long.

4. There is of course the manly march motif 56; with alternate hands giving the sense of 'walking' (M 18). The recitative chords of motif 48 are apt at the words 'sprach' and the following speech. The postlude with its tolling bass semibreves (M 29^{B}) may be compared with that of *Der Soldat*, where also a soldier falls and dies. The dominant-dominated passage at bars 53–58, about the granting of a request, has the wishful acciaccature of motif 16 (to be played expressively, not as quick grace notes).

48. (Op. 49, No. 2) Die feindlichen Brüder (The brothers' feud)

Heine – April 1840

High on the hilltop stands the castle, shrouded in night; but in the valley there are flashes of light, as bright swords clash in frenzy. Those are brothers, fighting a grim vengeful duel, aflame with anger. Say, how has it come about that brothers seek redress sword in hand?

It was the eyes of Countess Laura that sparked off their quarrel. Both fell passionately in love with the fair highborn maid. But to which of the two does her heart incline? If she cannot decide, then swords must.

So they fight with desperate courage, stroke on stroke crashes down. Take care, rash swordsmen; night brings cruel strokes of ill-fortune. Alas for the wounded brothers, alas for the blood-stained valley; both fighters are felled, each by the other's steel.

Many centuries pass, many generations die away. The deserted castle frowns down from the height as before. But each night in the valley the scene changes eerily; when the first stroke of midnight sounds the brothers appear, fighting.

Elsewhere Heine was a great myth-maker, with the Lorelei and the Flying Dutchman. Here he is less successful. The language of the poem is deliberately fashioned to create the mood of far away and long ago. Schumann's music is even more stilted, and unfortunately the means are more apparent than the end in each case. But the song has atmosphere and strength in the opening theme and a wholly Schubertian charm in the contrasting love-music of the Countess Laura; and the final page where the scene is evoked in a spectral whisper is admirably effective in its way.

NOTES. 1. Heine has 'der Bergesspitze' in bars 2–3. The repetition in bars 50–53 is Schumann's.

2. The prelude may be compared with that of *Warnung* (M 24).

3. The D major section devoted to Countess Laura has the thirds of motif 57 – sharing is certainly the idea here – and bar 29 the dominant questioning of motif 43. B minor is associated with the idea of enmity.

4. There are thematic affinities with *Belsatzar* (also something of a ghost-story) e.g. in the opening vocal melody of each.

Liederkreis von Eichendorff (Cycle of songs by Eichendorff) Op. 39 and other Eichendorff settings

In April 1840 the lovers were together in Berlin, planning their marriage. Mendelssohn heard the songs, and was impressed. Spring came early and profusely to Leipzig that year. When Schumann returned he wrote to Clara . . . 'It took me by surprise to see everything suddenly in blossom.' And early in May we hear . . . 'my head is still ringing with the happiness of our time together; I can't calm down . . . and such music I have in me that I could sing the whole day through.'

The music was these songs to words by Eichendorff, which include some of Schumann's greatest masterpieces. This cycle may not be deliberately linked by any story or idea; but most of the poems are about a scene, a season, and a time – sky or forest, in spring or summer, at dusk or night time. And at all these times, in all these scenes and seasons, there is an overwhelming personal emotion; and the feeling as if in a dream, that, with the slow passing of time, something momentous is about to happen, for better or for worse, for life or death. As if in response the music blends new moods and harmonies. In particular the piano style attains a new unity, where the prelude is treated as an inseparable and integral part of the musical structure (as e.g. in Nos 54, 56, and 60). In the first edition the first song was in D major (see No. 49, note 2); but in the final form of Op. 39 the key structure itself seems to reflect the idea of gradual evolution and change. The keys proceed from F sharp minor to F sharp major, much as in *Dichterliebe* (see p. 107) but with a quite different effect. The key centres here are mainly contained within the fourth from E major or minor to A major or minor, as the songs themselves are more self-contained and withdrawn.

As in *Myrthen* there is not only this conscious order but the insight afforded by the selection and arrangement of poems. In nearly every one there is an image of movement to the sky and beyond, the Romantic ecstasy of 'elsewhere' typified by a bird that sings as it flies into the empyrean. Schumann turns this metaphor into music, and the music back again into metaphor; for him the two were interchangeable. 'I have composed so much that it almost frightens me', he writes. 'But I can't help it; I'm having to sing myself to death, like a nightingale.'

The image is a fitting one for these love songs of ecstasy and despair, triumph and pain. 'The Eichendorff cycle is my most Romantic music ever, and contains much of you in it, dear Clara.'

49. (Op. 39, No. 1) In der Fremde (Far from home)

Eichendorff – *c.* May 1840

The clouds are coming from my homeland behind the red lightning. But father and mother are long since dead, and I am forgotten there.

How soon, oh how soon, the time of silence will come when I in turn shall sleep, under the sweet murmur of the lonely woods, forgotten here too.

The piano's deep thrumming arpeggios suggest that Schumann had read Eichendorff's story *Viel Lärmen um Nichts* (Much ado about nothing) in which this song is sung by Julie to a guitar accompaniment. Perhaps the sudden accents at the crest of each successive surge of notes reflect the occasional vivid lightning-flash. They die away once the scene is evoked. Then in contrast the lowest note of each group is elegiacally prolonged. This effect, together with the sad chromatics, erects a brief memorial in tone to the memory of mother and father. Then the long minims toll out in the bass as the voice sings of the quiet time to come. Here the voice part in perfect tranquillity of mind reaches a sustained high note. There follows a magical evocation. 'Rest, peace' sighs the piano melody; the whole song cries for it; and at the thought of sleeping in the forest the idea of the rustling trees inspires Schumann to spread his right-hand chords into fronds of sound at the top. This dark melancholy music lit by intermittent but vivid flashes of insight is wholly characteristic of the composer and his relation to poetry.

NOTES. 1. The relation to the actual words is typically casual, as exemplified by the repetitions at bars 13–15, 20–21, and 22–25, the last of which distorts Eichendorff's 'und keiner mehr kennt mich auch hier'.

2. This song was not published until 1850 (the first edition of Op. 39 began with the clearly inferior *Der frohe Wandersmann*); and the manuscript copy is in Clara Schumann's handwriting. So it has been suggested that the work may be hers. However, although the hand may be Clara's, the voice is clearly Schumann's.

3. Thus, the arpeggios throughout are entirely characteristic, not only as guitar accompaniment but as the nature motif 21A; while at bars 10–11, in clear association with the word 'Stille', appears motif 26:

4. At bars 13–15 is the Clara-theme P1, in the same notes as the opening of the next song; here associated with the solemn minims of motif 35.

50. (Op. 39, No. 2) Intermezzo

Eichendorff – May 1840

In the depths of my heart I keep a radiant image of you, looking at me all the time, fresh and smiling.

And my heart sings softly to itself an old sweet song that wings into the air and swiftly flies to you.

[*In the depths of my heart I keep a radiant image of you, looking at me all the time, fresh and smiling.*]

For Schumann in his wedding year it is as if the vision of the distant beloved inspired first the thought of her, and then the idea of a journey to her side.

The wistful reverie of the opening melody is transformed by barely perceptible gradations into an impassioned flight. The impatience of the syncopated rhythm is eager to be off and away.

'My song flies to you,' says the poem, and ends. But this same idea sets Schumann's music off again, quickening and enriching the love-song of the opening bars with the notion of seeing her soon. The piano now has the added assurance of deep bass notes and octaves. The word 'fröhlich', which in the first verse meant no more than happiness, is now set laughing for joy. In the postlude the imagined picture in all its beauty comes to life in a second voice, a new twining melody that shares in a singing to which there is to be no end; a musical vow and covenant.

NOTES. 1. The repetition of the last verse is Schumann's.

2. The motto-theme P^1 signifying Clara creates the song

This melody reappears two years later in the slow movement of the A major quartet, Op. 41, No. 3, as the second subject of the Trio, Op. 80, finished in 1849, (perhaps a clue to the emotive content of these works) and again in the Lenau song *Meine Rose*. Note also theme Q^2 as the left-hand melody in bar 6.

3. The amorous dominants of motif 64 appear at bars 3–4, etc.; the added bass notes in the last section have the calm of motif 35; the right-hand semiquavers at the first 'fröhlich' are expressive of pleasure (M 10), while the second (bar 23) laughs outright as in motif 15. A form of the 'departure' motif 45 falls pat at the moment of departure; 'eilig zieht'. The syncopated rhythms of the middle section give the idea of impatience (M 61).

51. (Op. 39, No. 3) Waldesgespräch (Overheard in the woods)

Eichendorff – May 1840

'It is late, and growing cold; why are you riding lonely through the woods? The woods are wide, you are alone, let me lead you home, fair lady.'

'Great is the cunning and the deceit of men; my heart is broken for lost love. I hear hunting horns faintly blowing here and there; fly, for you know not who I am.'

'So richly adorned are steed and woman, so exquisite the young body – now I know you, God shield me! – You are the witch Lorelei!'

'I am indeed. From the towering rock my tall castle looks silently down sheer on the Rhine. Yes, it is late, and growing cold; and you shall never stir out of these woods again.'

The Lorelei seems to have been a romantic invention of Clemens Brentano. In his poem *Die Lore Lay* she is a Circean witch-figure, a Belle Dame sans Merci caught in her own toils who hurls herself from a great cliff into the Rhine. The myth-making Heine posts her back to the summit, there to sing siren songs that lure ships to destruction, thus revenging herself on mankind. Eichendorff, the poet of the German woodlands, transfers her to his own ground; and here she is less Circe than Diana the huntress, Nature herself. Schumann's naïveté stands him in good stead. As his own choice of title shows, his immediate concern is with the scene as living reality of meeting and talking in a twilit wood. His music is an encounter of man and mystery.

The hunting horns that sound in the prelude express the young man, his attention quickened. But there is no hint of apprehension, as the calmly confident bass notes tell us. On the contrary, there is eagerness and panache in the long crescendo that warningly, even condescendingly, matches the length of the forest. At 'schöne Braut' (fair lady) the music leaps forward, offering itself as a squire of dames, catching at the bridle. There follows a catch in the breath. The word 'heim' (home) which should have been the most reassuring word yet spoken, falls eerily on an interrupted cadence in the wrong key; the chord stands astonished.

In these unexpected tones the Lorelei speaks, all witchery and sweetness, melody and harp-strings. A chromatic wavering comes into the music at 'Wohl irrt das Waldhorn', evoking the imagined atmosphere of twilight and autumnal woodsmoke. The horn-passages begin again as the young man replies, dominating his words and throwing the accentuation even more awry than before. Then comes the central moment of the poem, on which all the paths of the music have converged. It should not be over-dramatized. For Schumann the revelation is not terrifying; it is even perhaps expected. The music has a mild suggestion of dismay; but its main expression is rather one of heightened awareness at the word 'Lorelei'.

The revealed Lorelei sings again in the home key of E major, now that there is no need for further disguise. And in this key the voice soars to the real climax, a new range of high notes with new piercing sweetness, a glint of magic in the dark wood.

The music has clearly established man the eager hunter, woman the defenceless quarry. But in the last few bars of the declaimed, almost spoken, voice part, the prey leaps from ambush at the huntsman, rending and tearing. In the postlude the music is held across the bar, cut off by a chill wind; the voices die in the forest, the horns are still.

NOTES. 1. The main theme is clearly conceived as piano-music. But the splendid poem is treated with fair respect. In Eichendorff's *Ahnung und Gegenwart* it is sung as a duet. The repetitions at bars 29–30, 37–38, and 61–64 are Schumann's, as is 'ist' for 'wird' in bars 7 and 57.

2. One equivalent is as effective as anything in the Lied. 'Heim' at the end of the first verse strikes an odd note in the poem, because the unexpected assonance with the word 'allein' deceives and confuses the ear. In the result, what should have been an everyday word of reassurance is made to convey mystery and magic. Schumann makes the same effect in song. There are two sources of harmonic power, the home key of everyday, and the key a major third lower, for eeriness. The word 'heim' impatiently connects the two terminals, and the music fuses.

3. For further evidence that Schumann imagines this poem as the expression of human love see the thematic affinities with *Der arme Peter*. The central moment here is paralleled in bars 9–12 there; the dénouement here in bars 22–24 there. The mood of the music is much more akin to resignation than the awe or menace of Eichendorff. Indeed it might be argued from another obvious analogue in Beethoven's *Der Mann vom Wort*, Op. 99 (bars 8–9) that the mood here is hardly more than exhortation.

4. Schumann depicts his characters vividly. The hunting horn themes that dominate words and music alike are clearly associated with the young man (M 4). These passages are also inflected with the dotted manly rhythm of motif 56, which is intensified when the Lorelei is coveted (compare piano bar 5 with 33, 8 with 36). The dominants at 12–13 are motif 64; the decoration immediately preceding the word 'schön' in bar 14 is the beauty motif 65. The Lorelei's music is all feminine. The piano part suggests slow waves and also a harp-music associated with the legendary Rhine-maidens or Heine's siren. And it is surely

revealing that the spirit of the Rhine should sing a melody very like Schubert's *Du bist die Ruh*?

5. Two more general motifs are worth noting; the interpolated C major (M 47) for the unrecognized Lorelei, and at the end of the song a most effective use of the 'music dying' motif 46.

52. (Op. 39, No. 4) Die Stille (Silence)

Eichendorff – May 1840

No one knows or can guess how happy I am. If only he *knew; no one else ever should.*

My thoughts are calmer than the snow outside, more silent than the stars above.

Would I were a bird flying out over the sea and beyond, until I reached heaven.

[*No one knows or can guess how happy I am. If only* he *knew; no-one else ever should.*]

The music despite its apparent simplicity is closely-wrought. Lightly-touched chords suggest reverie; the vocal melody is all joy. There is a sigh from the piano; if only *he* knew, 'nur Einer'. The music flows elatedly on without a break into the next verse, where the piano sings quietly to itself the voice's first tune; 'how happy I am'. This is developed into a new melody which is then given back to the voice at 'Ich wünscht' (would I were). The first verse is repeated with slight alterations that add warmth to the music; the postlude is left murmuring 'how happy' . . . 'if only'. . .

NOTES. 1. Eichendorff's third verse is omitted and his first repeated.

2. The dreamy staccato accompaniment is motif 32 throughout. There is not only a sigh but a tear, if the progression at bars 6–7 and 30–31 is any guide (M 9). This is stressed on the second appearance by an extra accent and a portamento in the voice. The idea of the starry sky forces the music steadily flatwards (M 50) from bar 12 on; the horn-passage at bars 21–22 reflects the verbal sense of pleasurable freedom (M 4).

3. The end of the song in both voice and piano anticipates the end of *Wenn ich in deine Augen seh.*

4. Cf. Mendelssohn Op. 99, No. 6.

53. (Op. 39, No. 5) Mondnacht (Moonlight)

Eichendorff – May 1840

It was as if the sky had softly kissed the sleeping earth, so that she in her bright haze of blossom could now dream only of that kiss.

The air moved through the fields and the ears of corn swayed gently; the woods murmured softly, the night was so starry-clear.

And my soul spread wide its wings and flew over the silent countryside as if it were flying home.

By common consent this is one of the world's great songs, hard to speak of with restraint.

The poem sings the bridal of earth and sky, Just so in the music. Even the first two notes are deep in the bass, high in the treble, softly bound and blurred together. Even the look of the music on the page is expressive, with its long drifting slurs and musing repetitions. Its sound is the imagery and its emotion made audible. The prelude arches serenely down and unfolds, the tenderest of nightfalls. The profound calm of the music moves in preordained patterns.

Only at the end is there a slight change of mood. The gently insistent semiquavers are heard in both hands; the piano prelude melody appears briefly in the accompaniment at the mention of the spreading of wings. Finally the calm bass notes pronounce a heart-felt Amen, the prelude wings off, the music dies away.

NOTES. 1. The poem is about spiritual communion with Nature. But Schumann is expressing its bridal imagery. Thus, Eichendorff has 'nun träumen müsst' ' – must *now* dream of him, while Schumann's text wrongly reads 'nur', must dream of him *alone*. This may be a mistranscription; or a revealing error, as in other songs.

2. We know too from a letter to Clara that he thought 'Ehe' (marriage) was 'a very musical word' (H = the note B in German). This motif is surely worn too long, too openly and too often on the piano's left hand not to have been placed there deliberately? The fourfold pattern of sustained notes occurs four times.

3. Again, the opening vocal melody is a sister-version of the Clara-theme Q[1] as in the postlude to Nos. 12 and 16 of *Dichterliebe*, with the same harmonies, including the same semitonal clash. Even the omitted first note, here B sharp, is heard later, at 'Flügel aus', etc., to complete the Q[1] theme, in a passage which emulates *Du bist wie eine Blume* (cf. its bars 5–8, top notes of the piano part) again in homage to Clara.

4. Schumann's inspiration was always love, never religion. It would not be surprising if his music faltered, if only a very little, at a conclusion about the soul winging off to its home. Some may find the sweetness of motif 12 at

the B sharp mentioned above faintly cloying; or the flat seventh (M 50) and the Amen cadence, for the idea of higher things, a little too bland.

5. There is no doubt that the ending of the song gave Schumann much difficulty. Both the first publication (in a *Neue Zeitschrift* supplement), and a manuscript version written out for Clara's mother, try out different ways of repeating 'nach Haus'.

6. In the *Neue Zeitschrift* version the mordents in bar 12, etc., were printed thus:

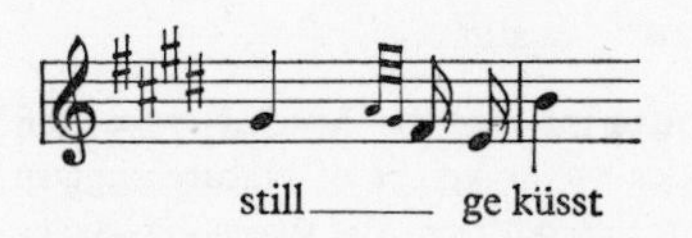

7. The prelude has the sense of 'twilight' in its key and chromatics; cf. the postlude to *Schöne Wiege*. The opening vocal phrase has the shape of the 'Stille' motif 26 to match the lulling effect of the text – 'still', 'leis', 'sacht' etc. The staccato is dream motif 32 throughout. The falling bass motif E H E, cipher or not, has the sense of deepening night (M 28). Humility (M 38) is in the repeated chords in both hands, e.g. bars 49–52, etc.; the postlude ends with the 'music dying away' motif 46, also a feature of this Opus – compare No. 9 and particularly No. 3, each in the same key.

8. The expressive use of tonality is especially important. Ears attuned to Schumann will hear in the first bars the dominant of the waking sky gradually emerging and resolving on to the home tonic of the sleeping earth at 'die Erde' all within the unity of E major; there is no question of actual modulation at any point in the song.

9. Brahms' early setting (without opus number) is worth comparing if only because its time-signature, repetitions, flattened seventh at 'nach Haus', and above all its mistake of 'nur' for 'nun' (note 1 above) show that his starting point is Schumann's song rather than Eichendorff's poem. For a similar note on Wolf, see No. 139.

54. (Op 39, No. 6) Schöne Fremde (A lovely land far away)

Eichendorff – May 1840

The branches stir and sigh as if the old gods had returned at this hour to troop around the half-ruined walls of their temples.

Here under the myrtle trees in the strange splendour of deep twilight, what is it you are murmuring to me as if in a dream, fantastic night?

All the stars look down on me with shining eyes full of love; the whole horizon cries out in ecstasy of some great joy in store.

In Eichendorff's novel *Dichter und ihre Gesellen* (Poets and their companions) the scene is set thus: 'Just then the moon came out and transformed everything into a dream. Then Fortunatus, opening the folding doors, took his guitar, and strode singing up and down through the long row of rooms.'

But Schumann's mind is already out of doors in the first bars, eaves-dropping on a conspiracy of night and trees. First the music expresses simply the idea of the night wind stirring among dark leaves. Then it is as if the secret listener hears and sees, and in turn imparts, an enriched vision of gods, twilight, starlight and a great joy in store, in a typical outpouring of romantic ecstasy.

NOTES. 1. The manuscript copy is headed 'sprechend, flüsternd' which in connexion with the idea of the voices of Nature suggests the poem of *Dichterliebe* No. 12. The affinities between the two song-cycles (see also notes to Nos. 52, 55, 58, 60, 69, and 77) may suggest that Schumann was working on both together.

2. The piano tune throughout is the 'Stille' motif 26 as in No. 49 above. The vocal melody at bars 8–9 has the contentment of motif 1. The echo of this phrase, a semitone lower, is a part of the evidence for a mystery motif 40 enhanced by the presence of the word 'heimlich' in bar 10; the D sharp minor of this sombre twilight hanging like a pall exemplifies the funeral associations of E flat minor. The 'Demut' motif 38 is made tremulous in the awe-struck music of the last section at bars 17 on; the postlude's mention and resolution of the sadness of motif 8 suggests the overcoming of doubt.

3. Brahms' *Meine Liebe ist grün*, Op 63, No. 5, seems deeply indebted to Schumann's postlude here; a tribute particularly fitting for a song the words of which were by Schumann's son Felix.

55. (Op. 39, No. 7) Auf einer Burg (An old castle)

Eichendorff – May 1840

The old knight has fallen asleep in his watch-tower. Rainstorms shower around it, and the forest rustles through the portcullis.

Beard and hair matted together, breast and ruff turned to stone, there he has sat for hundreds of years in his quiet cell.

Outside all is quiet and peaceful; everyone has gone down into the valley. Lonely forest birds sing in the empty window-arches.

Down on the sunlit Rhine a wedding party sails by; musicians are playing gaily, and the beautiful bride is in tears.

The quasi-modal tonality suggests antiquity, the static rhythm adds an oppressive quality; this is the very music of a ruined castle in a timeless heat-haze. Seemingly this treatment defeats the poet's intention of contrasting the two scenes. But the music's one impassive mood matches Eichendorff's essential thought, the slow indifferent passing of time and the river.

NOTES. 1. Something of this music's inert brooding quality was absorbed by Wolf into his setting of *Auf ein altes Bild* where also a picture is painted in quasi-modal tonality and inert rhythm.

2. This quality also owes much to the stillness of motif 26, which shapes the vocal line, e.g. at bars 10–13. The suggestion of E minor, the bass octaves, the slow movement in the part-writing (M 31, 39) remind us clearly of *Zwielicht* and vividly of *Im Rhein,* which indeed is almost the same music (compare the opening of each). The imagery is Schumann's rather than the poet's; in each case it is deeply felt. Here it even takes precedence over the 'unhappy wedding' theme which is in the poem (where the last word comes as a great surprise) but not the music, though elsewhere it is seized on by Schumann's musical imagination. It seems that the image-cluster of twilight, awe, stillness, an old building, the river Rhine, exerted a profound influence on his subconscious mind (cf. also the Rhenish symphony c. 1850).

56. (Op. 39, No. 8) In der Fremde (Far from home)
Eichendorff – May 1840

I hear the streams running in the woods, here and there; in the woods, to the sound of leaves and running water, I know not where I am.

The nightingales are calling here in the solitude as if they were singing about the lovely days of old.

In the fitful moonlight I seem to see the castle down in the valley; yet it lies so far from here.

And surely that must be my sweetheart waiting for me there in the garden filled with white and red roses? But no – she died long ago.

The piano's ceaseless flowing and sighing of semiquavers, first as melody then as accompaniment-figure, finely re-creates the sense and mood of the attractive poem, in which the half-heard sounds of the forest alternate with half-remembered memories. Against this chequered background of light and shade, sound and silence, the words are vividly evocative and colourful.

NOTES. 1, 'So' in bar 32 and the following repetitions are Schumann's.

2. The bar of piano prelude is the idea of 'rauschen', already at the outset full of the sadness of motif 8. The lightly-touched chords of the even-numbered bars are the dream motif 32 ('ich weiss nicht wo ich bin'). The staccato is indicated at bar 14 (30) and 16 (32) when the words most clearly express the mood of nostalgia.

3. The upward sixth for nightingale-song in bar 10 (M 19) recurs in *Wehmut* to the same notes.

4. Perhaps it was the idea of timelessness that made the opening melody quote that of *Auf einer Burg*.

5. Cf. Joseph Marx.

57. (Op. 39, No. 9) Wehmut (Sadness)

Eichendorff – May 1840

True, I can often sing as though I were glad; but then tears flow, relieving my heart.

So nightingales, when spring breezes blow, sing a song of yearning from the prison of their cage.

Then all hearts listen and all are glad; but no one feels the pain and deep sadness in the song.

In Eichendorff's story *Ahnung und Gegenwart* (Future and Present) the poem is introduced thus: 'When Frederick came to Erwin's door that evening he heard a voice within singing the following words, without any instrumental accompaniment, to a moving melody.' Of all song-writers Schumann was least likely to write for unaccompanied voice. But his setting embodies one of his most moving melodies, which certainly dominates the musical expression. In other ways too he surmounts with éclat the problems presented by this ostensibly simple lyric. 'Deep inside my song there is sadness;' says the poem 'but no one can tell'. So the music by sounding joyful must somehow convey the impression of sadness. Schumann's heart goes into the singing. In the piano part not only is the melody enriched but there is added expression. The rising sixths are the glad song; there is even a suggestion of tears. And when in the next verse a new melody is brought in, the rising intervals are still there but widened into the yearning octaves so typical of Schumann. Finally, with the return to the opening melody in the last verse, form enhances meaning in a wholly Wolfian way. Here the two ideas are interfused; the melody singing, the piano part yearning and sighing. In the postlude there comes at last the subtle and allusive hint that shows deep correspondence with the poetic idea. For a brief moment plaintive bass notes are added, scarcely audible in the depths of the left hand; 'deep sadness' indeed, and usually passing unnoticed as the poem says.

NOTES. 1. Eichendorff has 'so' not 'es' in bar 9 and 'Käfigs' not 'Kerkers' in bar 16.

2. The rising sixth associated with singing (M 19) occurs here also in the voice part, at 'Lied'; and, in the previous song, on the word 'Nachtigallen' (which may be part of the associative process). The yearning of motif 16 is ubiquitous, most obviously at bars 10–13. The E sharp at bar 6 moving on to the supertonic is explicable as a reaction to the word 'Tränen' and hence a variant of motif 13. There is motif 8 in the bass at the beginning of bar 26, no doubt the subconscious equivalent of the 'tiefste Leid' just mentioned. The preceding

dominants (M 64) suggest that this song is thought of as a love-song. In the last few notes is the 'music dying away' motif 46.

58. (Op. 39, No. 10) Zwielicht (Twilight)

Eichendorff – May 1840

Twilight is about to spread its wings, the trees stir and shiver, clouds drift by like oppressive dreams; what does all this dark mystery mean?

If you have a pet deer let it not graze alone; hunters are about in the woods sounding their horns, voices echo here and there.

If you have a friend in this world, trust him not at this hour; his eyes and lips may be smiling but in treacherous peace he is plotting war.

Whatever now goes tired to rest will rise again tomorrow; but many things can be lost in the night for ever, so keep awake, be on your guard.

In *Ahnung und Gegenwart* this song is heard sung as it were off-stage by a voice within a forest. There is dramatic point in its effect on the listeners in Eichendorff's story, where the verses are a warning against infidelity. Schumann's brooding symbolism seems to express an even deeper betrayal, a flaw in the fabric of the world.

The slowly-moving quavers of the piano prelude paint a grey twilight blackening into a deep bass night. This serves as a back-cloth for the vocal melody. In the next verse the bass octaves are deeper and darker still. Then at the idea of the treacherous friend the bass line rises in ominous syncopation and changes into the menace of jerking octaves. When the last verse points the moral the music undergoes a final and very revealing change. The wavering melodic figures stiffen into repeated quaver chords over a slow firm bass; the voice falls into a recitative suggesting the matter-of-fact tones of everyday speech, punctuated by sharply decisive chords. In every note we can hear Schumann privately resolving never to be taken unawares.

NOTES. 1. Eichendorff has 'müde gehet' in bars 33–34, and 'bleibt' for 'geh' and 'bleib' for 'sei' in bars 37 and 39 respectively.

2. This melancholy twilit effect of E minor quavers creeping along in Indian file is also a feature of *Mein Herz ist schwer* in the same characteristic rhythm (M 33). The semiquavers of *Muttertraum* have almost the same notes though in a different key, with the same nocturnal effect; cf. also *Im Rhein*.

3. Other obvious thematic points are the dominant question at bar 15 (M 43), and the perplexed effect of the diminished sevenths throughout (M 41) – particularly in their extended use in bar 26 and again in bar 32 to bracket off the moment of betrayal. The last section has the declamatory effect of motif 30 as in e.g. *Ich grolle nicht*. The closing chords are those of *Ich hab im Traum geweinet*,

and share their effect of dire finality. There is also, predictably, the recitative motif 48 in this concluding passage.

4. Much of the music derives from the Clara-theme P[1].

59. (Op. 39, No. 11) Im Walde (In the forest)

Eichendorff – May 1840

A wedding procession passed by the hillside; I heard the birds singing. Then riders came flashing by, sounding their horns; a gay hunt.

But before I had realized it the echoes had died away. Now darkness covers the land. The only sound I hear is the forest sighing from the hillside, and deep in my heart I feel afraid.

The first part of the poem is not description but recollection. So interpreted, the music can very powerfully evoke a reverie of the scenes it describes, and the awe and mystery of them.

The pattern of reiterated notes in the bass moves down stepwise from E to D to C sharp with a new long chord for the new mood at 'Eh ich's gedacht' (before I realized). There is a move up to D sharp and another long chord at 'Die Nacht'. Then the first note E is heard again, persistent as before, but now part of the dominant not the tonic; a question rather than a statement, a funeral knell rather than a marriage bell. At the end this pattern finally moves down stepwise on to a low A as the voice's falling octave goes down to the depths of the heart.

NOTES. 1. Schumann has 'schauert's' for 'schauert', and repeats the last line.

2. The opening melody recurs in the minor in *Der Spielmann*, also for a wedding.

3. It seems possible that Schumann had in mind Mendelssohn's *Jagdlied*, Op. 84, No. 3, which also deals with time passing into evening in the woods with a hunt, a horn, birdsong, twilight, and a feeling in the heart. Its melody that recurs at each mention of birds precedes and follows the one mention of birds in this song.

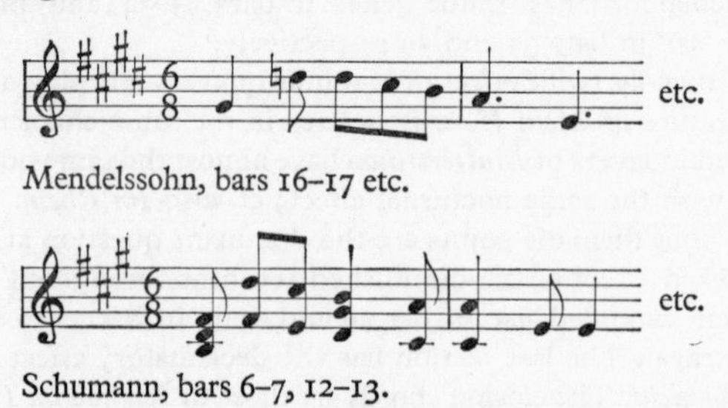

Mendelssohn, bars 16–17 etc.

Schumann, bars 6–7, 12–13.

4. Note the mysterious effect of contrasting tonality (M 40) at the mention of night in bars 27–30.

5. Schumann set the poem again for a capella choir nine years later with a middle verse added: Op. 75, No. 2. Cf. also Medtner Op. 46, No. 4.

60. (Op. 39, No. 12) Frühlingsnacht (Spring night)

Eichendorff – May 1840

Over the garden through the night air I heard the birds come flying in; that means spring scents soon, and already the blossoming is beginning in the garden.

I feel joy and tears together, as if it could only be a dream. All the old miracles come thronging back bright in the moonlight.

And the moon and the stars say, and the dreaming woods whisper, and the nightingales sing 'She is yours; yours!'

The poem typifies the Eichendorff vision; an ecstatic quickening of flowers, moon and stars, tears of joy, and a welter of returning wings far up in the stretches of a spring night, all to make a brief love-song. No composer could resist it, least of all Schumann in his wedding-year. His ecstasy is perhaps too clearly a pianist's rather than a song-writer's; but the song has moments of unexampled loveliness – the visionary wings in the prelude, the opening vocal melody, or the way in which the music dreams and glows at the mention of flowers and moonlight.

NOTES. 1. Eichendorff has 'übern' in bar 1 and 'in Träumen' in bars 20–21.

2. The most evident anomaly is the different scansion in voice and piano. Thus the vocal phrase begins as the piano's ends, in a way which was just right for Wolf but which in Schumann sounds like a miscalculation (athough this effect is deliberate in Op. 39).

3. The decorated melodic line of the piano's first two bars, heard again as the opening melody of *Und wüssten's die Blumen*, is the Clara-theme P/P¹.

4. This idea sustains the music for the first nine bars. Then the impulse slackens perceptibly; and when Schumann's own creative voice is silent his memory becomes audible. First he thinks of Beethoven's *Adelaide*, Op. 46 (perhaps because that fine song also has a garden in springtime in the evening air; e.g. at the piano interlude before 'Abendlüftchen'). At bar 14 the piano solo takes the form of Chopin's prelude No. 17. Bar 25 is a reminiscence of the sixth bar from the end of his own *Reconnaissance*, Op. 9, No. 14, while the last bar of the postlude is also in effect the last bar of his *Blumenstück*, Op. 19. Perhaps all these had special meaning for him.

61. (Op. 77, No. 1) Der frohe Wandersmann (The merry wanderer)

Eichendorff – May 1840

God's elect are sent out into the world to see his marvels by mountain, forest, river, and field.

The idle ones, the stay-at-homes, they are not quickened by the sunrise each morning; they know only the rearing of children, sorrow, worry and hunger.

The springs leap from the mountain, the larks on high sing for joy; and why should not I be singing with them, full-throated and fresh-hearted?

I place all my trust in God who holds brooks, larks, woods and field, earth and sky, in his hands; and that is the right way of life for me.

Ostensibly a brisk rousing folk-song melody and accompaniment. But somehow the setting despite its obvious attractions has never gained widespread acceptance; as with most of Schumann's attempts at the popular vein, the poem is better known and more widely sung to another tune. This may be because of a certain diffidence about the music, as if, despite its protestations, it could quite easily be persuaded to stay at home itself, or at least be back well before nightfall.

NOTES. 1. The final repetition is Schumann's, to make a rousing peroration. Eichendorff has 'Den lieben Gott lass ich nur walten' in bars 33–34. Perhaps the slip echoes the chorale title which Schumann had in mind in writing No. 10 above. This song reminds us of No. 11 (cf. e.g. bars 5–6 of each) and is also in debt to the F major *Novellette* (cf. the tune at bars 9–10 here with bars 3–4 of Op. 21, No. 1). Perhaps this music began as a sketch for Op. 24, a love-song with Clara-themes.

2. Schumann himself found it unsatisfactory; originally the first of Op. 39, it was replaced by *In der Fremde* from the second edition on.

3. Another unconvincing song of the open road is *Freisinn*, No. 13. (Cf. its bars 8–9 with bars 11–12 here.)

4. Most of the piano movement is in brisk marching quavers (M 56); but where the word God occurs (e.g. at bars 3 and 33–34) the music hastily reverts to even crotchets, as if other expressions were insufficiently reverent.

5. Note the musical response to the word 'träge' in bar 13, etc., which fires off a triple canon ending in bass octaves just for the idea of slothful dragging (M 59A). The horn passages (M 4) refer to the open-air theme. The quaver notation, especially at bar 23 et seq., suggests the reverie of motif 32.

6. The postlude shows that Schumann, though he may not have shared Eichendorff's gay vein of natural piety, had views of his own; and once free of the burden of conforming to the words he can make a very attractive thing out of the ideas of manliness, dream and joy (with characteristic motifs for each).

Dichterliebe, Liedercyklus von Heine (A Poet's Love, song cycle to words by Heine) Op. 48 and other Heine settings

Hardly were the Eichendorff songs sketched than the inspired Schumann began the Heine songs known as *Dichterliebe*, still in the same masterly vein. Again there is the same pattern of conscious order and subconscious revelation. First, there is harmonic diversity in the contrasts between the vocal and instrumental cadences. For example the voice may end on a dominant while the piano postlude continues on to a tonic, whether at once as in No. 2 or at length as in No. 6; or the tonal relationship between the two closes may be altogether more complex, as in No. 1 or No. 9. Conversely, the harmony may continue as a unifying force throughout two or more separate songs. For example, the tonics at the end of the piano part in Nos 2 and 3 can be conceived as dominants leading into Nos 3 and 4. Finally the large-scale harmonic scheme, instead of being confined to a few tonalities in a modest range, as in the Eichendorff *Liederkreis*, traverses a whole circle of keys from F sharp minor back to C sharp minor/major, to make a great cycle of songs. In these and other ways the music is to be a universal symbol of a love endlessly lost and endlessly renewed, like springtime and sunrise after dearth and darkness.

It tells the story of Schumann's own estrangement from Clara, and the bitter hurt it cost him; and then his reunion with her and their lifelong love. Perhaps he had already formed some ideas earlier in the year when he had turned to Heine's *Buch der Lieder* for the texts of Op. 24 and three songs of Op. 25, all for Clara. This opus has Clara-themes in common with both these works and with the *Davidsbündler*, Op. 6.

The personal approach would be clear from the music alone. But it could also be inferred from the title. In Rückert's *Liebesfrühling* (Love's Springtime) which Schumann had just used as a source-book for some of the songs of *Myrthen*, Op. 25, we find

> 'Dichterlieb' hat eignes Unglück stets betroffen.
> Hohe Götter, lasset mich das Beste hoffen!'

('A poet's love has always met with its own special misfortune; let me hope for the best, oh high gods!')

Schumann, we know, approved of the term 'Dichtungen' (=poetry, or fine writing) as applied to musical composition; and thought of himself as a 'Dichter', or imaginative writer, as in the piece entitled *Der Dichter spricht* in Op. 15. It seems then that *Dichterliebe*, Op. 48, could be expected to express Schumann's own knowledge of love, with its joys and sorrows, its hopes and fears; and certainly the impression left by the music after repeated hearings is an overwhelmingly personal one.

It happens that Heine's poems are the same in essence, if not in flavour. So worldliness is fused with innocence, irony annealed with passion, to make the uniquely bright and indestructible alloy which has been called the most perfect of love-song cycles.

62. (Op. 48, No. 1) Im wunderschönen Monat Mai

Heine – May 1840

In the lovely month of May, when all the buds were breaking into bloom, love rose up in my heart.

In the lovely month of May, when all the birds were singing, I told her of my love and longing.

Here is a perfect example of Heine's art; simple in words, clear in design, rich in allusion. Love unfolds like a flower, sings like a bird, with easy inevitability. Love comes in at the eye, as a received impression of beauty and wonder, and wells from the throat, as an outgoing expression of gratitude and joy. Love flowers with the season, as if flowering were the world's way of falling in love; and sings with the birds, as if bird-song were the world's way of declaring its love. Reality itself is expressed as a symbol of feeling, with all creation flowering and singing in spring sunshine.

Such a lyric calls out music. Yet Schumann varies the plain sense of Heine's poem. That, on any level of meaning, is all love and joy. But the song begins and ends on a *discord* in a *minor* key. The happiness is over and done, and is remembered with aching regret. The prelude is the music of the past tense; wistful in its minor tonality, hesitant in its uneven rhythm, with fitful gleams of remembered melody. The voice enters as reminiscence, not actuality. True, the tonality has lightened into Schumann's springtime key of A major: there is a new singing melody. But its first notes recall the plaintive prelude. The discords, the hesitation are still there. Further, each verse is framed in this sorrow; the prelude is repeated as interlude and postlude, finally breaking off unstilled on an unresolved dominant seventh. The love finds no answer, the longing no response.

NOTES. 1. Schumann is expressing a time when Clara's love seemed lost to him. His treatment of the words is a perfect match for this meaning; note how the ostensibly joyful opening melody has a poignantly dissonant appoggiatura on 'wunderschön'. Conversely, the rising of love is celebrated with a rising sequence which despite its modest compass has a skylark lift and lilt; and the piano's unexpected B flats, at each mention of love ('Liebe' in the first verse, 'Sehnen' in the second) warmly enhance the meaning of the words.

2. The piano prelude is in F sharp minor, as required by the key-sequence of the cycle as a whole; and yet there is not one single tonic chord in the song, even at the end. The sorrow that suffuses it remains unspoken. Against that evocative background the voice's A major remembers past happiness – in effect the harmonic interpolation of motif 47.

3. The tiny changes undergone by the prelude are worth noting, e.g. how the jerky rhythm of the right hand in bar 2 is smoothed out in bars 13 and 24, while semiquavers are added in the bass in the later passages. In this music germinate the ideas of Nature (M 21) of singing (M 19) and sadness (M 8 in the bass); together suggesting a love lost in spring, and so ending on the pleading dominant seventh of motif 44. See also No. 70, note 3.

4. Cf. Franz, Op. 25, No. 5.

63. (Op. 48, No. 2) Aus meinen Tränen

Heine – May 1840

From my tears there will spring many a flower in bloom; my sighs become a choir of nightingales.

And if you love me, little one, I'll give you all the flowers; and the song of the nightingale shall be heard at your window.

In the poem, flowers and bird-song are elemental symbols. They also have an evident figurative meaning, namely Heine's own poems (in the *Lyrisches Intermezzo*).

But Schumann's more literal imagination is moving in the sunlit garden and the moonlit glade, creating a music first of bright certainty then of shadowy doubts. The opening phrases are offered as simple diatonic statements of fact. Then the tonality clouds over at 'wenn du mich lieb hast' (if you love me); and when the simple brightness of the first music resumes it has a lingering trace of rhythmic diffidence, of chromatic wistfulness, turning 'if' into 'if only'. This easy inevitability of musical expression is pure Schubert of the golden age; and with it goes a sighing fervour that is inimitably Schumann's own.

NOTES. 1. The engaging aptness of motif 45 for the bestowing of flowers at bars 11–12 shows both the literal-mindedness of the music and its underlying sadness; that motif depends for its meaning on the use of the dominant, which confirms the key at that moment as the F sharp minor of the previous song. Similarly the slight chromatic alterations of the flattened seventh at bars 12–13 and the flattened sixth at bar 14 suggest reverence and sadness (M 50 and 8). As if in explanation the left hand at 'if you love me' in bars 9–10 pensively adds 'Clara' (theme X).

2. Note the dream motif 32 in the staccato in bars 1–2 etc. (which is worth comparing with the opening bars of Op. 24, No. 1) and the typical lingering mediants of Eusebius (M 63) in the opening melody (cf. the opening of *Volksliedchen*, No. 42, also about a garden).

64. (Op. 48, No. 3) Die Rose, die Lilie

Heine – May 1840

The rose, the lily, the dove, the sun, I loved them all once in the bliss of love. I love them no longer, I love her alone, my little sweet gentle love, my own one; she herself is the source of all love, she is rose and lily, dove and sun.

Heine's flowers and birds and sunlight have now lost much of their cosmic force, and are little more than decorative. But they are still attractive, and they set the composer an exacting task. The song must conjure up an excitement of colour, fragrance, brightness and wings; and then go on to express a greater radiance within which all others are dimmed. Schumann does just this. The small miracle works more easily at first hearing than later, more readily in youth than after; but with a freshness renewed for each new hearer, so that the shortest-breathed song in the history of the Lied may be among the longest-lived.

NOTES. 1. Heine has 'Bronne' not 'Wonne' in bar 10.

2. Note the change from the decorative pattern of semiquavers to the expressive quavers at bar 9; and the correspondence between bar 13 etc. and Op. 24, No. 1, at 'träumend wie in halben Schlummer'.

3. The Clara-theme P[1] appears at bars 10–11 and again at 12–13.

4. This song, like No. 72, sounds a little surprising in its context; the music of both runs counter to the prevailing mood of the cycle.

5. Cf. Franz, Op. 34, No. 5.

65. (Op. 48, No. 4) Wenn ich in deine Augen seh

Heine – May 1840

When I look into your eyes all my sorrow and pain vanish; when I kiss your lips I am healed and whole again; when I lay my head on your breast the bliss of Heaven steals over me. But when you say 'I love you' I cannot choose but weep bitterly.

The insistent self-effacing rhythm of the piano part, the gentle melodic murmur of the voice, give the music a calm sweetness which absorbs and counters the venom of Heine's last line. Schumann offers tears of humility and unworthiness.

The piano rhythm begins as a docile echo of the opening phrase; then it moves forward with a kissing eagerness at 'wenn ich küsse'; then it is given added melody and added harmonic tension with a sustained dominant chord leaning across the barline at 'wenn ich mich lehn' etc.; and then it stands still in wondering perplexity after 'wenn du sprichst', before resuming in the meditative postlude.

NOTES. 1. Heine means that 'Ich liebe dich' was a lie. But Schumann is innocent of innuendo. His music's meaning is not even discontent, let alone distress. The key to it is the humility of motif 38, coupled with the expressive use of harmony. Thus the tonality is flattened reverently in what is for Schumann a dizzying plunge of self-abasement from the tonic to the subdominant side of the subdominant in only a few bars (4–7). (This unusually dramatic version of motif 50 is perhaps under the influence of the word '*Himmels*lust' later on.) The quasi-religious strain persists in the organ-like chords of the postlude. This, together with the tense diminished sevenths of motif 41 awaiting the release of 'ich liebe dich', and the lack of any musical equivalent for a rather obvious verbal point suggests that Schumann's sole idea is that of adoring and humble devotion. The opening mediant melody is again very Eusebian (M 63).

2. Note the aptness of motif 45 at 'so *schwindet* all mein Leid und Weh'.

3. Since the songs are essentially piano-music, the voice has every reason to sing the higher notes in bar 7.

4. Cf. Franz, Op. 44, No. 5: and an early setting by Hugo Wolf.

66. (Op. 48, No. 5) Ich will meine Seele tauchen

Heine – May 1840

Let me plunge my soul into the chalice of the lily. Then the lily will resound and breathe a song of my beloved.

The song will tremble and quicken like the kiss her mouth once gave me in a magically sweet hour.

The previous song was hardly more than wistfully perplexed, though the words hinted at tragedy. In this one, where the words are blissfully erotic, the music, especially in the postlude, is frankly sad; the next song too has a more sombre colouring than the words require. In Schumann's mind these are poems about lost love.

The shivering delicacy of the demisemiquaver piano part responds to the idea of tremulousness in the words; its effect is to draw a veil of sound over Heine's erotic symbolism. The harmony may come from deeper sources; it is the progression associated with the memory of past happiness in the first song of the cycle. Once again past joy is seen in vision through present tears; the postlude is all regret.

NOTES. 1. Perhaps Heine's symbolism escaped Schumann; see No. 79. Yet the melody is obviously thinking only of Clara; the song begins with her theme Y thrice, followed by her theme P^1. The B minor form of each is strongly reminiscent of the running theme in the *Davidsbündlertänze* Op. 6, also heard in Op. 24.

2. For harmonic parallels with *Im wunderschönen Monat Mai* compare bars 1–2 (3–4) and 9–10 (11–12) here with 9–10 (20–21) there; and bars 5–6 (13–14) here with 11–12 (22–23) there.

3. The postlude has the sorrow of motif 8 and something of the nobility of motif 51 in the minor, suggesting a conscious (almost self-conscious) renunciation.

4. Cf. Franz, Op. 43, No. 4.

67. (Op. 48, No. 6) Im Rhein, im heiligen Strome

Heine – May 1840

In the holy river Rhine there is mirrored the great holy city of Cologne with its great cathedral.

In the cathedral there is a picture painted on golden leather; into the wilderness of my life it came smiling in like sunshine.

Flowers and angels float round Our Lady; her eyes, her lips, her cheeks are just like my beloved's.

Slow tempo, dark E minor tonality, insistent dotted rhythm, suggest a sombre and awe-struck twilit reflection, a great cathedral mirrored in a great river. In the flowing treble the slow waves of the Rhine heave endlessly down; the bass octaves stand up in strength and majesty.

After the first verse has set the scene Schumann's mind moves in procession into the cathedral, where the piano's new theme of organ-tones in thirds now appears within the opening cathedral-music. Again the images converge as the vision narrows from the broad and dark-coloured canvas of the first verse to the charming and colourful miniature of the second. By the words 'freundlich hinein gestrahlt' we are already in a different setting, a different world.

The way back leads through chromatics, as vivid and mysterious as the painting itself. The piano thrice has a supplicating gesture of rising octaves; the rhythm is stilled at the final mention of the beloved; the harmony is for a while poised questioningly on the dominant for the first and only time in the song.

But the only answer is the continued inexorable movement back to the vast and sombre opening scene. In the postlude the music emerges to contemplate the vision of moving water and unmoving stone, bringing with it from the poem the memory of a love as selfless and as eternal as they, until finally the images waver and blur into silence.

NOTES. 1. Schumann repeats 'die Lippen' in bar 38.

2. Schumann's genius is for making sonorous images in the light of the verses; and here his focus is so intense that the image is apparently inverted as the poem suggests. The sombre left-hand octaves stand like stone for the cathedral, the right-hand figurations flow like water for the river.

3. In a sense Heine's meaning is also inverted. In the words of Franz, whose Op. 18, No. 2, is worth comparing, Schumann 'depicts Gothic arches and columns; however, it is not these but the picture that is the main point of the poem'. True enough; but then Franz and his music and his acumen are all lost in the shadow of this masterpiece (see also No. 95, note 3).

4. It is possible that the Clara-theme X is inverted or otherwise alluded to at the words 'gleichen der Liebsten genau', (compare 'Lied von der Liebsten mein' in the previous song).

5. The opening bass semibreves have the notion of courage in adversity expressed by these notes elsewhere in the 1840 songs (M 5). The right-hand waves are motif 21; the rising octaves and tenths in the piano at bars 35, 37, 39 are the yearning motif 16. Note also M 31 and M 39, e.g. in the postlude.

6. For the passage said to have strayed in from some different world of song see No. 42, note 2.

7. Cf. Liszt (two versions).

68. (Op. 48, No. 7) Ich grolle nicht

Heine – May 1840

I shall not chide you, though my heart break; oh love forever lost, I shall not chide.

What though you shine in the splendour of diamonds; no ray falls into the night of your heart, that I have long known. [*I shall not chide you, though my heart break.*]

I saw you in vision, and saw the serpent that gnaws at your heart; I saw my love, how truly wretched you are. [*I shall not chide you.*]

The words speak of sympathy, forgiveness, even a measure of reconciliation. But under the music lies a different story. The vehement accents, the hammered chords, the declamatory style, all suggest the Old Testament rather than the New; the brooding tread of the bass minims sounds almost menacing or retributive. And yet the song begins with heartbreak; and at the word 'Herz' the poignantly flattened sixth and the tense harmony contradict the natural notes and plain chords of the previous bar. So throughout the song it is as if anguished chromatic harmonies are being forced into a stoic C major. The music seems to express an unconquerable resolve never again to be made to suffer through weakness.

NOTES. 1. Tension between music and words is heightened by Schumann's insistence on the phrase 'ich grolle nicht', which he has six times to Heine's twice, thus protesting too much. The repetitions of 'ewig verlornes Lieb' and 'wenn das Herz auch bricht' are also his.

2. The authenticity of the alternative high notes in bar 27, etc., has been questioned. They do not appear in the manuscript version, and so may be an afterthought; and they are arguably inappropriate to the poem. On the other hand, they are authentic; they are the piano's melodic line, and therefore a first choice for the vocal line in any Schumann song; they are clearly motivic (the logical continuation of the ascent begun at bar 23, and deriving from the idea of 'ewig verlornes Lieb' at bars 5–8); they are appropriate to the sense of the poem as Schumann conceives it; and they are undeniably more effective. Of course they should be sung.

3. There is sorrow (M 8) at the flattened sixth on 'Herz' and strength (M 53) in the dominant–tonic movement at bars 12–16. The postlude hammers home the rhythm of 'Ich grolle nicht' yet again, with perhaps a slightly self-conscious air of self-denial, complete with the nobility of motif 51.

69. (Op. 48, No. 8) Und wüssten's die Blumen

Heine – May 1840

If only the little flowers knew how deeply wounded my heart is, they would weep with me to heal my pain.

And if the nightingales knew how sad and ill I am, they would make the air ring with song to restore me.

And if the golden stars knew my sorrow they would come down from the sky and comfort me.

But none of these can know my grief; it is known to one alone, and she it is who has torn my heart asunder.

Flowers, birds, and stars had cosmic significance in the earlier lyrics. Here they are imaged as comforters in grief. Schumann sees them also as decorative pictures, to which he responds with demisemiquaver broken chords that flutter and twinkle over a mood of minor melancholy. At the same time the harmonic foundations of these chords give the music a strength and stability that enhances the poem. This lends life to the mysterious moment where new expressive sighing melodies steal into treble and bass as the poem turns aside to say, ruefully and realistically, 'no, they cannot help me'; while for the climactic 'zerrissen' (torn) that smooth texture is split apart to reveal an underlying music of dark and wild despair.

NOTES. 1. Heine has 'die', not 'sie', in bar 24. Some older Peters editions misprint 'Trotz' (defiance) for 'Trost' (comfort) in bar 23.

2. Perhaps the second verse was a main source of the music; the scansion is apter, and the sad flat supertonic fits the word 'krank'. If so the musical imagery may be the idea of birds' wings; which would explain the analogy with *Frühlingsnacht*. Both begin with the Clara-theme P/P[1] (see No. 60, note 3); here the two following bars are filled, for good measure, with the Clara-theme Y; and her theme X is twice used almost accusingly in the closing words (an interesting contrast with the identifying use of this theme as the opening of the lotus flower in *Die Lotosblume*).

3. There is much evidence in the songs of the bitter hurt that Schumann suffered during his quarrel with Clara; rich music still wells freely from that source three and four years later. Here this obsessive personal involvement can be heard in the music, distracting it from the poem. Thus in Heine the last verse chills with reality. But its mention of 'one alone' elicits what in Schumann's terms is a *warmer* expression of major third and dominant seventh; which is in turn contradicted by the startling vehemence of the postlude. This is not explicable by reference to the poem; the composer's mind is elsewhere.*

4. With the postlude cf. the beginning of *Kreisleriana*, which may have a similar expressive meaning.

5. Cf. Franz, Op. 12, No. 6: Mendelssohn Op. 9, No. 10.

70. (Op. 48, No. 9) Das ist ein Flöten und Geigen

Heine – May 1840

There's a blowing of flutes and a scraping of fiddles, with trumpets blaring in; my own true love must be dancing there at her wedding feast.

And among all this tinkling and booming, this pounding and puffing, you can still hear the angels weep.

The piano prelude compresses song and poem into one brief statement. Under the stamping and swinging of the wedding dance one bass note is

* For a suggested explanation see the *Musical Times*, August 1965, pp. 586–7.

unobtrusively repeated, hinting at the self-torturing images that distilled their jealous rage into Heine's fine verses. This music expresses not so much the imagined sound of the wedding music as its imagined effect on a rejected lover listening outside. In the resentful mind the harmonies have become discordant, the melodies distorted – the musical equivalent of Heine's contemptuous description. When the scene is identified at 'Herzallerliebste mein' (my own true love) the dormant dominant pedal notes awaken in rage as accented octaves hammering out despair. In the postlude the harmonic clashes are more acrid than ever as the taste of the hated wedding music and its meaning rises like bile in the mouth. Finally the lover is imagined as wrapping his cloak around him and departing into the night, the music still a jagged hurt to the jealous mind until at last the sound of the festivities dies away.

NOTES. 1. This is the music of Schumann's jealous fantasies about Clara's marriage to another (perhaps also the source of his frequent choice of poems on this theme). His personal emotion, though congruent with the poem, is expressed first as piano-music, on which the vocal melody has somehow to be grafted, regardless of Heine's scansion. Hence the repetitions at bars 12–15, 28–31, 42–46, 58–62, to make up the required phrase lengths; hence four alterations of the words to preserve the dactylic rhythm of the music, viz, 'darein' for 'drein' at bars 10–11, the insertion of 'wohl' at bar 21, the change from 'von Pauken und Schalmein' at bars 46–49, and the substitution of 'lieblichen' for 'guten' at bar 63.

2. The accompaniment is fashioned entire from the Clara-theme X; while at 'Herzallerliebste' (my best beloved) occurs the longest linking of that theme found anywhere in Schumann. We have heard such links before in *Ich wandre nicht* and *Mit Myrthen und Rosen*: but the record eightfold repetition here is worth quoting:

3. The opening vocal phrase is kin to the 'wedding' melody of *Der Spielmann*. The opening piano phrase is, consciously or not, related to that of the first song of *Dichterliebe*, which may account for the sadness already in that song. This melodic cell (example E on p. 2) seems to have some special meaning for Schumann; cf. the opening of *Aufschwung*, Op. 12 and bars 12–13 of *Der Dichter spricht*, Op. 15.

4. Wedding music suggests instrumentation; just as in *Der Spielmann* and Op. 29, No. 3, the texture is quasi-orchestral, prefiguring Mahler and Strauss. In particular compare e.g. bars 33–34 with Mahler's *Des Antonius von Padua Fischpredigt*, though of course the material is used quite differently.

5. The major third of the final chord well exemplifies the 'music dying away' motif 46.

71. (Op. 48, No. 10) Hör ich das Liedchen klingen

Heine – May 1840

When I hear the song that once my true love sang, my heart seems to burst with a wild leap of pain.

A dark longing drives me out to the high woods; and there my overwhelming grief finds its relief in tears.

In the poem the song is heard from time to time, by chance. Schumann's music finely conveys that it is there in the bereaved mind all the time, unforgettable. The right hand of the prelude suggests the lingering memory of it, with its wistful syncopations. The voice begins with this same melody now made manifest. As the vocal line briefly changes at 'so will mir die Brust zerspringen' (my heart seems to burst) so the piano recalls the song with tearful harmonies. The next verse quietly speaks of escape to the high hills. But no sooner is the voice there than the song comes bursting out again in the piano part, as it were involuntarily; and it breaks in before the voice has finished its phrase, so that both halves of the tune sound together in the piano as in the distraught mind. Then it seems that the postlude tries to be rid of this too painful memory. Two bars of thrusting and tightening syncopations labour to wrench the thoughts elsewhere; unsuccessfully, as the last bass notes show.

NOTES. 1. Heine has 'vor' not 'von' in bar 10.

2. The brilliant intuitive organization of this masterly song presages Wolf. Its intensity again suggests a strong personal emotion of grief for Clara. The main 'Liedchen' theme sings of her, and her theme in its enchained X form as in No. 70 dominates the postlude.

3. The passage at bars 24–25 may have had some cryptic meaning for Schumann: it occurs in the *Abegg* variations, *Papillons*, *Carnaval*, and elsewhere, in contexts suggesting the idea of remembered music.

4. Cf. Franz, Op. 5, No. 11.

72. (Op. 48, No. 11) Ein Jüngling liebt ein Mädchen
Heine – May 1840

A boy loves a girl who prefers another; but he in turn loves another and marries her. So the girl, out of pique, marries the first man that comes along, and the boy takes it badly.

It's an old story, yet always a new one; and when it happens to someone it breaks his heart.

Perhaps this eternal pentagon really happened to Heine; but not to Schumann. True, he knew about being jilted and jealous, and this knowledge is important for *Dichterliebe.* But here he is in a more detached, even amused, frame of mind. The song is all dancing high spirits – until the key phrases; first 'der Jüngling ist übel dran' (the boy takes it badly) and then 'und wem sie just passieret' (when it happens to someone). Here suddenly the music, for all its reticence, unmistakably says, with a ritardando and wistful chromatics, 'Much the same has happened to *me.*' So the accompaniment figure has throughout been a synonym for simulated gaiety, affected nonchalance; and in the postlude, once the secret is out, we can hear the coarse and angry emphasis of jealous despair.

NOTES. 1. Heine has 'heuratet' not 'nimmt'.

2. This song was a favourite of Wolf's. On occasion it suited his own mood. Moreover it is a direct (perhaps the only) forerunner of one of his extensions of song-writing, the expression of ironically opposed viewpoints. Schumann, no ironist, achieves this as it were by accident; the modulation at the key-phrase in bars 29–30 is an instinctive expression of regret (M 25).

3. There is laughter in the falling octaves (M 15) as in *Schlusslied,* and joy in the resolution of motif 2 throughout, as in *Venezianisches Lied II.* The postlude sounds like a deliberately clumsy parody of that to *Die Rose, die Lilie.*

73. (Op. 48, No. 12) Am leuchtenden Sommermorgen
Heine – May 1840

On a bright summer morning I go walking in the garden. The flowers talk and whisper together, but I walk on in silence.

The flowers talk and whisper together and look up at me in sympathy – 'Be not angry with our sister, you sad pale man.'

The verses though maudlin are likeable; for once the poet is not harping on his own misfortunes. Schumann goes further still; for him there are only the flowers and the plea for forgiveness. The piano's preluding arpeggios express a wind-stirred movement of tall flowers nodding, painting a picture in which the opening harmony is mysteriously bright and alien to the key into which it instantly fades and vanishes. Melody and harmony are Schumann at his most tender and relaxed. The bright chord returns and is again resolved. Then the flowers begin to whisper and speak. Imagination, the poem suggests, or at most imagery. But for Schumann, as we have seen, the image *is* the meaning. They really spoke; and it was magic. So the other-wordly brightness that the music has been hinting at is now heard from a remote key far away over the other side of the cycle of fifths.

The first two lines of the music are now repeated. Then again a new tonality, this time nearer home, is suggested for the idea of 'our sister'; the magic flower idea made more familiar but still embowered with harmonic change. The postlude is firmly in the home key, reverting to the everyday language of flowers in order to convey more clearly the final message as the music moves from forgiveness through reconciliation to undying love.

NOTES. 1. Schumann is thinking of flowers in colour. For example the chord in the second half of bar 19 is sadly pallid in flats ('blasser Mann'), but in bar 8 it is magically bright in sharps ('sprechen die Blumen'), while in bars 1, 6 and 11 it is deliberately ambiguous in both. The same chord has a different expressive quality in each context. The transitory modulation at bars 8–9 notated in sharps (though flats would have been easier) suggests the idea of brightness in the composer's mind, while the implied new tonality of E major at the furthest possible remove from the home tonic of B flat major gives a sense of mystery (M 40).

2. Schumann is also thinking of Clara and love-song. There are the amorous dominants of motif 64 at bar 10 and memories of *Ich sende einen Gruss* throughout (compare e.g. bar 16 here with bar 24 there). The postlude is explicit in its sonorous image of a voice sighing and singing hidden among flowers (the variegated chord mentioned above, the syncopated notation of the melody, the nature-arpeggio motif 21A in the outdoor key of B flat). The air is redolent of *Du bist wie eine Blume*.

3. All this, as an expression of Heine, would be bewildering. But as an expression of love for Clara, it would be clarity itself. All the evidence is against the former and in favour of the latter. Music, by Schumann in 1840, heard as a love song against the sense of the poem, new-composed in the postlude like a typical allusion, must mean Clara; it is her theme Q^1. As such it reappears in the postlude to the last song of the cycle, No. 77 q.v.

4. Cf. Franz, Op. 11, No. 2.

74. (Op. 48, No. 13) Ich hab' im Traum geweinet

Heine – May 1840

I wept in my dream; I dreamed you were lying in your grave. I woke, and my cheeks were still wet with tears.

I wept in my dream; I dreamed you had left me. I woke and went on weeping bitterly for a long time.

I wept in my dream; I dreamed you were still in love with me. I woke, and yet my tears are still flowing.

The painful point of the poem is in the last verse (cf. No. 65). But Schumann's mind was elsewhere. Perhaps Heine's 'du lägest im Grab' (you were lying in your grave) caught his imagination; his mind was abnormally sensitive to ill-omen.

The voice begins alone, an awe-stricken mourner leading a cortège where muffled drums beat in an ominous E flat minor. Then sharp chords suggest waking. But each time the implacable vision returns, its processional effect made even more vivid by canonic imitations in the last verse. There, at the climax, grinding chromatics express a cruel grief before the dark drums file past for the last time.

NOTES. 1. A song of great originality; voice and piano react to the visual and auditory imagery of the poem (cf. also *Lieb Liebchen*, which has in common not only the silences and solo voice but the equation of E flat minor with death). A possible pointer is the Clara-melody X at 'du lägest im Grab'.

2. The drums are heard in dream, as the staccato shows (M 32). The sharp chords for waking are also expressive, as in Schubert's *Frühlingstraum*. It is not clear why the chords at bars 19–20 should be unaccented (so in the first edition).

3. At bars 10–11 is the 'going away' motif 45, standing for 'floss . . . herab'; each 'geweinet' is motif 8.

4. Cf. Franz, Op. 25, No. 3.

75. (Op. 48, No. 14) Allnächtlich im Traume

Heine – May 1840

Every night in my dreams I see you and your friendly smile of welcome; and I sob aloud and throw myself down at your sweet feet.

You look at me sadly, and shake your fair head; from your eyes steal teardrops of pearl.

You whisper a soft word and hand me a wreath of cypress; I awake, and the wreath is gone and I cannot recall the word you spoke.

Both poem and song are enigmatic. There is an occasional fine point.

Thus the third line of the poem, instead of being set to four leisurely bars of two-four time, as it was entitled to expect, is suddenly flung into one precipitate bar of three-four, rushing and falling as the words suggest. But this device has lost much of its relevance by the second verse; and some of the other responses seem formular, as in the tearful music of the interludes.

NOTES. 1. Perhaps the halting presentation of the words is expressive of the confused dream state. On the other hand Schumann is having to repeat words as early as the second line in order to fit his music ('freundlich', like 'schüttelst' and 'den Strauss' later). Preconceived piano-music in B major suggests a sketch contemporary with Op. 24 (e.g. *Ich wandelte*), perhaps even with Op. 6.

2. The key-structure of the cycle suggests that this song is used as a transition from the dream-tragedy of No. 74 to the sharper awareness of No. 76 (cf. also the part played by No. 122 among the Kerner songs). Certainly any suggestion of independent rhetoric or tragedy goes well beyond what the music can sustain.

3. Note the expression of tears (M 9) in bars 11–13 after 'aufweinend' and in bars 24–26 after 'Tränentropfchen': but there is hardly any sorrow elsewhere in the music. As in No. 74 there are strong accents for the moment of waking, here at bars 35–36.

4. Cf. Franz, Op. 9, No. 4; Mendelssohn, Op. 86, No. 4.

76. (Op. 48, No. 15) Aus alten Märchen

Heine – May 1840

From old fairy-tales a white hand waves; there are sounds and songs of a magic land where brightly coloured flowers bloom in the golden light of evening, and glow sweet and fragrant with a face like a bride's. There, green trees sing ancient melodies, and in them the winds echo mysteriously and the birds trill for joy; and misty shapes rise from the very ground and dance airy dances in strange chorus; and blue sparks burn on every leaf and twig, and red lights run wildfire all around; and singing springs gush from wild cliffs of marble, and strange reflections shine in the streams.

Oh, if only I could reach that land, and set my heart at ease, and be relieved of all pain, and know freedom and joy. Oh, that land of delight, often I see it in dream; but with the morning sun it blows away like a drift of foam.

As in No. 72 this is the music of illusory happiness, which calls for great care in performance. In the whole of this long song there is hardly any suggestion of a minor key or harmony; all is unrelieved and almost incongruous brightness save for the wistful reverie of its last page. There the suddenly slower basic rhythm at 'ach könnt ich dort hinkommen' is a brilliantly apt musical imagery for being as it were earthbound, too slow to reach the enchanted land promised by the first version of the melody, and its fiery pace. In the last bars this slow pace is slowed down still further, almost to a standstill; the pulse is faint, the nerves numb. And almost tauntingly the music of this land of lost content is heard in the distance; perfect, unattainable, and snatched away by an unfriendly wind.

NOTES. 1. Apart from the repetitions at 'Ach' and the last four lines, the text follows Heine's first edition, which was later substantially revised, and thus confirms it as the source probably used by Schumann (see No. 11, note 1).

2. Schumann transfers this song out of its order in Heine to make the climactic final song more effective by delay and by contrast.

3. Note the rhythmic construction, e.g. the off-beat quaver used first in the prelude and interludes as a gay skipping rhythm, in the last section as a sad knell and in the postlude as a fleeting memory.

4. There are the joyous arpeggios (M 23) at bars 5–6 and the dream staccato (M 32) at bars 17–24.

5. The vocal melodies and harmony of the peroration recall the similar close of *Mit Myrten und Rosen.*

77. (Op. 48, No. 16) Die alten bösen Lieder

Heine – May 1840

The old ugly songs, the grim wicked dreams, let us now bury them; bring me a great coffin. I have much to lay to rest in it, though I shall not yet say what; it must be even bigger than the great vat at Heidelberg. And bring me a bier made of tough thick timber; it must be even longer than the bridge at Mainz. And bring me twelve giants; they must be even stronger than the strong St Christopher in Cologne cathedral on the Rhine.

They are to carry the coffin away and sink it deep in the sea; so large a coffin needs a great grave. Do you know why it is that the coffin will have to be so huge and heavy? I am burying in it my love and my pain.

Heine's hyperbole expresses the crushing strain of an intolerable burden. Just to lift it will take prodigious strength and resolve; to be rid of it will take superhuman effort.

Schumann begins by stating the resources as well as the task. The two-bar prelude summons a giant strength. Then the vocal melody, also stated in the left-hand octaves and implied in the right-hand figuration, proclaims, repeats and emphasizes the home key and key-note, inserting inflexible resolve.

Then the task is approached, each lever set in place. Here the mood and motifs rise to meet the challenge, about to heft a massive burden. The music now leaves the tonic and alludes to other keys: but only to convey, both in its short-range and long-range harmony, an insistence on the dominant. The tension thus generated discharges with titanic violence at the words 'die sollen den Sarg forttragen', as in the composer's imagination twelve giants march off in procession, to an accompaniment of crashing chords as if from full orchestra. In seven strides of slow march they reach the sea's edge; and there, to a dramatic diminished seventh chord, they heave the coffin out of sight into an awe-struck silence.

Once that burden has vanished the whole structure of the song lightens. First the key, though still notated in four sharps, eases into the major at 'wisst ihr warum der Sarg wohl'. Then the vocal melody moves upward without a hint of effort or strain, culminating in a long floating portamento. Finally the previously taut and knotted rhythm rests and relaxes. Now the voice is released from the accompaniment to sing the final moving phrases: then the piano in turn is free to meditate on this blissful deliverance from the tyranny of love and its pain. First it recalls the postlude to No. 12 of the cycle, *Am leuchtenden Sommermorgen*, which speaks of reconciliation and continuing tenderness. Then it breaks into an impassioned rhetoric before finally fading into acquiescence and acceptance. And this ending, beautifully controlled and poised, is on the dominant of the first song; the whole cycle is heard as an endless renewal, an eternal beginning again in Maytime, a virtual image of love in the world.

NOTES. 1. Heine has 'schlimm' not 'bös'' in bar 6 and 'von Brettern' in bars 21–22. More interesting is Schumann's 'senkt'' for 'legt'' in bar 48. This, together with the deep left-hand octaves at this point, might suggest that his mind was already dwelling on the deep sea (M 29A).

2. The harmony is worth noting. In the first part of the song the supertonic, dominant and tonic of each successive key are remorselessly hammered home. On the second page two dominant climaxes converge on to 'die sollen den Sarg' at bar 36 – not only the obvious dominant of bars 32–35, but the conclusion of the previous eight-bar phrases from bar 4 on. The chords of C sharp minor in bar 11, E major in bar 19, F sharp minor in bar 27 and G sharp major in bar 35 form a larger pattern which also adds its weight to the climax.

3. The prelude theme is associated by Schumann with the idea of the giant strength of St Christopher (M 55). This is related to the strength of motif 53 in bars 19, 27, 35, with the chords noted above. Then it becomes the march theme into which these chords lead, in a grand processional style analogous to the march movement in the *Fantasia*, Op. 17.

4. The expressive content of the piano postlude is so clear and direct that it

can be heard contradicting the plain sense of the poem. 'I am burying and drowning my past love, casting it off forever,' says Heine. No sooner are these words out than the piano begins a blissful love-song, essentially:

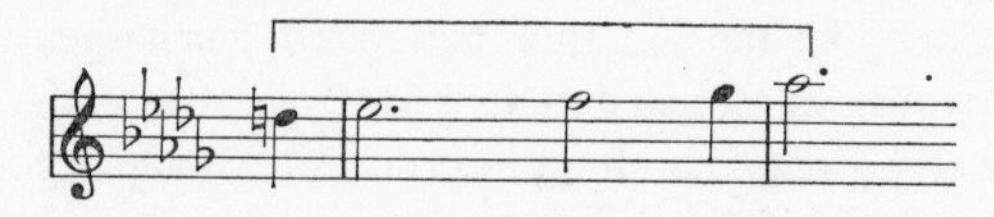

The feeling is inescapable that this melody and the way in which it is hidden among the barlines had some personal and private meaning for Schumann. If so, it will be the same meaning as in the postlude to *Am leuchtenden Sommermorgen*, since it is the same music. Its likely meaning at any time would be love for Clara, let alone a few months before their marriage; it is her theme Q^1.

5. This was already heard, complete with the same left hand countermelody as here, as the bridal music of *Mondnacht* No. 53 (q.v.). It reappears as the bass line that informs and controls the whole musical expression of the rest of this postlude

See also No. 35, note 2.

6. As a further pointer to the deliberate use of meaningful themes, it may be felt that the postlude has a more deliberate and rhetorical effect than the rest of the song (cf. the use of similar material in the eloquent cadenza of the piano concerto, also written for Clara, of the following year).

78. (Op. 127, No. 2) Dein Angesicht

Heine – May 1840

In my dreams last night I saw your dear beautiful face; it is so gentle and angelic and yet so pale, so deathly pale.

And only your lips are still red: but soon death will kiss them white, and the heavenly light will be darkened that now shines from your eyes.

[*In my dreams last night I saw your dear beautiful face, so gentle and angelic and yet so pale, so deathly pale.*]

The setting shares the pale life of the poem. The slow semiquavers of the right hand are resigned, the bass octaves tranquil. The music contemplates, with a thrilled lift in the voice at 'schön'. At first it finds no reason to grieve. Then 'engelgleich' (like an angel) strikes an uneasy note; and at 'doch so bleich' (yet so pale) the hesitant syncopations show disquiet. A warmer pulse returns at the mention of red lips; but at the following repeated phrase the first note is suddenly eerie and ominous, with alien harmonies and sepulchral bass notes. So far this is among Schumann's most impressive evocations; but now the life of the music seems to fade in sympathy. The pattern is completed by a formal return to the first theme, with a new melodic peroration; the last page, down to the unctuous final chords, wears an uncomfortable air of formal mourning apparel.

NOTES. 1. Heine has 'schmerzenbleich', not 'schmerzenreich'. His text ends at bar 17; the repeats are Schumann's. The song was intended for *Dichterliebe*, but no doubt the words seemed too ominous for a wedding year. It was not published until 1854, with No. 80 below.

2. The sad modulation from the E flat to the G flat region is motif 25. *Ein Jüngling* has this and the same final chords. It was to be expected that the harmony would at least allude to the sombre E flat minor (bars 25, 28); the reluctant syncopations are motif 59[A], the bass at bars 11–13 motif 29[B].

79. (Op. 142, No. 2) Lehn' deine Wang'

Heine – May 1840

Lean your cheek on mine, so that our tears mingle: press your heart to mine, so that their flames beat together.

And when the river of our tears flows into that towering flame, and when I clasp you with the full strength of my arms, then I shall die of the bliss of love.

The lush eroticism of the lyric clamours for Wagner or Strauss. Schumann at least finds the right direction, 'leidenschaftlich' (passionately), but seems unable to follow it; his naïve triplet rhythm and bland sequences never stir beyond an innocent domestic affection.

NOTES. 1. This was intended as part of *Dichterliebe*, and omitted presumably because of its tameness; it is also derivative (cf. Schubert's *Sehnsucht*). It was published posthumously, with No. 81 below, in 1858.

2. Schumann replaces passion by sadness (sequence a minor third higher, bar 9 (M 25), with the falling semitone of motif 8 in bars 14–15). The climax in those bars, such as it is, obviously needs the higher notes, which also follow the piano line. In its reference to beauty, motif 65 in bar 33 has the same wistfulness as in the postlude to *Mit Myrthen und Rosen*, while the unstilled ending on the dominant is motif 43. Even without her theme P[1] in the close of the vocal line we should detect the presence of Clara.

3. Cf. Jensen, Op. 1, No. 1.

80. (Op. 127, No. 3) Es leuchtet meine Liebe

Heine – May 1840

My love shines in dark splendour like a sad tale told on a summer night.

Two lovers are walking in silence in the magic garden; nightingales sing in the shifting moonlight.

The maiden stands still like a picture; the knight kneels before her. Then up comes the giant of the wilderness; the frightened girl runs away. The knight sinks bleeding to the ground, the giant goes stumping home.

When I am buried, the story will end.

There is much excitement and invention in the music of this rarely-heard song, which is well worth a revival of interest. Perhaps the vivid and sinister poem had some personal meaning for Schumann. The tense jerking chords of the piano prelude resolve into mellower music for the dreaming garden. But the menace returns; and in the piano interlude after 'flieht' (runs away) the bristling spikes of the first theme are lifted up in both hands and brought down again, like a mace, for the *coup de grâce*. Then the accompaniment goes crashing off in triumph while the voice dies in despair.

But just as in other Heine songs the music seems too innocent and innocuous to make its intended effect.

NOTES. 1. The 'unhappy wedding' theme suggests that Schumann chose this poem as an epitome of his own frustration, with old Wieck as the villain of the piece (cf. also *Die Löwenbraut*). If so, psychologists may have an explanation for his odd mistake of writing 'Ritter' for 'Riese' in bar 15. The repetition at bars 25–26 is also Schumann's.

2. This was also omitted from *Dichterliebe* (see No. 78, note 1). The music is evidently instrumental in conception: the same material serves with little change as the Scherzo of the A minor string quartet Op. 41, No. 2, of 1842.

3. Bar 11 provides clear evidence of the meaning of motif 26, at the word 'still'. The main theme has the distress of motif 8, with the idea of strength (M 53) varied to include tense diminished sevenths (M 41) instead of dominants. The left-hand figure of the *coup de grâce* at bars 21, 24, 26, has the virile dotted rhythm of motif 56. The graphic illustration of the giant's departure is kin to the 'giant' motif 55 in *Dichterliebe*.

81. (Op. 142, No. 4) Mein Wagen rollet langsam

Heine – May 1840

My carriage rolls slowly along through the pleasant green woodlands, through flowering valleys magically bright with blossom in the sunshine.

I sit and dream and think of my beloved.

Then three shadowy figures come into the carriage wagging their heads in greeting; they hop and grimace, mocking yet evasive; they whirl together like mist, then snigger and flit past and away.

The poem is Baudelairean in its personification of evil thoughts. Schumann introduces his setting with the unique direction 'Nach dem Sinn des Gedichts' (in accordance with the meaning of the poem). He then proceeds to repeat the poem arbitrarily, misquote it senselessly, and, to judge from the curiously innocent music, misunderstand it completely. At the same time he feels and expresses a part of the poem's essential content with consummate insight and mastery.

We can hear his thoughts taking musical shape. The piano has the slow rhythmical turn of the carriage wheels. This embodies not merely a sound or a picture but the expression of a mood. There is peace and relaxation in the deep bass octaves of the left hand; the right hand adds the idea of being gently carried along, an effortless momentum.

Into this music the voice enters, sharing the murmured melody of the left hand, all relaxed contentment. Then the piano figure ceases, and we hear in the music the new idea that has at that very moment entered the passenger's mind. He is no longer conscious even of being on a coach-journey; his whole thought is devoted to a dream of the beloved. With a sadly tender modulation a minor third higher the music enters a new key and a mezzo-staccato dream-world. Then this vision briefly fades and the idea of the carriage wheels returns. But this remains in the new key; the awareness of the environment is now suffused with the warmth of the thought.

Into this subtly-changed background there now come stealing in, almost unnoticed, the three phantom figures. They seem at first to be harbingers of more profound thoughts of love, as the bass octaves suggest. But they are not reassuring after all; the music then explains by reverting in an outlandish tonality to the dream-motif just heard, that their presence is unaccountable, their passing a relief. In the postlude the carriage-music resumes in the higher register. Dream returns, tinged with sadness. A new melody is heard offering brief reassurance over the turning wheels. There follows a relapse into grieving reverie, but the rest of the postlude reassures completely. It must be all right, the music says, it was only my own foolish fancies after all: the final chords are anxiety relieved.

NOTES. 1. The repetition of 'und sinne' and 'zum Wagen' is the composer's, whose mood of dreaminess at this point may account for his writing 'huschen' thrice (the first two should read 'grüssen', bar 31 and 'hüpfen', bar 39).

2. Heine's imagery is erotic; cf. *Les Fleurs du Mal* CXV. But the music says that Schumann has read into the poem no more than the uncertainty of love. Its omission from *Dichterliebe* (see No. 79, note 1) meant that some of its ideas could be used again in *Ich hab' in mich gesogen.*

3. The dream-motif 32 begins at 'träume'; the sadness of motif 8 in the right hand at bars 59–60 is foreshadowed in the left at 53–54; there is the joy of motif 2 in the last bars. The right-hand melody, e.g. in the postlude, is eloquent of Clara (her theme P) throughout.

4. Cf. Richard Strauss, Op. 69, No. 4.

Frauenliebe und -leben; (A woman's love and life) Op. 42 and other Chamisso settings

In June 1840 Schumann again had to rest from music. Clara was back in Leipzig; the pair were fighting her father in the law courts for their right to marry. There was the wedding to plan, a home to find.

Now the songwriting takes a new and revealing turn. Of course it is still an outpouring of love for Clara; there is the same harmonic structure, the same unity of themes (including motif 20, as in the Heine *Liederkreis*). At deeper creative levels appear further signs of objectivity. As in *Dichterliebe* an idea was seeded by *Myrthen*, Op. 25. There Clara appears in her own right, as girl, bride, wife, mother and widow. At that time too Schumann had been looking at the poems of Chamisso (cf. No. 40). Now these ideas are to be treated with even greater sympathy and understanding. A woman's love and life was the obvious choice (Loewe's setting had appeared a year or two before); nor is it just coincidence that each of the other Chamisso poems set at this time is about a woman (Nos 90–92). But of course the inspiration of *Frauenliebe*, as before, is the composer's own awareness of the world of life and feeling, which is exactly Chamisso's relation to the poetry; so words and music are excellently congruent, and suitable for direct simple expression.

In the result this cycle is among Schumann's finest achievements. Yet it has been deprecated. Some complain that it makes women seem inferior. Others explain that Chamisso's words are in fact inferior. But among Schumann's poets he ranks high; and these lyrics if homespun are durable wear. The social disparity is part of the imagined situation. The girl sings of herself as a lowly maid because she was one, if that helps. In any event, the objection that a modern woman takes a quite different view of her love-life seems hopelessly irrelevant; what these songs express is the quality of love that Robert and Clara Schumann in fact had for each other.

82. (Op. 42, No. 1) Seit ich ihn gesehen

Chamisso – July 1840

Since I first saw him I have been blind to all else. I see him only, wherever I go; by day in vision, by night in a dream made brighter still by the darkness.

All else is dark and grey; I have no heart for my sisters' games, I would rather sit and weep all alone in my room, blind to all else since I first saw him.

As in *Dichterliebe* there is an unexpected sadness in the first song. Here Schumann is responding to the verses; blindness and weeping and darkness have more than their share of attention. The troubled harmonies at the end of each verse even express uncertainty and apprehension, so outspokenly that the plain chords of the prelude, returning as interlude and postlude, sound perfunctory in comparison. But the lasting impression goes far deeper than this, to the visionary blindness of a trance. Love is blind; the melody is amorous, the harmony troubled. Impulse is blind; the slow rhythm is compelling. So the music despite its doubts and fears goes along quietly and obediently, like a good child, towards the light.

NOTES. 1. The repetition of 'heller' is Schumann's.

2. Further pointers to this interpretation:

(*a*) The dream-motif 32 begins and ends the song; the music takes its rise from 'wie in wachen Traume' as well as 'blind'.

(*b*) At that phrase is the Clara-theme P^1, followed by X in the voice and accompaniment.

(*c*) The preponderance of altered or minor chords suggests irresolution and melancholy, enhanced by the drooping sevenths of the melody in bars 12 and 28.
(*d*) The solemn bass octaves are motif 29C.
(*e*) It appears from Schumann's manuscript that the surprising interrupted cadence at the climactic moment of each verse (bars 15 and 31) was an afterthought, for expressive effect.
(*f*) The processional effect of the three-four rhythm is self-evident.
(*g*) The A flat G movement in bar 4 (both hands) and again in bar 5 (voice and right hand) together with the G flat F in the following bar suggests the melancholy of motif 8.

3. The music's derivation from the first verse has some odd corollaries. Thus, the meaningless accent on the word 'begehr' makes sense in the first verse (on 'ihn' in bar 7). The second verse has no word like 'heller' which can conveniently be repeated to fit the tune, so a crotchet rest appears instead. The vocal line is clearly subordinate to the piano melody.

4. Schumann refers to this song in the first version (for two pianos, horn and cello) of the *Andante and Variations* Op. 46, more familiar in its later arrangement for two pianos only.

5. Cf. Loewe, Op. 60, No. 1.

83. (Op. 42, No. 2) Er, der Herrlichste von allen

Chamisso – July 1840

He is the finest of all men; how gentle and loving he is; sweet lip, bright eye, clear head, true heart. As stars shine in the blue depths of the sky, so he is a star in my sky, bright and glorious, high and far.

Go on your way, just let me gaze on your brightness; humbly to think of that is all my sorrow and all my joy. Heed not my silent prayer said for your happiness; you must not know so lowly a maid as I am, you high and bright star.

Only the finest of all women is worthy of your choice; and she shall have my thousandfold blessing. And I shall be glad and joyful, joyful, though I weep; what matter if my heart should break?

[*For he is the finest of all, gentle and loving; sweet lip, bright eye, clear head, true heart; gentle and loving.*]

The one-bar prelude starts a pulse of eight light quaver chords which beats in quick elation throughout the song. Over this the voice or the piano treble sing their shared melodies of joy; under it the strong bass octaves seem to picture the lover himself. At the mention of the bright star 'in blauer Tiefe' (in the blue depths) the accompaniment chords lighten. In the preceding and following piano interludes the theme of joy leaps high and ecstatic, finally rejoining the opening piano melody.

This gives place to a new mood of hushed reflection. Go on your way, without me if you must, says the voice, 'wandle deine Bahnen'; but the piano melody endearingly follows after, only a pace or two behind. New themes and variations express humility and prayer; the music is heard at its devotions. The main theme is repeated; and now the mood of humility culminates in total renunciation at 'brich o Herz, was legt daran?' (what matter if my heart should break?). Again this renunciation is belied by the music, while the passionate harmonic tensions gather and break softly against the idea of tenderness and goodness as the opening words are repeated for the last time. The postlude, without relaxing the unremitting quaver pulse, takes a further new and unexpected turn. The rhythm becomes a melody; the heart sings.

Of course, a description of the song in these terms exaggerates its sentiment, which is not universally acceptable. But to reject it is to lose one of the most consummate expressions of love in song.

NOTES. 1. The repetitions at bars 36–38, and 57 on, are Schumann's. Chamisso has 'hoch' not 'hehr' at bar 16, 'soll' not 'darf' at bar 40, and a second 'segnen' at the crotchet rest in bar 44, where the tune leaves no room for it.

2. The tempo indication 'lebhaft' seems only partly apt to the music. The joyous melody (M 23) has evident elation; but the expressive quality of the sustained bass notes (M 30) suggests a slower tempo.

3. The bass seems related to the subconscious (left-hand) idea of the lover; note the manly rhythm of motif 56 announcing itself at bar 6, etc.

4. The canon 'following' is motif 59; in the same bars is the yearning of motif 16.

5. The use of repeated chords in both hands (M 38) for humility or devotion occurs (*a*) for four bars at the word 'Demut', (*b*) for three bars at 'das Herz auch brechen', i.e. in contexts which have only this verbal idea in common. At these last bars is also the dominant question of motif 43.

6. The association of the flat seventh with heaven or prayer (as here at bar 29) is motif 50.

7. The affectionate dominant chain of motif 64 at bars 54–59 is the longest in Schumann (and hence no doubt in all expressive music); note how the returning first phrase in the voice and piano at bar 57 et seq. is remodelled for inclusion in the chain.

8. Other musical images correspond to going one's way with joy and sorrow. The four descending notes, at 'wandeln' in bar 21, are associated with that word elsewhere, as in *Frühlingsnacht* and *Ich wandelte*; motif 20. There are two expressions of joy; motif 1, in bars 37 and 65 right hand, and motif 2 in the last bar but one.

9. Cf. Loewe, Op. 60, No. 2.

84. (Op. 42, No. 3) Ich kann's nicht fassen

Chamisso – July 1840

I cannot fathom it, cannot believe it; I must be dreaming. How, from among all women, could he possibly have chosen to honour and bless me?

I thought I heard him say 'I am yours for ever', but I must still be dreaming, it cannot be true.

Oh, let me die in this dream, cradled in his arms; what bliss so to die, in tears of endless joy.

[*I cannot fathom it, cannot believe it; I must be dreaming. How, from among all women, could he possibly have chosen to honour and bless me? I cannot fathom it, cannot believe it; I must be dreaming.*]

Dramatic tension is increased as the reverie of the first song is inter-stressed with the excitement of the second. Again there is more joy in the words than in the music, which is in its minor mood. Chamisso's 'It cannot be true; I must be dreaming' is rhetorical. But Schumann takes it literally; his music doubts, ponders, yearns, repeating those words over and over again. The piano with its first sustained chord has unsteady harmonies, a catch in the breath, at 'berückt' (deceived). The following recitative passage has sweet simple chords set apart from the rest as if by quotation marks at 'Ich bin auf ewig dein' (I am yours for ever). But the harmonies are incredulous and finally sad; it cannot be so. Then the bliss of the imagined death converts the tonality into the major. The minor resumes as the first verse is repeated. Now follows a self-contained piano interlude with new material. 'Ich kann's nicht fassen' the voice has said; but oh, cries the piano melody, how I wish I could; if only it were true. Not until the last two bars is the truth finally accepted with fervent thanksgiving on a falling arpeggio of C major.

NOTES. 1. The poem ends at 'Lust' in bar 51. Chamisso has 'seligsten' not 'seligen' in bar 45. Perhaps the former seemed too much of a mouthful to articulate at the required speed. 3/8 may also be Schumann's way of expressing a quick light movement; the music rather suggests 6/8.

2. The piano interlude is built up from the yearning of motif 16. Its typical leaps increasing from a fourth to a sixth and finally to an octave decorated with a twelfth form a musical paradigm of wishful thinking.

3. The staccato is the mezzo-staccato of the dream motif 32, not the martellato effect sometimes heard. The sadness of motif 8 is at 'nimmer so sein'; the recitative chord of motif 48 for 'er habe gesprochen' is at bar 18, etc.

4. Note the Clara-theme X at 'Adagio', a direction which often introduces a quotation or allusion in Schumann.

5. The sustained F on 'dein' clashing with the F sharp in bar 24 cannot surely have been what Schumann intended.

6. Cf. Loewe, Op. 60, No. 3.

85. (Op. 42, No. 4) Du Ring an meinem Finger

Chamisso – July 1840

Ring on my finger, dear golden ring, I press you devoutly to my lips, to my heart.

I woke from the peaceful dream of childhood and found myself alone in the wide world. But you, ring on my finger, have opened my eyes to the real truth of life.

I shall live to serve him, to be his alone, surrender myself and become transfigured in the light of his love.

Ring on my finger, dear golden ring, I press you devoutly to my lips, to my heart.

This justly famous song is the passive counterpart of No. 2 of the cycle, drawing on its themes for musical material but transforming them from an elated outgoing expression of adoration into a withdrawn mood of rapt contemplation.

NOTES. 1. Schumann changes 'werd' to 'will' in bar 25, repeats 'an die Lippen' in bars 7 and 39, and 'und finden verklärt mich' in bar 31; and invents the words 'schönen' and 'tiefen' in bars 12 and 24 to fit his tune.

2. Much of the music is adapted from *Er der Herrlichste*. Thus bars 3–4 here are bars 27–28 there; the imperfect cadence at bars 15–16 here is at bars 45–46 and 53–54 there; bar 16 and the postlude here are in the postlude there; the descending four-note scale at bar 12 and bar 29 is found at bars 21–22; bars 29–32 are bars 25–28; the melody at bars 39–40 is at 37–38 and 65–66.

3. There is the brief joy of motif 2 at bar 10; and motif 10 at bar 16 and in the postlude, which also has the flattened seventh of motif 50 (for 'fromm'). The expressive variants at bars 37–38 (lower bass octaves, lower right-hand notes) are worth bringing out as peroration. The Clara-theme Q^1 is unobtrusive here, like X in the voice at bars 7–8 and 23–24. The latter may have been the reason for changing the words.

4. cf. Loewe, Op. 60, No. 4.

86. (Op. 42, No. 5) Helft mir, ihr Schwestern

Chamisso – July 1840

Help me, my sisters, with my bridal wreath, tend me on this my happiest of days; twine the myrtle blossom about my brow.

When I lay happily in my loved one's arms he would always tell me how impatiently he longed for the dawn of our wedding-day.

Help me, dear sisters, help me to dispel my foolish fears; let me receive him, the source of all my joy, with undimmed eyes.

And are you here, my love? Sun, do you shine? Let me bow to my lord in all reverence and humility.

Spread flowers for him, sisters, offer him rosebuds. But to you, my sisters, I bid a sad farewell, though I leave you with joy.

The prelude's arpeggios crest and break in light waves, with a small skip on the last beat; the music of delicate and elated impatience. On the scale of restraint thus established the following upward movement at 'als ich befriedigt' (when I happily) arches high and bright with warmer harmonies up to a top note at 'ungeduldig' (impatient) before reverting to the main theme in words and music. The insistent arpeggios seem to take on added meaning at each repetition; a bridal arch, the twining of a wreath. Perhaps Schumann has gone too far in this mood to be successful in the abrupt change that follows at 'Bist, mein Geliebter'. The sudden prostration in devout quaver chords seems incongruous.

But this contrast enhances the unaffected delight of the original theme, which is taken up with real pride to a high sustained F at 'mein'; and this in turn makes another finely effective contrast with the real regret that comes into the music at the moment of final farewell. At the end is a brilliant Schumannian invention. The wedding march heard in the postlude is a variant of the main theme. It is as if the composer had begun by imagining the scene, with organ music, and a procession down the aisle. In the elated mood of the verses that music is dissolved into fluent melody and running arpeggios, from which the wedding-march finally crystallizes, as the whole assembled scene moves off and away out of sight and sound.

NOTES. 1. Chamisso has 'freudige*s* Herzens' (bar 12), 'heut'gen' (bar 18), 'gibst du Sonne mir' (bar 29), and 'bringt' (bar 39). Schumann adds 'sonst' (bar 13) and 'lass' (bar 33) for his tune's sake.

2. The song's two interpolations will sound ruinously intrusive without the utmost care in performance. First, bars 27–32, constructed from the motif 38 of 'Demut' (the word appears at bar 32) are yet another reference to *Er der Herrlichste* (compare its bars 15–16 with the echo at bar 29 here). Second, the bars at 41–52 can sound like an inexplicable switch to the *Novellette* in F (e.g. its bar 290) unless they are played with all possible hesitancy and delicacy.

3. The whole song is fashioned from the joyous arpeggio of motif 23, like the first section of *Widmung*. (The further implication of twining or winding is in the piano duet *Beim Kränzewinden* Op. 85, No. 4.) There is a dominant question

(M 43) at bar 30. The processional effect in the postlude is enhanced by the use of canon (M 59) and the walking motif 20.

4. The march tune is the opening melody differently barred, which suggests that the time-signature may properly be 2/4.

5. Cf. Loewe, Op. 60, No. 5.

87. (Op. 45, No. 6) Süsser Freund

Chamisso – July 1840

Dear friend, you look at me in surprise, you cannot understand why I weep. Let the unaccustomed glory of wet pearls quiver in my eyes, for they shine with joy.

How anxious my heart feels, yet how blissful; if only I knew how to say it in words. Come and hide your face here on my breast, let me whisper all my joy.

Now do you know why I am crying? should you not see my tears, my beloved husband? Stay by my heart, feel how it beats; let me hold you close, closer.

Here by my bedside there is room for a cradle, silently hiding my blissful dream; and one morning the dream will wake and look at me laughing with your eyes. Your eyes!

Now Schumann seems diffident. Down to 'alle meine Lust' (all my joy) all goes well enough, with a calm sweetness that reflects the composer's own essential nature. But the change to C major – via a piano interlude to allow time for whispering – seems staged. After 'weisst du nun' (now do you understand?) the left hand is allotted the melody of the opening phrase 'Süsser Freund'. After 'geliebter Mann' the right hand, understandably at a loss for a reply, solemnly quotes from (of all things) *An die ferne Geliebte*, a favoured reference to Schumann's love for Clara. The repeated quaver chords add their touching devotion.

No doubt this music is sincerity itself; but it seems to come from a more conscious creative level than the rest of the song. The contrast certainly adds radiance to the serene assurance of the first strain as it resumes at 'Hier an meinem Bette' (here by my bedside). The words now wear this melody with a new dignity; and the final coda with a repeated 'Dein Bildniss' (your image) incorporated into the postlude has a quite unexpected emotive force.

NOTES. 1. Chamisso has '*freudenhell* erzittern in den *Wimpern* mir' at bars 10–11. The repetitions at bar 31 and bars 41–42 are Schumann's. A verse telling how mother was consulted is omitted (after bar 21).

2. The melody (Ex. C, p. 2) is typical, cf. *Zum Schluss.* Its augmented interval is perhaps derived from 'Süsser', motif 12.

3. The allusion in bars 33–34 and 37–38 is rather to Schumann's own previous quotations of *An die ferne Geliebte* (e.g. in the fourteenth bar from the end of the first movement of the *Fantasie*, Op. 17) than to Beethoven's text. However, it seems deliberate enough, and is perhaps the reason for the change to C major. All this section (particularly the sequential passages from bar 38 on) has the humility of motif 38.

4. There are the affectionate dominants of motif 64 throughout, with the yearning grace note, or rather grace-chord, of motif 16, in the postlude, where the sudden introduction of new material suggests a conscious allusion to the Clara-theme P^1 (bars 56–57). The word 'Traum' calls for the staccato marking of motif 32 in bar 52.

5. Cf. Loewe, Op. 60, No. 6.

88. (Op. 42, No. 7) An meinem Herzen

Chamisso – July 1840

On my heart, at my breast, my child, my joy. Happiness is love, love is happiness; so I have always said and so I say still. I once thought myself boundlessly happy, but now I truly am. Only a women loving the child at her breast, only a mother can know the real meaning of love and happiness. How I pity a man, who cannot know the joy a mother has.

You dear angel, looking at me and laughing: come to my heart, my breast, my child, my joy.

Chamisso shows both by precept and example that a man cannot know mother-love. Having nothing to express, the verse offers no sustenance to the composer. His music, though joyous enough, is hardly specific enough to be viable without interpretation of the highest order. But with the postlude comes a new expressiveness. The piano's cheerfully awkward yet tender rocking strain audibly envisages the holding and hushing of a real breathing child; so that when the last four right-hand notes are heard saying 'Dein Bildniss' (your image) from the previous song, we understand that the dream has come true down to the last detail.

NOTES. 1. Chamisso has 'überglücklich' in both bars 10 and 12, and 'Du schauest mich an und lächelst dazu, Du lieber lieber Engel, du!' in bars 26–29.

2. If the postlude is Schumann's own reaction, as suggested above (and perhaps confirmed by the earlier parallel of *Hochländisches Wiegenlied*), it is agreeable to note the compound of (*a*) tenderness (M 16), (*b*) perplexity (M 41), (*c*) affection (M 64), and (*d*) stillness (M 26), thus:

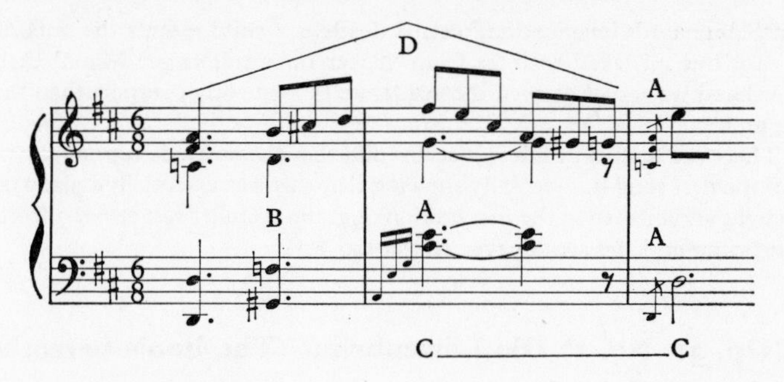

3. The yearning at bar 38 is remembered from bar 57 of the previous song.
4. There is an evident if unintentional relation between the last page here and No. 3 of this cycle passim.
5. Cf. Loewe, Op. 60, No. 7.

89. (Op. 42, No. 8) Nun hast du mir den ersten Schmerz getan

Chamisso – July 1840

Now for the first time you have hurt me, but this hurt is grievous; hard, pitiless man, you are sleeping the sleep of death.

Left all alone, I survey an empty world. I have lived and loved, and now my life is done. I withdraw silently into my inmost soul; the veil falls. There I have you and my past happiness, you my whole world!

After a flow of tragic recitative, a piano postlude rounds off both song and cycle by recalling the music of the first song, 'Seit ich ihn gesehen'. By this means Schumann seeks to re-establish the mood of first love in youth as the final truth and message. This is his own conclusion, rather than Chamisso's, just as the postlude to *Dichterliebe* expresses his own feelings rather than Heine's. The beauty and poignancy of the music and its deep personal feeling are its justification.

NOTES. 1. Chamisso has a ninth poem which finds final consolation in the continuing life of children and grandchildren. Schumann would have found this difficult to set, since his 1840 songs were of innocence, rather than experience; hence perhaps the expedient he adopts. His alteration of 'vergang'nes' (past) to 'verlor'nes' (lost) in this poem neatly illustrates the dichotomy; Chamisso's whole point is that the happiness is *not* lost, though gone before.

2. The melancholy opening triads are characteristic (M 7). The recitative of motif 48 was only to be expected. The rising minor thirds may have the idea of resentment as well as courage (M 5). This foreshadowing of the theme of *Fremder Mann* of 1848 (Op. 68, No. 29) suggests that the widow, still a young

girl in Schumann's imagination, resents death as a child resents the unfamiliar. It is easy but mistaken to infer from 'harter unbarmherz'ger Mann' that the late husband was cruel or even inconsiderate in some other respect than that of dying first.

3. There are textual puzzles; it seems odd that the postlude repeats the piano part of the first song (incidentally showing that this was essentially a piano piece) with slight variants (so in the first edition) e.g. the crotchet rest at bar 7 from the tempo primo and the semiquaver rest at bar 8.

90. (Op. 31, No. 1) Die Löwenbraut (The lion's betrothed)

Chamisso – *c.* July 1840

Adorned with her wedding wreath and jewels the keeper's young daughter, the rosy maid, goes into the lion's cage. He lies at the feet of his mistress, and fawns before her.

The powerful beast, but now wild and fierce, looks up at her, all innocence and understanding; the tender and radiant girl fondles him softly and weeps the while.

'In days that are no more, we were playmates, like two children; but those days are long since past. Before we could believe it, you were mightily shaking your kingly head with the mane waving around it. And I grew up too; as you see, I am no longer a child with a child's mind.

If only I were that child again, and could stay with you, my strong, faithful and devoted lion. But I am forced to marry a stranger and journey far. He thought me beautiful; I was betrothed to him; so now, my true friend, you see me with orange-blossom in my hair, and tears that dim my eyes.

Do you really understand? You look angry; but I am resigned, and you must be too. Now I see him coming whom I must follow; I must give you, friend, one last farewell kiss.'

As the girl's lips touched him, the cage was seen to tremble. As the bridegroom appeared the troubled bride was seized with terror. The lion forces her away from the door of the cage, lashing his tail and roaring hugely. She implores, orders, threatens him, but he will not let her pass.

Outside a confused shouting is heard. The young man cries 'Bring arms; I'll fire point-blank, I'll shoot him down!' The lion rears and foams, berserk with rage. The luckless girl tries to reach the door; but the changed beast attacks his mistress. The fair form, a fearful prey, lies torn and bloodied in the dust.

And having shed that dear blood, the lion lies darkly down by the body, sunk in sorrow and remorse, until the fatal bullet strikes his heart.

Here is a very different Chamisso. In his last sick years his verse took on a strange and violent turn. This dark poem is not without a certain power, despite its superficially ludicrous aspects. It no doubt also had a special significance for Schumann, whose piano teacher and prospective father-in-law, Friedrich Wieck, was opposing his marriage tooth and nail. The implacable ferocity and bestial cruelty of which, as the letters show, Schumann believed him capable, assort well with the grim head and wild mane of the Wieck portraits. In the circumstances the almost total failure of the setting, despite the power in the leonine tread of the first bass octaves, is a tribute to the composer's good nature.

NOTES. 1. Chamisso has 'taten's mir' in bar 36, 'und nicht vor Tränen' at bars 45–46, and 'Gitter' not 'Zwinger' at bar 61.

2. The song is undated; but may be attributed to July with the rest of the Chamisso songs.

3. The theme of the 'unhappy wedding' is here given its most disastrous statement.

4. The recitative motif 48, at bar 4, suggests that for Schumann these words are introductory; the song proper begins with the voice of the central character at bars 15 et seq. Revealingly, what she sings is the opening melody of *Widmung*, over and over again (bars 15–23) and variants of it thereafter.

5. A motif confined to this song is the love-music of bars 7 ('schmiegt'), 14 ('liebstreichelt') and 54–55 ('den letzten Kuss'). The verbal associations and the treatment, which is expressive to match the words, e.g. at bars 54–55, alike confirm this link; Schumann may not have been conscious of it himself, or he would have hardly used the same music for the terror in bar 62.

6. Well roared, lion; but it takes an uncommon devotion to Schumann's harmonic language to be awed by the chromatics at the Grand Guignol climax in bars 75, etc. They must however have sounded very striking and powerful in their day, and have still not entirely lost their compulsion. Among other aspects of the idea are the nobility of motif 51 at bars 71 and 72; and the strength of motif 53 in the last chords of the piano prelude, etc.

7. The lion music may be compared with the musical bestiary in *Der Handschuh*.

91. (Op. 31, No. 2) Die Kartenlegerin (The fortune teller)

Chamisso, after Béranger – July 1840

Mother's gone to sleep at last over her book of sermons, so I can stop this hateful sewing. I'll set out the cards and tell my own fortune.

Something tells me I shall first of all see my own true love. Fine, just as I thought; here he comes, the knave of hearts. But who's this? A rich widow? Yes; and he marries her instead, the brute. Now I see heartache and weariness, a convent school with high walls. But the king of diamonds is sorry for me, comforts me, takes me away with him; I'm happy and rich.

Now, I expect this king of diamonds will turn out to be at least a prince in real life, so that makes me a princess. But what's this? an enemy – a fair man in my life – a secret discovered – an escape – what a blow! That's goodbye to all my comforts.

And now another man, several, a crowd, I can't tell how many; and – what's this? An old woman coming to scold me and ruin all my love and happiness? Yes, well, I might have known it; mother's awake, and starting to grumble. That just shows the cards don't lie. No indeed; the cards don't lie.

The French original is graceful and gay; Chamisso's occasionally rather inept translation adds bite and acerbity. Schumann's music, between the two, sparkles in contrasting lights.

The kittenishly tentative opening motif introduces a vivid character-sketch. The reduced note values of 2/8 time, and the sharp little piano chords, suggest a petite determination. Flouncing demisemiquavers express wilfulness as the sewing is put aside at 'nähen, immer nähen, nein!'; there is independence in voice and piano parts, even to the extent of contrary motion. All this is repeated as the fortune-telling begins. Then, as excitement mounts, the recitative element dominates; the harmonies, like the cards, are played out in sequences.

For the king and his attractive suit there is a suitably ceremonious interlude followed by the cheerful return of the first themes. But then follow more sequences, this time tragic ones, as the harmonies show. Again the music dwindles with dismay and the voice takes charge with impassioned dramatic recitative, though still on the same tiny scale. Now we hear the original motif transformed from gaiety, by a few deft touches, first into bewilderment and then into near-desperation

Interlude (b)

presaging the interruption so accurately foretold. For this, the original theme returns for the last time, rounded off by a peroration and the good-humoured exasperation of the postlude.

NOTES. 1. Béranger's original *Les Cartes, ou l'Horoscope* is still well worth reading. Schumann omits the sixth verse of Chamisso's translation, thus obscuring the point that the old woman in the last verse turns up first of all as a card, say the queen of spades. The alteration of 'Kommt das grämliche Gesicht' into 'kommt das dumme Frau'ngesicht' is no doubt designed to help with this. The omission of a whole line, presumably by inadvertence, as still faithfully reproduced in the Peters Edition, could be rectified: after bar 12, read 'Legen will ich mir die Karten' and then 'Ei, was hab ich zu erwarten?' at bars 15–16. Other corrected readings are 'Ahndung' in bar 23, 'Tag' in bar 100 (to rhyme with 'Schlag' in bar 112) and 'kaum sie' in bar 120. The final repetitions are Schumann's.

2. The motivic transformation quoted above, and indeed the whole song, are a wholly novel contribution to song-writing. Here Schumann approaches as near as his nature permitted to ironic objectivity. The music smilingly explains that the situation is not too tragic after all; and it contains so loving and detailed an observation of the nature of a young girl's caprice that one cannot but speculate on its emotive source. The opus as a whole was dedicated to Ernestine von Fricken, but the model was surely the young Clara Wieck. Something of the kind, a decade and three daughters later, is heard in *Singet nicht* and *Weh, wie zornig*.

3. The demisemiquavers in 2/8 time are clearly motivic as an expression of the petite, but are heard (regrettably) nowhere else in the songs. The staccato is here sharp and decisive, not motif 32. The contrary motion is heard again in the B flat symphony, a work on which Schumann was to begin later in the same year; an interesting link between an objective song and the objective approach that symphonic writing is traditionally held to demand. At bars 6 and 19 here is the dominant question of motif 43; the recitative motif 48 with falling semitones in the bass at bars 96–115, from which this component is abstracted as the direct expression of sorrow (M 8) at bars 127 and 129.

92. (Op. 31, No. 3) Die rote Hanne (Red-haired Jane)

Chamisso, after Béranger – July 1840

She had a child at the breast, another on her back, and leads by the hand a third, who is half-naked, barefoot and freezing. The father has been arrested, and is cooling his heels in jail. God be with you, red-haired Jane, your poacher husband is under lock and key.

I knew her in happier days, as the schoolmaster's dear little daughter, singing at her spinning, reading and sewing, a sweet child, neat and charming. At the village dancing on Sundays under the linden trees how cheerful and gay she was! God be with you, red-haired Jane, your poacher husband is under lock and key.

A handsome young farmer courted her, promised her a better fortune; but people laughed at her red hair, and her rich wooer jilted her. Others came and went – she had no dowry. God be with you, red-haired Jane, your poacher husband is under lock and key.

Then up came a scoundrel – 'I'll marry you,' said he, 'red-haired or not. I have three guns, I know the trails, the gamekeeper can't catch me, I can even pay the preacher for the wedding.' God be with you, red-haired Jane, your poacher husband is under lock and key.

She did not refuse him; the gentle promptings of nature urged her on; and thrice alone in the forest she knew the bitter joys of motherhood. The children, fresh and hardy creatures, grew and thrived. God be with you, red-haired Jane, your poacher husband is under lock and key.

But now the faithful woman finds comfort, the nights have a brighter gleam. She smiles; the children will have curly black hair like their father. She smiles; and her smile gives him fresh courage in his prison. So God be with you, red-haired Jane, your poacher husband is under lock and key.

Chamisso's verses, from Béranger's *Jeanne la Rousse, ou, la Femme du Braconnier*, are naïve enough: but for both poets the source of the work is a deep feeling for human misfortune. This may help to explain its attraction for Schumann the liberal; which in turn may account for the pious and moralizing tone of much of the music.

NOTES. 1. 'Ich nehm' dich zum Weibe' is Schumann's change from 'Ich nehme dich', presumably to fit the impatient rhythm (M 61) and strong melodic line at bar 67. Chamisso has 'hübscher reicher' at bar 45.

2. It may be that Schumann's deepest sympathy was subconsciously reserved for the poacher. In the prelude to this song (for a bass voice) the manly motif 56 in single notes, to which are added semibreve notes and chords, is taken down to successively deeper levels (M 28) – an apt expression, in Schumannian terms, of a prisoner patiently waiting in solitary confinement.

Fünf Lieder
(Five songs to words by Hans Andersen etc.) Op. 40

Schumann sent a presentation copy of Op. 40 to Hans Andersen with a revealing letter. 'Perhaps the settings will seem strange to you. So at first did your poems to me. But as I grew to understand them better, my music took on a more unusual style.'

'Your poems' means Chamisso's German versions, which Schumann had found in the volume containing *Frauenliebe*. 'A more unusual style' means the continuing trend away from the purely lyric impulse into narrative, character-study and drama (a trend which owes much more to Chamisso than to Andersen). In the result each song is more of a separate entity, the unifying key-scheme is less evident, the impulse is more objective. Within three months of these songs, the diary records the first sketches for a symphony (cf. No. 91, note 3).

93. (Op. 40, No. 1) Märzveilchen (Sweet violets)
Andersen (trans. Chamisso) – July 1840

The sky arches blue and clear, the frost makes a flower-garden on the window-pane. A lad stands there admiring it. And on the other side are two laughing blue eyes; sweet violets, the sweetest ever seen. Warm breath will melt the flowers of frost; and may the good Lord have mercy on that young man!

The Danish original is bittersweet, all love-longing and dismay. Chamisso's translation loses a little of this, and Schumann's setting the rest. But the latter's alternative, a shy and elated tenderness, is wholly delectable; and the pictorial aspect, at least, of Andersen's poem lives again in the music. The clarity and precision of the right hand's lightly-touched semiquavers, the semitonal sighing in the left, assort well with the idea of a vision seen through frost. This provides the background to a warm melody until at 'Augenpaar' (two eyes) the piano joins in affectionately. The opening strains are repeated; and the song might now have been rounded off with a concluding chord and still be a delight. In fact it does even better. The composer's vision goes through to that young pair, as theirs has to each other. The piano, always Schumann's ideal medium of self-expression, now takes over the melody, as if identifying itself with the young man. Two bars of interlude sing a love theme. The last words are repeated in folk-song fairy-tale vein, and the postlude sings another love-theme; in this music they live happily ever after.

NOTES. 1. The repetition is Schumann's.

2. The musical articulation in rising semitones is worth study; the kinship with the Sonata in F sharp minor (1–4 l.h. here, 6–11 r.h. there) dedicated to Clara may suggest that further homage is in mind.

3. The accentuation of the third verse (bars 17 et seq.) suggests that Schumann's music relates more directly to that part of the poem; the vocal line at Der Reif wird, angehaucht, zergehn' echoes that at bars 51–54 and 63–66 of *Mit Myrthen und Rosen*, where also the words are about thawing into life.

4. There are the affectionate dominants at 'Augenpaar' and the postlude at bars 29–30 (M 64); the yearning leap of motif 16, also in the postlude; and the dream-staccato of motif 32 in the prelude and throughout (though here it might well be played with a crisper touch).

94. (Op. 40, No. 2) Muttertraum (A mother's dream)

Andersen (trans. Chamisso) – July 1840

The mother prays and looks with joy at her little son asleep in the cradle all snug and warm; to her he seems like an angel.

She kisses and holds him tight in her joy, forgetting all her past sorrows. Her hopes and wishes hover in the future, for this is how all mothers dream in their hearts.

But outside the window the raven and his brood croak a different refrain – 'your angel, your angel, will be our prey; we shall be pecking at the robber on the gallows'.

The music tours a Schumann picture-gallery. First comes a drooping and ominous twilight. Then in the lit room there is a rocking cradle. Next, the gazing music loves and dreams, while the piano prelude returns as an interlude to say that it is still twilight outside, and that this bodes ill. Now the figure of rest and peace is given a solemn and sinister turn. To repeated semiquaver chords over tolling bass notes the croaking ravens pronounce sentence of death and dissolution, fittingly low and hoarse. In the postlude the deepening bass notes take on an increasingly gloomy view as they fade into dark inaudibility.

NOTES. 1. Chamisso has 'so' not 'und' in bar 10.

2. The prelude is the twilight music of motif 33, as in *Zwielicht*. In the first

eight bars the bass has the hesitation of motif 59^{A} together with the deepening gloom of motif 28, which in the postlude becomes dark night. The mention of a cradle starts a rocking theme in the right hand over the idea of rest and sleep (M 35^{A}) which is later given a sinister inflexion in bars 29–30. There is warm affection at 13–16 (cf. bars 9–12 of *Im wunderschönen Monat Mai*) leading at bar 19 to the dreaming staccato of motif 32 solely for the one bar in which the word 'träumen' occurs. At bars 28–31 is the typically solemn utterance of motif 30 as in *Du bist wie eine Blume*, etc., while a version of the recitative motif 48 makes its predictable appearance in bar 31.

3. Schumann's main Bach studies are said to have been concentrated on the year 1845; but here is that influence already assimilated.

95. (Op. 40, No. 3) Der Soldat (The soldier)

Andersen (trans. Chamisso) – July 1840

We march to the sound of a muffled drum. How far away the place, how long the road! If only he were at rest and it were all over. My heart will surely break in two. He was my only friend in the world, and he is to die today. The firing squad paraded with full band; I was ordered to be one of the party. Now he is looking for the last time on the light of day, now he is being blindfolded. God grant him eternal rest. Then the nine of us loaded and aimed. The others were so trembling with fear and grief that their bullets missed. But mine struck him square in the heart.

Schumann asks his music to stand respectfully aside as destiny marches past to a rolling and tapping of muffled drums. The implacable slow-march theme treads through and over the scansion and even the sense of the poem; everything is subordinate to the image of the cortège, the tragic inevitability of fate. This treatment, though undeniably effective, loses some dramatic tension as the company is halted to aim and fire. The piano part cannot halt too; instead it is redeployed to suggest anxiety and distress in a way not entirely congruent with the rest of the song. But if this is a weakness it is more than compensated by the finely imagined climax, where recitative at last takes over, in an awe-stricken whisper of grief and remorse. In the postlude, with a barely audible gasp and groan and a few pathetically drooping chords, the figure of a dead soldier sags and slumps in its bonds.

NOTES. 1. Chamisso has 'Trommel' in bar 6, 'die Neun' in bar 40, and 'ins' in bar 48. Schumann repeats 'ich traf' and 'dazu'.

2. The obsessive march-rhythm exemplifies a favourite march theme often used figuratively for manliness (M 56) but here as

it were literally. The drum-roll is obvious throughout; the music at 21–27 has also a suggestion of cymbals ('bei klingendem Spiele'). The recitative motif 48 introduces the spoken climax aptly at bar 36 (perhaps the Cs in bar 38 should be C sharps to complete the parallel?). The diminished seventh tremolo at the end is expressive of the numb shock of dread (M 41).

3. The song was described by Franz (whose Op. 52, No. 2, may be compared) as 'a picture of the execution; whereas it is the soldier's sorrow that is the essential and characteristic thing'. An exactly similar comment is recorded at No. 67, note 3. Just so; but for Schumann, as we have seen, the image *is* the meaning. The postlude is seen in vision as clearly as in *Die Grenadiere*.

4. The dominant ending leaves a question unresolved (M 43).

96. (Op. 40, No. 4) Der Spielmann (The musician)

Andersen (trans. Chamisso) – July 1840

There's dancing and singing in the village tonight; they're celebrating a wedding. The red wine sparkles among the happy guests; but the bride is as pale as death.

Yes, dead to the one she will never forget, though he is not the bridegroom. There he stands drinking his wine among the guests, playing his violin cheerfully enough.

Yet as he plays, his hair turns grey, the strings whip and screech; he crushes the fiddle to his heart, not caring if it too breaks into a thousand pieces.

It is terrible for a man to die of grief while still young; I cannot bear to watch, it will turn my brain. But why are you all pointing at me? Have mercy, Lord, let not any man be mad. I too am just a poor wretch of a musician.

In this neglected masterpiece Schumann has not only imagined the scene and the protagonist in music of vivid directness but also expressed the central experience; and like the poet, he has made that experience his own.

After four bars of wild stamping prelude for the rough dancing, the music hushes for the opening vocal phrase. This is immediately echoed in single notes in the upper register of the piano. 'A wedding' the voice explains, and again there is an echo, now unmistakably arranged as a fiddle-tune, fiercely gay in double-stopping. At 'Wein so rot' (wine so red); the violin echo is refreshed and lyrical, a lilting waltz. 'The bride looks pale'; and at that instant the music changes dramatically back to the harsh and desperate stridency of the prelude. In this way the whole sense of the poem is brought out, extended and emphasized, between the lines.

The same music is repeated a fifth lower so that the voice re-enters on a low note at 'tot' (dead). For the following violin-playing fresh sources of power are unleashed; the interludes are incorporated in the piano accompaniment, so that the effect is of scene and mood together, a dancing despair. This culminates after 'zerbricht' in the great outburst of the prelude once more.

Then the scene fades, the mood changes. The voice ruminates on so terrible a fate. The words are dispassionate, objective; but the broken snatches of fiddle-tune remind us of what has gone before. The voice continues its pretence; the piano again denies it. Then comes the moment of truth, in the wild outcry and wrenched harmony at 'Wer heisst euch mit Fingern zeigen auf mich?' (Why are you pointing at me?). With this the music seems to give itself up, acknowledging the futility of further pretence or protest, and goes quietly. This slow turn to the major tonality is unforgettable in its expressive meaning. Now the broken phrases are the voice of a broken man. Bass octaves plumb these depths of despair. At the last revealing words, 'bin selber ein armer Musikant', a new theme appears, in a song already prodigal of thematic material. It is a wistful, smiling, uncertain theme, seeking reassurance. It is followed by a questioning hopeful pause. Then we hear the music, still smiling, being taken inexorably down into the comfortless dark.

NOTES. 1. Chamisso has 'springen', not 'schwingen' in bar 69.

2. Again the theme of the unhappy wedding; and there are thematic resemblances with *Das ist ein Flöten und Geigen*, e.g. the key-signature and the melodic curve at bars 17–20 here, and bars 5–8 there. The opening melody here is a minor version of *Im Walde*, which begins with a wedding procession.

3. The recitative harmony of motif 48 is implicit at bars 115–116, as if to indicate that the preceding words are a special self-revelation: the deep bass notes are motif 28.

97. (Op. 40, No. 5) Verratene Liebe (Love betrayed)

Anon (trans. Chamisso) – July 1840

No one saw us, my love, when we kissed at night – except the stars, and we thought we could trust them. But one star fell and told the sea; the sea told the rudder, which told the helmsman, who sang of it to his sweetheart – and now all the boys and girls are singing about it in the market-place and in the streets.

The attractive music is a smiling response to the words. Beginning with a few confided notes, it gradually gets more busy and elated as the secret spreads, until finally the piano postlude sets the theme laughing and chattering to everyone in cheerful unconcern. The singer, in this music, shares in his own secret, happily at one with stars and sea and people in a cosmic glee.

NOTES. 1. The text, although 'from the modern Greek', was probably drawn from a French translation by C. Fauriel in his *Chants populaires de la Grèce moderne* (1825). Chamisso has 'Mädchen und Knaben' in bar 25.

2. The serene gaiety of the postlude (in which motifs 2 and 3 abound) pleased Brahms, cf. his *Sandmännchen* (bars 26–27 here, fifth bar from the end there). Motif 2 is heard earlier (bars 2, 4, 8) and motif 3 in bars 6–7.

3. The mediant in the bass at the end of a song describing the end of a song is motif 46.

4. The expressive qualities of the happy sigh at the end of the piano postlude (right hand last two bars) can be compared with those of its minor equivalent at the close of *Mädchen-Schwermut*.

Sechs Lieder (Six songs to words by Robert Reinick) Op. 36

The Chamisso and Andersen songs had the seed of a new objectivity, and a new style. But German romantic verse in 1840 was not the ground for it; and Schumann in his marriage year would have to write more of his personal love-lyrics. We are fortunate that he did. Yet after the miraculous month of May 1840, the self-expressive love-cycles lose impetus, and slow down gradually into the static Op. 37. Then the song-writing stops altogether, to yield place to the more mature and developed art of the symphonies, the concerto, the quartets.

In the meantime we have the new objective Schumann setting subjective lyrics. The dichotomy is reflected in the increasing lack of unity in the song-cycles. The taut key-structures slacken; there is either no central theme or figure, or there is an obviously artificial attempt to provide one; and when Schumann chooses his poetry in this more detached way his taste is seen to be indifferent.

98. (Op. 36, No. 1) Sonntags am Rhein (Sunday by the Rhine)

Reinick – July 1840

How good to walk beside the Rhine on a Sunday morning, with the church bells ringing to matins all around. A little ship sails by on the blue waves, amid singing and rejoicing; how pleased it must be to be sailing among so much happiness.

From the village organ-music resounds, hymn-singing is heard, reverently the procession comes out of church. And the castle looks down on all the magnificent scene, eloquent of the good old days when men built upon firm rock.

All this the mighty Rhine offers on its vine-covered shores; and so it mirrors in brightest reflection the whole fatherland, the dear faithful fatherland in all its glory, blessed by the good Lord with joy and song.

Schumann in his song year could outbid most of his poets with ease; but his superiority over this fourth-rate poem does not amount to more than second-hand music.

NOTES. 1. Reinick has 'stärker' at bar 31, 'hellem' at bar 40.

2. The second half of the melody sounds like a discarded sketch for *Im wunderschönen Monat Mai*. This reminiscent mood suggests that Schumann was thinking more of a riverside walk than of the closer and stranger associations with the Rhine suggested by other songs.

3. The wide-ranging melody and the contrived peroration suggest *Der Page*; the middle section echoes *Süsser Freund* and its similar use of the humility motif 38. There is the idea of procession both in the canon (M 59) and in the middle section at bars 18 et seq. The postlude has motif 2 for joy, together with the heavenward gaze of motif 50 and the final plagal cadences.

99. (Op. 36, No. 2) Ständchen (Serenade)

Reinick – July 1840

Come to me in the silent night; my love, why delay? The sun has long been down, the world's eyes are closed; only love is awake.

My love, why delay? Already the stars are bright, the moon is in her place; but they move so fast, you must make haste too.

Only love is awake, calling for you everywhere; hear the nightingale, hear the sound of my voice, and come to me, my love, in the silent night.

The verse though vapid is at least unobtrusive. The song rivals some of the classic serenades of the Lied; Strauss' and Brahms', if not Schubert's *Ständchen*, or *An die Laute*, which it somewhat resembles. The idea of a serenade sends Schumann into one of his brightly-coloured dreams of sound. In his piano-pictorial imagination the night becomes taut and sonorous like a great guitar, with spread chords thrumming warm and dark while melody notes twinkle and shine above. This is music of such ease and elegance that one marvels at not hearing it sung more often.

NOTES. 1. Schumann's omission of the third and fourth verses vitiates Reinick's laborious rhyme-scheme.

2. Motif 65 pays homage to beauty in the left hand throughout. In the only variant (bar 12) the change to the Clara-motif Y (A G♯ A B C) will not be accidental. A pause on the dominant in bar 6 points the question (M 43) as well as the delay; the vocal melody at bars 7–10 is the finality of motif 49; the affectionate dominants in bars 11–12, etc., are motif 64; the recitative motif 48 at bars 25–26 emphasizes the quasi-parlando idea behind the words.

3. Cf. the early setting by Hugo Wolf.

100. (Op. 36, No. 3) Nichts Schöneres (Nothing more beautiful)

Reinick – July 1840

When I first saw you and saw how sweet and beautiful you were, I could never have dreamed in all my days that there could be anything more beautiful than to gaze into your dear eyes for ever.

Then I gazed so long that you became my sweetheart, and again I could never have dreamed in all my days that there could be anything more beautiful than to kiss your red lips for ever.

I kissed so long that you became my wife; and now I can be quite certain that there can be nothing more beautiful than to be at one, body and soul, with a dearly-loved wife.

Melodies in voice and piano sing agreeably of love; but as in No. 98 the music has not enough leverage to budge the dead weight of the poet's ineptitude.

NOTES. 1. The change from 'das gar nichts Schöneres kann sein' at bars 43–44 and 'ein' to 'und' in bar 48 (together with the following repetitions) are Schumann's. But the form 'Weibchen worden bist' (later 'Weib geworden bist') at bars 39–40 occurs in the first separate print of this poem (in the *Deutscher Musenalmanach* of 1836) so this song may be earlier than the others. It is still evidently at the rudimentary stage where musical material is lugged on to the poem regardless of the fit. Schumann's accentuation may not be specially refined, but he does not often emphasize unstressed words so remorselessly as in the odd-numbered bars of this song ('als, wie, da, dass, als, hin, da, bis,' etc.).

2. The idea

of two converging voices in a love-song may have given a pointer to Hugo Wolf. The top voice is the Clara-theme P¹; and the incidence of the melody notes C B A G♯ in bars 8–9, etc., may not be coincidence.

101. (Op. 36, No. 4) An den Sonnenschein (To the sunshine)

Reinick – August 1840

Oh sunshine, sunshine, how you shine into my heart, waking thoughts of love, so that I feel constraint in my heart.

I feel constraint too in my room, in my house; and when I run out of doors I see that you have tempted out into the fresh air many of the most beautiful girls ever seen.

Oh, sunshine, you must think I ought to follow your example and kiss every fair flower now unfolding to your warmth?

But you, who have watched the world for so long, must know that this is not for me; so why do you torment me so, sunshine, sunshine?

The poem is a bad one; but the musician is in the song-writing vein. The poem is a sad one; but the musician is in elated mood. So the text is consumed in the untroubled serenity of youth and summer, and a contented Schumann writes in the margin of his manuscript 'As I wrote this there was radiant sunshine – in my life too'. The song is associated with the warm-hearted Jenny Lind, of whose interpretation the composer once said that when she sang it you could feel the sunshine warm on your back. Some fifty years later she is said to have sung its opening bars in a frail whisper on her death-bed when a ray of sunshine came into the sickroom. It has been for many years since a favourite work, and the direct source of more than one popular song. The shadows are longer now; but it has given a fine light in its day.

NOTES. 1. Reinick has 'wie' not 'wenn' in bar 15; the repetition of 'die allerschönsten Mädchen' is (revealingly) Schumann's.

2. The sun is bright in A major; the arpeggios' melodies are motif 23. Note the freedom octave of motif 16B in the bass at bars 9 and 13 at the first mention

of going out into the fresh air; this motif is writ large in the yearning of the octave lift in the piano five bars from the end.

102. (Op. 36, No. 5) Dichters Genesung (The poet's recovery)

Reinick – July 1840

Once again I thought of my beloved, hitherto seen only in dreams; and the thought drove me out into the moonlit night, through silent valleys. Then suddenly the valley began to gleam eerily, like a hall full of ghosts; the river and the winds roared and whistled together in a dance melody. There came dancing past a fleeting throng from rocks and vales, from waves and woods; in the moonshine, like a white wreath, the elves were dancing their rounds.

In their midst was an airy maiden, their queen, and I heard her sing: 'Leave your heavy earthly body, leave foolish earthly things; only in the moonshine is true life to be found, only floating in dreams is true immortality. I am she whom you have often seen in dreams, I am she whom you have often hymned, I am the queen of the elves; you desired to see me and now your wish has come true. Now you shall be mine for ever; come and dance with me in our fairy ring.'

Then they were all fluttering and flying round me. Then suddenly the wind of dawning blew and brought me to my senses. Farewell, queen of the elves, for I will choose another love; free from trickery and deceit and pure of heart, there will surely be such a one to be found for me.

The Lorelei or witch-woman in various guises has haunted European story and song for many centuries, claiming most of her victims in the nineteenth. It seems fitting that the egregious Reinick should be the only one to escape. For whatever reason, his clumsy verses find Schumann exceptionally responsive to the contrast between sacred and profane love. Schumann also hoped for redemption in this year of his marriage: it is not only longed for, as in the verses, but known and almost named. The opening bars for the piano say to Clara with unobtrusive tenderness, 'Du bist wie eine Blume'. This solemn music also suggests a purposeful departure in the calm night. The word 'rauschten' sets off semiquavers of leaves and winds, the elves' dance floor. This theme is extended for the dancing itself, with an added idea of the grace of their young queen. The fairies, though on the same melodic lines as Mendelssohn's, are more sturdily built; the music relishes the rather innocuous temptations of the elvish Venusberg. Indeed, the transition from the amorous darkness of E minor to the broad daylight and righteous renunciation of E major seems in comparison unconvincing, while the postlude is decidedly perfunctory.

NOTES. 1. Reinick has 'Mond*en*glanz' (bar 22); 'ein ewig Sein' (bar 44); 'die in Träumen dir oft erschien' (bars 45–46); 'die in Liedern oft du besungen' (bars 47–48); 'hin' not 'her' at bar 59; 'will ich ein andres Lieb mir erlesen' at bars 63–64, and 'in Sonnenschein, und von Herzen', etc., at bars 65–67.

2. The poetic form is also disregarded by Schumann; but singers should know for example that 'einmal' in bar 10 is the rhyming end of a short line, and that 'Sein' in bar 44 is the end of a verse.

3. The semiquavers beginning at bar 13 are the windy tremolandi of motif 22. They broaden at bar 22 to a dance-theme made queenly by the apt minor form of motif 51 at bar 26, which is later given added oddity by the interpolation of the 'wrong' chord at bar 34.

4. The elves announce their kinship with Mendelssohn's by appearing in the same notes and the same key, though in a more solid register; cf. bars 35–36 here and bar 8, etc., of the *Midsummer Night's Dream Overture*. E minor often means a twilight emotion to Schumann.

5. The vigour of motif 56 appears in force at bar 62, etc; the horn passages at bar 64 are also characteristic (M 4). The tenths of the penultimate bar may be the companionable motif 57.

6. The piano part begins as *Du bist wie eine Blume* with the right-hand chords an octave higher and the harmony slightly altered by the sharp fifth on the fourth beat (M 12) – an idea also used at bar 9 of the earlier song, which is even more redolent of Clara. Her theme finally emerges into major daylight in the *Novellette* music of bars 65, etc., and the typical cadence at bars 69–71, where E♯ F♯ A B in the left hand is the Clara-theme Q^3.

103. (Op. 35, No. 6) Liebesbotschaft (A message of love)

Reinick – August 1840

Clouds scudding eastwards to where my only love lives; all my hopes, my wishes and songs go flying with you, guiding you to my sweetheart so that she may think of me.

If she is still dreaming, drift softly down into her garden as dew in the still dark dawn, strewing pearls on flowers and trees, so that if then my darling comes walking by she will see all the fair flowers budding in brighter beauty.

And at evening in silent peace sail away to the setting sun, in crimson and gold, in a sea of bright fire so that she thinks you are singing angels; and indeed my thoughts would be angels if my heart were as pure as hers.

[*All my wishes and hopes and my singing fly with you, guiding you to her, my sweet, my only love.*]

'Soon you will be getting another love-letter, one that I wrote for you yesterday, and it may be a musical one' says a letter to Clara on 24th August. And in the margin of the manuscript Schumann wrote 'the day of the second reading of the banns'.

It would be churlish to resist this song. Reinick's usual fervent fustian is unusually highly-coloured; nothing was better calculated to set Schumann dreaming. As ever his heart is in his piano-music. The opening strain is perhaps oversweet; the octaves and tenths in similar motion faintly cloying. But the long tune sent billowing off is evocatively right for its purpose; and the effect of the following piano interlude that sends heartfelt greetings flying after is in its way novel and beautiful. It must be confessed however that the contrived peroration, which is the last if not the lasting impression, mars the total effect.

NOTES. 1. The repetitions of 'die Eine' (bar 3), 'gleich ihrem' (bars 49–50) and on the last page, are Schumann's. A verse is omitted after 'Prangen' in bar 33; as if in compensation he omits the expected piano interlude at bar 41, because the sense runs on from 'Strahlen' to 'leicht'.

2. The lovers really did share the opening melody, which is that of Clara's own *Liebeszauber* from her Op. 13.

3. The canon at bars 33–34 has the processional idea of motif 59 for the march of clouds; the tune at bar 3, etc., is a love-theme (M 10A); the tenths are motif 57 passim; the acciaccature of the yearning motif 16 appear at the words 'Wünsche' and 'Hoffen' (wishes, hopes) in bar 52; the final cadence has the joy of motif 2.

4. The purity mentioned at bars 50–51 is matched in music which later became another hymn of praise for Clara – *Mein schöner Stern*. The Clara-theme Q^1 in the left hand at the last words is no surprise.

5. Cf. the early setting by Hugo Wolf.

Drei Gedichte (Three poems) von Emanuel Geibel Op. 30 and other Geibel settings

Again the presence of character sketch or story puts life and mettle into the music, while their absence leaves it spiritless and dull (as in e.g. 111 and 113). The three men of these Op. 30 songs are perhaps a deliberate counterpart to Chamisso's three women in Op. 31. Relieved of the responsibility of serious expression, they are 'in lighter vein', as Schumann himself described them. Geibel's characters have a certain family resemblance, and a common background of light-hearted romance and chivalry; but the music shows an impressive and original talent for this entirely novel genre.

104. (Op. 30, No. 1) Der Knabe mit dem Wunderhorn (The boy with the magic horn)

Geibel – August 1840

I am a merry fellow, who on earth could be gayer than I? My swift steed bears me like the wind into the wide world, trara, into a world in flower.

As I ride, I blow my sweet silver-sounding horn for hours together, setting the echoes ringing from hill and forest, trara, far and wide.

And when I come to holiday dancing, to sport and play in the sunlit wood, where languishing glances shine and flowers crown the wine-cup, then I leap down, trara, down from my steed.

Sweetly the guitar calls to the dance, I kiss the girls, drink the wine; but when the crimson sun sinks behind blossoming trees then I must make my bow, trara, and take my leave.

For I feel the call of faraway lands; I spur my fleet steed. Farewell! I would willingly stay, but already other stars are beckoning, and my horn sounds its greeting for the last time, trara, hail and farewell!

The poem has freshness and verve; and Schumann fashioned it into a finely effective song.

The prelude announces in one brief figure the gay horseman and his horn: picture, sound, and mood in a flash of music.

In the same way, the themes which express the vigour of man and steed in the first verse speak as a silver horn-call and echo in the second. But already the music is softening towards the subdominant, dismounting as it were before the poem does, half-hearing the sound of lilting guitars. In the composer's imagination the following scene in the sunlit wood is vivid from dawn to dusk, first with the guitar chords thrumming among the trees, then with a silver horn winding in the twilight as the opening strains return to end the song.

NOTES. 1. The title refers to the collection of German folk-poetry made by Arnim and Brentano, *Des Knaben Wunderhorn* (The boy's magic horn), itself the source of many other songs. Schumann alters Geibel's text to suit his tune e.g. by curtailing the refrain's repeats ('blühende' omitted in bar 13, 'antwortet' in bar 26) or conversely by repeating e.g. 'trara' in bars 61–62 and the words from bar 66 on. It might be worth while restoring 'muss *es* geschieden sein' at bars 45 and 47 since there is a note available. At the end Schumann thoughtfully inserts an 'Ade!' of his own to provide an effective close.

2. The opening phrase quoted above is not only obviously evocative of the sound of the horn, and the motion of the rider, but also of the jerky rhythm of the manly motif 56 and the dominant-tonic of Florestan (M 62).

3. At bars 8–11, etc., are delightful examples of the joyous arpeggio of motif 23. There is the rising octave of freedom (M 16^{B}) in the last few bars.

105. (Op. 30, No. 2) Der Page (The page)

Geibel – *c.* August 1840

Since I must now renounce all my heart's desire, let me kiss the ground where your feet have trod. And if I may never stride proudly by your side as your cavalier, then let me always go with you to mass as your page. I will be for ever faithful, ever silent; by day alert for your least sign, by night lying before your gate, even in storm and hail.

Every morning I will bring roses with a modest greeting; and every evening I will lie at your feet and sing you songs to my guitar. And I will bridle the white coursers for you when it is your pleasure to go gaily hunting; I will carry spear and falcon as your equerry in the wide woods. I will even carry a torch for you to light your steps to your lover, and, while you are in his arms, guard the door with a shining dagger.

And all this will be without a single murmur of complaint or pleading so long as at the day's end I have but one smile as my reward, one glance from afar, like a gleam of light from my guiding star.

For once the voice is dominant. It begins first and alone, as if involuntarily. The piano is the faithful follower, attentive and devoted. At 'will ja treu sein' (I will be for ever faithful) the music is elated yet steadfast, becoming sweeter and smoother for the bringing of roses. Then piano and voice ride off together in a cantering rhythm with long arpeggios like lances for hunting and adventure. But at the end of the song this verbal impulse falters, as if the poet's conclusion were unbelievable; and the contrived peroration beginning at 'wenn gleich einem Segensterne' (when like a guiding star) is correspondingly unconvincing. The brief postlude seems more hopeful than the words suggest it has any right to be.

NOTES. 1. The poem is better known in a later version; but Schumann faithfully follows the text of the first edition, except for his repetitions.

2. Some of the many variants may be just inconsistencies (thus it is not clear why bars 25–26 should differ from bars 35–36) but some correspond closely with the detailed meaning of the poem. In bars 3–4 and 11–12 for example the difference is dictated both by the sense (the former is sad, and hence attracts the flattened sixth of motif 8) and by the sound ('Seite' suggests a wider interval than before). No doubt the poem had special meaning for Schumann: his submissive devotion is a frequent theme. There is also Clara's frequent theme P^1 at bar 2, etc., and over the barline at bars 5–6, etc.: and her main theme X makes the postlude.

3. Similarly the motivic equivalents are very sharply defined. The recitative motif 48 is everywhere, as if the creative mind imagined itself as speaking these words to someone. Affectionate dominants abound (M 64); the horn passages are characteristic (M 4). The joyous arpeggios at bars 40–43 (M 23) are the longest in Schumann, and have the clearest association with the open air (as in bars 22–23).

4. The postlude manages three canonic entries in two bars (i.e. 'following' M 59) and a left-hand decoration of the final chord (i.e. 'beauty', M 65): the expression of beauty's follower or cicisbeo could not be more succinct or apt.

5. In this atmosphere the vaguest associations may have meaning. For example the falling fifths on the second page may be under the influence of the word 'Rosen', motif 27. Their continuation at 'will die weissen Renner', etc., recalls Schubert's *Der Wanderer* at 'Das Land wo meine *Rosen* blühn'; the same notes in the same key. For some confirmation that Schumann had this song in mind at this time, see 107, note 3; which in turn might help to confirm August, with the other Geibel songs, as the likely date of this one, of which no dated manuscript exists.

106. (Op. 30, No. 3) Der Hidalgo (The hidalgo)

Geibel – August 1840

How sweet to jest with songs and hearts, with life and death. When the pale moon gleams I leave my room and roam the streets far and wide, ready for romance or for a duel. [*How sweet to jest with songs and hearts, with life and death.*]

The ladies of Seville, with their fans and mantillas, look down the river; they listen in delight to the sound of my songs and my mandoline, and dark roses fall from the balcony in thanks.

When I sing I always carry my blade of Toledo steel as well as my mandoline. My bold serenades praise the ladies and mock their cavaliers; so the mandoline is for the ladies, the sword for my rivals.

Then away to adventure! already the sun's fire is quenched behind the mountains. The hours of twilight and moonrise bring tidings of love, or they bring mortal combat; and it will be either with flowers or with wounds that I return home tomorrow.

In the margin of the manuscript Schumann wrote 'Am Tage des Consenses', i.e. the day, 1st August 1840, when a civil tribunal gave Clara Wieck permission to marry him despite her father's opposition.

He celebrates with this most brilliantly original love song, which has a tense ambiguity between the ideas of the first Geibel song above, or Schumann in fancy dress, and the second, or Schumann in deadly earnest. Lace ruffles at throat and wrist, long pale hand on a silver sword-hilt; and, at the same time, heart on sleeve.

The one-bar prelude is an aphorism. Grandiloquent gesture, lilting refrain, bolero rhythm, mandoline chords; a character-sketch in a handful of notes. Soon the music yearns with and for the ladies on the balcony; at 'blicken den Strom entlang' they and we together hear from afar the faint anticipation of a wind-blown serenade. The thrumming of the mandoline becomes nearer and more insistent. Then the serenader arrives in the music as his reward arrives in the words; his rising song in the piano mingles with the slowly falling phrase in the voice at 'dunkle Rosen fallen' as Schumann's imagination lingers blissfully in a trance of dark roses.

For the last verse the first theme returns in the strength of added bass notes, with a final series of plumed flourishes by way of peroration.

NOTES. 1. The repetitions at bars 17, 19–26 and 75 ff., are Schumann's. Geibel has 'vo*n* Toledan'sche*m* Stahl', 'de*r* Dam*e*' at bars 53–54; and 'Dämmerstunden' at bars 65–66.

2. 'Kokett' here means 'jauntily'; the rhythm which helps to create this impression is a version of the manly motif 56. The gay arpeggii of motif 23 are minor at 'mit dem ernsten Streit' as if to indicate only modified rapture. The I–IV–I movement of motif 51 is apt for a Spanish nobleman; the amorous dominants of motif 64 abound, e.g. where love is first mentioned, bars 15–16. The octaves yearn in motif 16 at bar 27, etc.; the dark roses induce the dream-staccato of motif 32; the added bass notes of motif 29 add strength and firmness of purpose at bar 58 et seq. The sharpened fifth of motif 12 appears in association with the word 'süss' and the grace notes of motif 65 with the word 'schön'. Even the variants (e.g. the minim and sharp in bar 19 but not in bar 2, or the difference between bars 31–32 and 47–48) seem to be evidence of verbal response.

3. In 1837 Schumann had described Clara's performance of Chopin's *Bolero*, Op. 19, as creating a picture of her beloved, which may account for certain affinities, e.g. of rhythm, between that work and this. Clara herself is serenaded; note her themes P and P[1] in voice and piano in e.g. bars 31–34, and X in the piano motto-theme (bar 1) throughout.

4. See No. 213, note 2.

107. (Op. 51, No. 1) Sehnsucht (Longing)

Geibel – August 1840

I look into my heart, and then I look into the world; and the tears fall from my eyes. Far-off lands shine in golden light; but the north holds me prisoner. My life is so narrow and the world so wide; and time so fleeting!

I know a land where the grapevines bloom among sunny foliage around overgrown temples, where the purple waves foam on the shore, and the laurel dreams of poets to come. Far lands shine and beckon to my yearning mind; and I cannot go!

Oh for wings to cleave through the blue of the sky; how I should bathe in the fragrance of summer. But all in vain; the hours pass by. Mourn for lost youth; bury the songs. My life is so narrow and the world so wide; and time so fleeting!

A letter to Clara of 9th August says, 'I have written a song in these last few days that I think will make a special appeal to you; it strikes me as quite exceptionally inventive.' That phrase would certainly describe this song. The piano's dithyrambic outburst in alternating hemidemisemiquaver octaves must have sounded outlandish in 1840, and is still surprising. Even more so however is the comparative tameness of the song that follows, which for all its emphasis of passionate chords repeated is curiously sedentary and passive. The scene of the poem becomes a framed lithograph, contemplated amid the cosy contentment of some of Schumann's most lovable domestic melodies.

NOTES. 1. All the repetitions are Schumann's. Geibel has '*be*schäumt' in bar 18 and '*ver*traure' in bars 30–31.

2. The prelude is aptly compounded of motifs for yearning (M 16), freedom (M 16B) and discontent (M 11) in Schumann's melodramatic key of D minor.

3. The inspiration is recognizably Schubertian. Thus the combination here of 'Ufer', 'Grün', 'Woge (Welle)' and eyes troubled with tears evoke Schubert's *Des Mädchens Klage* (Op. 58, No. 3) which provides its semiquaver triplets and stately bass line, and characteristic rhythm (at e.g. bars 17–19 here). Then the idea of cold northern yearning for summer sunlight suggests the theme of *Aus Heliopolis I*, Op. 65, No. 3; its sad minor second at the word 'Norden' yields Schumann's motif 8 at bar 7 here at the words 'hält mich der Nord'. Finally the chords of *Der Wanderer* at 'immer wo?' and 'Land, wo bist du?' are heard here at bars 23–24 – 'kann nicht hin'.

4. Cf. Spohr, Op. 103.

* * *

On the 12th September, the eve of Clara's twenty-first birthday, the two were married. Then the music too turned to duets (Op. 43); and thence to sketches for a symphony. The song-writing continued to derive its strength from the idea of shared experience and the life of others, as the following songs show; the most personal and lyrical, No. 111, is by far the weakest.

* * *

108. (Op. 53, No. 1) Blondels Lied (Blondel's song)

Seidl – October 1840

Scanning the barred window in the bright moonlight a minstrel stands before the castle of Dürrenstein, lute in hand. He tunes it softly and begins his song, for a foreboding whispers to him 'Seek in faith and you shall find'.

King Richard, hero of the crusades, can you really be lost? Must your sword rust in the sea, a far grave hide you? Your minstrel seeks you through the world, taking no rest, for a voice speaks to him 'Seek in faith and you shall find'.

Hope, Richard, and believe; faith guides and leads me, and in the far lands of home your loved ones pray for you. Blondel follows your paths, Margot beckons you longingly, and your minstrel's foreboding says to him 'Seek in faith and you shall find'.

And hark; from the castle's dungeons a soft song, a well-known air meets Blondel's listening ear. Like the greeting of a dear friend he hears his own song echoed; and his foreboding says, more strongly than ever, 'Seek in faith and you shall find'.

He sings again, and again there is the echo, sweet and distinct beyond all doubt, an assured joy. It is the voice of his king, long sought after, that he hears; not in vain was his foreboding 'Seek in faith and you shall find'.

He flies homeward with the tidings, which bring both great sorrow and great joy; returns with a noble entourage; and ransoms his beloved king. All stand in amazed delight as the hero embraces his minstrel, his saying at last proved true; 'Seek in faith and you shall find.'

This was a contribution to the Vienna music annual *Orpheus*. Though occasional it is not negligible; the verses are agreeable and the technique is assured. Schumann wrote that it had given great pleasure in his own domestic music circle; so it can still.

NOTES. 1. Richard I, the Lionheart, was held to ransom by Leopold of Austria, and traditionally found and released by his minstrel, as the poem describes. It is possible that Richard's wife Berengaria is confused with Margot, also of Navarre. One verse, the third, is omitted, after bar 40; 'hervor' should read 'empor' at bar 68.

2. There is an interesting resemblance at bars 65–68, which describe a half-heard song, to bars 37–42 of *Frühlingsfahrt*, where the same notes in the same tonality are used for the same purpose.

3. The yearning of motif 16 occurs e.g. just after the word 'sehnend' in bar 56; the impatient rhythm of motif 61 is at bars 47–48, etc.

109. (Op. 45, No. 1) Der Schatzgräber (The treasure-seeker)

Eichendorff – November 1840

When all the woods were asleep he began to dig. Within the depths of the mountains he was digging deep down without respite in search of buried treasure.

God's angels were singing the while in the silent night. Then, like red eyes, precious metals burst shining out of the shaft. 'Mine at last, all mine!'

And he burrows down ever deeper, in a frenzy.

Suddenly rocks came crashing down in ruin over him and his folly. Wild mocking laughter echoed from the collapsed shaft; the angels' song died sorrowfully away in the air.

This neglected song is buried treasure, well worth winning. The prelude is all spade and pickaxe, effort and impact, yet already subtly presaging doom. The voice narrates, the piano imagines, each in its turn. Then they come together and contemplate, listening hopefully to the angels' song. But there is to be no redemption. The digging goes deeper; and at the moment when the treasure is claimed the music changes from the dark G minor to the mellower F sharp minor, a gleam of glimpsed gold. Back in the original key the digging goes yet deeper, in a frenzy the more impressive for its restraint, with all the dignity of Tom o'Bedlam. The last page is full of hollow mockery and sad singing from the piano, until in the postlude the treasure-seeker theme is stifled and silenced.

NOTES. 1. Eichendorff has '*der*weil' at bars 18–19, 'de*m*' at 40, and 'Kluft' and 'Engel*ge*sang' at bars 45–46. The repetitions at bars 26–28 and 32–34 are Schumann's.

2. The digging motif is one aspect of motif 16. The angels may have suggested motif 50 in the flattened sevenths of bars 17 and 19, and their song the rising sixth of motif 19 in the same bars.

3. The minor triad at bars 4 and 11 means melancholy (M 7). There is the laughter of motif 15 at bars 42 and 44 (at 'Hohnlachen') interestingly combined with the mystery and tension of motifs 40 and 41.

110. (Op. 45, No. 2) Frühlingsfahrt (A spring journey)

Eichendorff – October 1840

Two lusty lads set out from home for the first time, embarking on the clear-sounding and singing waves of the full tide of springtime.

They were striving for great things; regardless of their own fortune or misfortune, they wanted to achieve something fine in the world, and all hearts and minds laughed with them as they strode by.

The first found a sweetheart with a dowry of house and farmstead; and soon he was holding his own small son, and looking out from his comfortable room over his fields.

But to the second the waves of the sea sang their siren song with a thousand voices, luring him out over the great deeps and coloured oceans of the world.

And when he returned from the deep seas he was tired and old, his ship a sunken hulk, with silence all around and a chill wind blowing over the waters.

The waves of spring are singing and sounding now all around me; and when I see lads like these setting out in life, my eyes fill with tears – Oh Lord in thy great mercy bring us to thee.

Voice and piano stride out together as if impatient to be away; the brisk unison melody has spring in its step. Then the music swings into broader harmonies for the sung farewell and the full tide of springtime, and the whole is repeated for the second verse.

The rest of the poem now tells how the spring fails, the light dies. At the mention of cosy domesticity ('der erste, der fand ein Liebchen') the music becomes mellow and sedate. The elated march rhythm droops and fades, and thereafter is heard only softly and intermittently in the left hand like a regretful memory, except for the engaging moment when it returns with an added rocking movement in both hands for the idea of nursing a small son ('wiegte gar bald ein Bübchen').

The fate of the second young man is vivid and harsh in the minor, as the music changes from smile to frown at 'Dem Zweiten'. Bass notes toll sea-deep for the lost ship and the lost hopes; the monotonous repetition of quavers and semibreves speaks of desolation.

So far the music has been beautifully expressive in clear images. But now Eichendorff's natural piety sets a problem. After the story, the departure in youth and springtime, comes the moral, the departure of youth and springtime. In poetic terms there is both change and the fullest unity. But Schumann's mind is fixed in fair weather. He is wholly at one with the young men in the first part of the song, comfortably at home with the idea of domestic bliss in the next. But the sailor is already at the limits of his horizon, and the pious moral is beyond it. In the result the music feels constrained in peroration and postlude to express a new idea of pious homily; and perhaps the constraint is more apparent than the piety.

NOTES. 1. The title is Schumann's. He adds 'in die' in bar 6 and remodels 'in der buhlenden Wogen/farbig klingenden Schlund' at bars 47–50 to preserve his melody. Eichendorff has 'in *die* Runde' at bars 53–54, 'über die Wasser' at bar 55 and '*s*ingen und *kl*ingen' in bar 57. The final repetition is as usual part of the musical peroration.

2. Manuscripts show that bars 39–46 gave Schumann a great deal of difficulty. The first version has the piano part in minim chords with bass octave suspensions (M 31) as in *Im Rhein* or *Auf einer Burg*. The reason for the uncertainty may lie in the poem. Verse 4 is certainly about the sailor; but its words speak of the sea. Schumann's mind reacts directly in music of slow dark depths. But this makes too great a contrast musically; so, after much thought, the music of the fifth verse is made to serve here also.

3. The manly motif 56 was mandatory. The lifting sixths at 'so jubelnd' suggest via motif 19 that Schumann thought of the lads as themselves singing. The tenths in this and the following bars go well with the companionship of motif 57. The blend of this singing with a new rocking movement in the piano part is apt and delightful at bars 31 et seq. The upward striding turn given to the main theme at bars 12–13 is typical of the open-air march movement of motif 4, complete with horn passages. This is also a reminiscence from *Der frohe Wandersmann*, confirming the motivic association. Even when drained from its earlier version the sea-music still has its characteristic bass notes (M 29[A]), perhaps recalled from *Abends am Strand*. The rather owlish solemnity of the typical motif 30 texture at bars 57–58 serves well enough for the final verse, which Schumann thinks of as preaching.

111. (Op. 27, No. 5) Nur ein lächelnder Blick
Zimmermann – November 1840

But one smiling glance from your bright eyes, and I feel my inmost being illumined. So on an overcast day a friendly sunbeam cheers me, breaking through a veil of cloud. [*But one smiling glance from your bright eyes, and I feel my inmost being illumined.*]

But one dear word from your rosy lips and my whole being is restored and refreshed. So a drop of aromatic oil distilled from the rose can diffuse its fragrance through locks and bosom and robe. [*But one dear word from your rosy lips and my whole being is restored and refreshed.*]

Schumann, apparently under the influence of Mendelssohn here, might have wished to distil a drop of chromatic oil in his music. Over the years this has become something musty, but not everyone will find its period flavour disagreeable.

NOTES. 1. There is no discernible family or social reason (as there was for e.g. *Lorelei* and *Mädchen-Schwermut*) why Schumann should have set such stuff as this; he may have admired it. The repetitions are his.

2. The verses were called *Distichon*, as an obvious attempt to render a classic metre. The setting gives no inkling of this, Schumann being content to let his melody ride smooth-shod over the metrical stress. Indeed one suspects that the material is a remnant of previous piano music being thriftily used up.

3. Some further confirmation of this is provided by the form in which the song was first published, as a supplement to the *Neue Zeitschrift für Musik* of December 1840. The music was made even more mellifluously genteel by two piano interludes in each verse (between what are now the two halves of bars 8, 12, 39, and 43) and a descending phrase for the voice to fill up bars 16 and 47.

4. The accent at 'plötzlich' is one aspect of motif 61. But the corresponding accent at bar 45 seems pointless and might well be omitted. There are other editorial problems, e.g. why an accent in bar 28 but not in bar 59?

5. The last page of Brahms' *Auf dem See*, Op. 106, No. 2, owes much to bars 25–27 (56–58) here.

112. (Op. 49, No. 3) Die Nonne (The nun)

Fröhlich – November 1840

The nun stands in the garden framed among the rose-trees in the sunshine, so that the roses make a garland for her, to left and to right.

From over the way there come sounds of festivity from a wedding party; there's dancing and singing, everyone wants to dance with the bride.

The bride comes out on to the balcony to cool her flushed cheeks; the nun looks across and her eyes brim with tears.

'She, happy, like a rose under her white wreath; I, joyless and pale under my garland of red.'

Fröhlich had some repute as a writer of gnomic verse. This sample is typical both in its symbolism of isolation and in the odd antitheses of its last lines, intended as a stylish apothegm. Schumann clearly likes it and in consequence makes a most acceptable song, full of inventiveness and interest. The opening, quiet as a nun, with its hint of smooth organ harmonies, makes a fine contrast with the louder staccato wedding-music, a memory of which steals reflectively into the piano accompaniment to the closing recitative.

NOTES. 1. 'Möcht'' in bar 29 should read 'will'. The final repetition is Schumann's, whose slip in writing 'herüber' instead of 'hinüber' might indicate that his mind in this year is dancing attendance at a wedding. Nevertheless he chooses the 'unhappy wedding' theme yet again.

2. This theme, with a nun as the central figure, suggests the contemporary and far finer *Stirb Lieb und Freud*; and this seems to have been the source of some of the music. There is a general similarity of key and mood; the opening melody here quotes the actual notes of 'Alsbald der Glocken', etc., at bars 28–29.

3. Perhaps another such reminiscence accounts for the relation of the E major wedding-tune here to that far more famous and striking wedding dance in *Das ist ein Flöten und Geigen* (at bar 4).

4. There are other interesting affinities with *Dichterliebe*. Thus the D flat major/C sharp minor relation is found in the last song of that cycle; and the device of ending on an unresolved dominant seventh (M 44) is found in the first.

5. There is the manly motif 56 at bars 26–30, where everyone wants to dance with the bride; the three-part harmony used for a girl's grief (M 34); the idea of reverie (M 32) in bar 37 at 'ihr gehn die Augen über'; and sadness (M 8) in the bass semibreves of the last two bars.

113. (Op. 142, No. 3) Mädchen-Schwermut (A girl's melancholy)

Lily Bernhard – November 1840

The dew shining on the flower-cups looks like tears; to sad eyes, even flowers seem to be weeping.

The wind breathing along the fresh green leaves sounds like a lament; to sad ears, even spring breezes seem like a sigh for lost love.

Yet to the sad soul the stars in the night sky do not seem like the presence of God; there can be no gleam of comfort in this joyless world.

The music captures not only the languid and anæmic charm of the verses but also an authentic quality of sharp despair; the crying dissonance at 'Himmelszelt' (the canopy of the sky) in the last verse is unusually expressive even for Schumann. But for the most part the music is derivative and supine; and it was rightly left unpublished in his lifetime.

NOTES. 1. The verses are amateur, though better than most by the Schumann circle. The text has been ascribed[1] to Lily Bernhard, a friend of Clara's.

---

[1] Paula and Walter Rehberg, *Robert Schumann* (1951).

2. The main musical material is much the same as that of *Fürchtemachen* from Op. 15. Perhaps that title was a misnomer; or perhaps to the depressive Schumann melancholy and fear were closely akin. There is a later echo in the 'un poco adagio' section of the second movement of the quartet Op. 41, No. 3 of 1842.

3. The three-part harmony (M 34) and the key of E minor, complete with falling semitone (M 8) seem often to be an expression of the sorrow of a girl – here identified by the Clara-theme X in the vocal melody at bars 10–11, 19–20, 30–31 and 39–40.

Zwölf Gedichte (Twelve poems) von Justinus Kerner Op. 35 and other Kerner settings

It was the poetry of Justinus Kerner, with its overtones of mysticism and tragedy, that had drawn from the seventeen-year-old Schumann his first songs. So it was natural that at the height of his song-writing powers, in May 1840, he should think of Kerner again; and a letter to Clara of that time asks her to bring a copy of the poems for him to set.

Meanwhile they had married. In the twelve songs of Op. 35, his first major work thereafter, the love-song-cycle is wedded to the maturer style. As in the two *Liederkreis*, *Myrthen* and *Dichterliebe* the key sequence is significant (the main function of No. 9 for example is as a structural link).

The selection of poems hints at a story of lost love and separation. But the verse, acceptable though much of it is, will not stand this treatment; not even Schumann's art can make a unity out of this material. True to his new style the most memorable songs are on the whole those with some element of drama or conflict (Nos. 115, 116, 119); though the lyrics are also very beautiful in their way.

114. (Op. 35, No. 1) Lust der Sturmnacht (Joy in a stormy night)

Kerner – November 1840

When rainstorms gust and squall over hill and plain, making inn-signs and windows rattle with their violence, and wayfarers are lost in the night, how sweet to be at peace within doors, blissfully lost in love. All the golden shine of heaven floods the quiet room.

Richness of life, have mercy; let me be held safe in soft arms. Then spring flowers stir, clouds are blown away, and birds sing. Never end, oh wild night of storms; let the window shake, the inn-signs clash, the waves roar; the radiance of heaven shines all around me.

The song is a whole-hearted response to the poem. The dark storm rages in the piano part, grim and gusty until 'ruht es sich so süss' (how sweet to be at peace) where the heavy chords are drawn aside to let in a flood of melody. This adds a new note of joyous exhilaration to the storm music until finally storm and brightness mingle, the dark thunder shines; sorrow and love, light and dark, life and death, are illuminated from within the music by one continuous light.

At least, this is the aim of poetry and music alike. It may be that they too are a little exaggerated. But given the necessary virtuosity, they can achieve that effect; and once heard, however briefly, it is not easily forgotten.

NOTES. 1. Schumann repeats the last five words, changes 'ziehen, Vögel' to 'zieh'n, und Vöglein' in bar 32; and the first word from 'wann' to 'wenn'.

2. The rocking movement of *Schöne Wiege* (M 35^A) is excitingly quickened; thrusting syncopations are added (M 61 transformed by the sforzandi into the strength of M 53); the tenths in voice and piano suggest propinquity (M 57); the joyous arpeggios (M 23) stand up strongly in the subconscious regions of the left hand where the long bass notes have their own distinctive meaning (M 35). All this melts and blends together in the cataleptic music of a trance of flowers, clouds and birds in bars 29–33 (the dream of M 32).

3. Even the notation has special interest. Thus the main thematic material is in the key of E flat minor, but is written as E flat major with accidentals; an intuitive symbol of the poetic interplay of bright and dark.

115. (Op. 45, No. 2) Stirb, Lieb' und Freud' (Die, love and joy)

Kerner – November 1840

In Augsburg stands a tall house, not far from the old cathedral. From it one fine morning comes a devout girl; amid loud singing her dear figure enters the cathedral.

There she kneels and prays before the image of Our Lady. Heaven has filled her heart; all worldly pleasures fade. 'O pure Virgin', she prays, 'let me be yours alone.'

The muffled tolling of the bell recalls her from her prayers. She walks through the great nave, heedless of the crown of lilies shining in her hair.

All the congregation gaze in wonder at her halo of bright flowers. But she only moves on a little way, as far as the high altar. 'Take me poor maid to be a nun; die, love and joy!'

God grant that this girl wear her veil serenely. She is my own true love and will be so till doomsday. But now she will never know; my heart is breaking; die, love and light!

Schumann finds in this poem his most fertile ground; vivid pictures, keen emotion. The inward eye sees in the great cathedral one small figure; the inward ear hears among the chanting and the carillon one lonely cry. All the musical ideas are seen in a diffused religious light; the tranquil dedication of A flat major, the tolling bass bell notes, the old-world ceremonial, the archaic time-signature CC, and over all the massive power of a Bach organ prelude treading the ears to symbolize an inexorable fate. And this background gives an impressive emotive tension to the high notes on the last page; 'Zur Nonne weiht mich arme Maid' (take me poor maid to be a nun), like the echo of a child's cry heard drifting down from the dome.

NOTES. 1. Kerner has 'a*n* helle*m*' (bar 6), 'Mariä' (bar 15), 'Glock*e*' (bar 28). Schumann repeats 'die liebe' (bar 13), amends 'auf dem' to 'am' (bar 36) and adds 'Herz-' (bar 63) for the sake of his tune.

2. The last of these changes may have a deeper explanation. 'Herzallerliebste' occurs in the *Dichterliebe* song *Das ist ein Flöten und Geigen*, the prime example of the 'unhappy wedding' theme with which Schumann was obsessed; and this form may be an unconscious link between the two songs. For both poet and composer the theme is tragedy though the marriage is to Heaven; cf. also *Die Nonne* written at nearly the same time.

3. Motifs; the tenths at bar 22, etc., may be motif 57; the melody is the 'walking' idea of motif 20; the bell is obvious enough in the crotchet-minim rhythm of bars 28–39, 32–33, 44 and 47–48.

4. The three-part harmony has sad overtones, for Schumann (M 34), even though the tonality is mainly major. By the end it is the relative minor; and the ending on the dominant of that key is shared (perhaps by coincidence) with another song lamenting the passing of a loved girl, *Die Sennin* (some ten years later).

5. The girl's cry of 'Stirb, Lieb' and Freud'' uses four notes from the final chorus, *Herr Jesus Christ erhöre mich*, of Bach's Passion according to St John, which Schumann heard in 1840.

116. (Op. 35, No. 3) Wanderlied (A traveller's song) (Song of travel)

Kerner – December 1840

Come, a last glass of sparkling wine, and then goodbye friends, we must part; goodbye mountains, goodbye home; a strong force drives me away, into the wide world.

The sun does not stand still in the skies but is driven on over land and sea; the wave does not tarry on the lonely beach, the storms rage over the countryside.

The bird flies with scudding cloud and sings of home in distant lands. So a young man is driven out into the woods and fields to wander like his mother, the wandering world.

There he is greeted by birds well-known from across the sea; they flew there from the meadows of home. There the flowers have well-known scents; they were blown there by the winds of home. The birds know his ancestral home; the flowers are those he once planted as a garland for his sweetheart; and love follows him, goes with him hand in hand; and so even the farthest of far away places becomes home to him.

[*Come, a last glass of sparkling wine, and then goodbye friends, we must part; goodbye mountains, goodbye home; a strong force drives me away, into the wide world.*]

Schumann was a reluctant adventurer, more the poet of the fireside than the roadside. The words, like those of his other attempts to write in the folksong vein, are better known to a different tune. The main theme comes at least once too often, the final repetition is unimpressive, the transition to it is weak, the music is derivative from earlier and better songs.

But the work survives indestructibly fresh and bright; in this year of 1840 even the second-order music has a wealth and quality of invention that preserve it against criticism and against time.

NOTES. 1. 'Die' in bar 43 should be 'einst'. Kerner's poem ends at bar 48.

2. The manuscript is dated 29th December 1840. That may have been only the fair copy, or perhaps this is an afterthought among the Kerner songs. The music itself testifies that Schumann's creative powers are slowing down; their separate components can be observed. First, outdoor life suggests the key of B flat major. This, together with the idea of a character role, as it were assuming the guise of a traveller, recalls the opening fanfare of Schumann's own *Zigeunerleben*, Op. 29, No. 3, written earlier the same year (for small choir with piano accompaniment and tambourine *ad lib*). This is an adumbration of the manly motif 56; that motif itself appears as the main thematic material, together with the joyous arpeggio of motif 23 at e.g. bar 4. Similarly the middle section is derived (perhaps because of the interpolated idea of birds in each) from that of *Ich wandelte unter den Bäumen*, with similar music after a similar modulation (M 47). When this material runs out in bar 41, *Zigeunerleben* again supplies more; cf. pp. 9–11 of the Breitkopf edition with the quaver movement here at bars 41–50. Perhaps 'so wird ihm zur Heimat das ferneste Land' here reminds Schumann of 'sie schauen im Traume das glückliche Land' in the earlier setting. At least the staccato of motif 32 suggests a dreamy mood hereabouts. The following chromatics (M 48) suggest the idea of reported speech, again as if the idea were a dramatic scene rather than a self-contained lyric. There follow four bars of time-filling, awaiting the return of the first theme. This recurs with the predictable peroration on the lines of *Der Hidalgo* and *Der Page*. Finally the new melody introduced to make a dramatic finale recalls the end of *Ich wandre nicht*, before marching off to the strains of the wedding-march from *Frauenliebe und -leben*.

117. (Op. 35, No. 4) Erstes Grün (First green)

Kerner – December 1840

You fledgling green, you fresh grass, how many a heart you have healed that was made ill by the winter's snow; oh, how my heart longs for you.

Already you are waking from the night of earth; how my eyes laugh in delight at the sight of you! Here in this quiet valley I press you, green of spring, to my heart and mouth.

I am impelled to shun humankind; no word of man will ease my pain; only young springtime green laid to my heart will make it beat more calmly.

The poem contrasts human debility with the restoring freshness that dwells deep down in nature. Schumann contrasts a melancholy minor song-music with a joyous vision of springtime in the major piano interludes. In the result the words and their music are at different stages of recuperation. Thus the ecstatic second verse is sung to the same tune as the first. But this Schumannian treatment is effective; the feelings of assuagement and healing assigned to the piano interludes are thereby symbolized as lying too deep for words. The final postlude is subtly varied for a brief moment at one altered chord which falters and doubts for a while before believing again in the grass-green Avalon of the composer's imagination.

NOTES. 1. The title in Kerner (who was a doctor) is *Frühlingskur* (Spring cure), – perhaps too clinical for Schumann's hypochondria. His 'brichst' in bar 15 seems preferable to Schumann's 'wächst'.

2. The opening minor triad is characteristic (M 7); and the rising minor horn passage in bar 4 is a good example of its sense of courage in adversity (M 5). The staccato throughout is the dream motif 32, especially during the piano interlude's vision of spring (cf. the analogous interlude in *Ländliches Lied*, Op. 68, No. 20). Its cadence here is motif 2 just as in the prelude to *Wenn durch die Piazzetta*. This elated G major music of an idealized springtime has clear affinity with that of *Märzveilchen* and *Der Nussbaum*; it contrasts effectively here with the G minor winter of discontent.

118. (Op. 35, No. 5) Sehnsucht nach der Waldgegend (Longing for the forest lands)

Kerner – *c.* November 1840

Would that I had never left you, forests, high marvellous woods; you surrounded me lovingly many a long year.

Where in the shade of your branches birds sang, and the silver stream, many a song flowed fresh and bright from my heart too.

Your waving, your echoing, your unceasing murmur, all your melodies awoke those songs of mine.

But here in these distant plains all seems silent and deserted, and I scan the blue skies for clouds in vain.

And in enforced silence song seldom stirs, as a caged bird only half sings, sundered from brook and tree.

Whatever their poetic merits, Kerner's words come straight from real experience of a transition from woodsman (at Welzheim) to plainsman (at Gaildorf). Schumann's joy in Nature here, real and beautiful though it is, at first sounds cautious, like a townsman's excursion. But he is at home with the image of birdsong and love-song in the shadowed woods, and the piano's brief twilit reverie and bright melody are open and moving until the rhetoric closes in again.

NOTES. 1. Kerner has 'In den Busen eingezwinget' (which seems to suit the melody rather better); 'Halle' in bar 12 and 'Bach' instead of 'Blatt' in bar 25.

2. 'Euer Wogen' suggests waving foliage (M 21). This, with the added idea of distance – '*weiten* Triften' – brings back the music of *In der Fremde*.

3. This song profoundly impressed Brahms, as a comparison with his Op. 72, No. 1 shows (*Alte Liebe*, also in G minor), and Clara Schumann, who to the end of her days numbered it among her own special favourites (her theme X in canon ends the song).

4. No. 122, note 1, applies.

119. (Op. 35, No. 6) Auf das Trinkglas eines verstorbenen Freundes (To the wine glass of a dead friend)

Kerner – November 1840

Fine glass, you now stand empty; glass that he raised so often and so joyously. The spider has spun dark webs around you.

Tonight you shall be filled moonbright with the gold of Rhenish grapes. I look into the hallowed gleam of your depths and tremble.

What I see there is a secret not to be told to ordinary mortals. But it tells me clearly that nothing can part friend from friend.

In this faith, fair glass, I drain you with high heart. Clear in your precious blood, oh chalice, is mirrored the bright gold of the stars.

Silently the moon goes down the valley. Solemnly midnight chimes. The glass stands empty. In its crystal depths the hallowed echo still sounds.

We may or may not relish Kerner's attempts to tune the mind to a preposterous pitch. But within its conventions this poem is eloquent and even moving, combining a very real grief with an impressive sense of the ceremonial mourning rituals of white magic. Schumann's own close friend, Ludwig Schunke, with whom he felt an almost mystic kinship, had died young a few years earlier; this music has deep earnestness and rich sentiment.

Full chords followed by solemn octaves set the scene. The second verse sends the tonality twice flatwards, the melody lower, the harmonies choral, in a mellow oblation of golden wine. The following music perhaps offers mystery rather than the poet's certainty. But the hollow octaves at 'was ich erschau' (what I see) and 'wird mir klar' (it tells me) are an impressive evocation. Then Schumann's vision makes superb images of dark valley and riding moon; low chords followed by high chords, in harmonies moving from dark to bright over twelve bars of midnight. A final hymn-like affirmation of faith ends the song.

NOTES. 1. The poem commemorates Stierlein von Lorch, a minor official and the poet's friend and patron. Kerner's title is *An das Trinkglas*, etc.

2. The manly motif 56 comes at the mention of raised glasses; the staccato of the opening bars is the reverie of motif 32. The falling semitones in octaves at bars 17–18, 21–22, is the sad motif 8 writ large; these passages are a clear example of Schumann's mystery motif 40.

3. The key-shift from the note F considered first as a dominant and then enharmonically as the mediant of D flat major occurs for the stars in majesty in Beethoven's Op. 48, No. 4, *Die Ehre Gottes aus der Natur*, which Schumann may have had vaguely in mind.

4. Midnight is allotted exactly twelve bars (33–41); cf. the more striking effect at the end of the *Davidsbündler*, Op. 6.

5. It is not clear why the bass at the last two crotchets of the first bar should differ from that at bars 5, 25 and 29; perhaps the E flats should be restored.

120. (Op. 35, No. 7) Wanderung (Wandering)

Kerner – November 1840

Arise and travel with a light heart into unknown lands. Many a cherished bond must be broken today.

You wayside shrines of home, where I have often knelt in prayer; you trees and hills, give me your blessing as I go.

The wide world is still asleep, no birdsong wakes the grove; but I am not forsaken, I am not alone.

For at my heart I carry the dear token of her love; I press it, and all earth and heaven are near and dear to me.

A muted horn call; silence; then a brisk trotting movement, full of open-air alacrity. The music assumes a not wholly convincing piety as the blessing is asked. Then the brisk movement resumes, all the brighter for this momentary contrast; and the last page of the song is full of a new exhilaration, in the higher registers of voice and keyboard.

NOTES. 1. Schumann has 'frisch' instead of 'froh' in bar 3; and repeats the last four words.

2. The staccato is not motif 32, but a much lighter touch; a distant horn call. The composer's direction is 'Die Begleitung leicht und zart'.

3. The dominant chain of motif 64 in bars 19–20, and the sad key-shift to a minor third higher (M 25) suggests a farewell to the loved one, rather than a greeting to the shrines of home.

4. B flat is the outdoor key; the horn passages (M 4) reinforce that impression. The word 'Himmel' yet again sends the music flatwards, bars 35 etc. (M 50). The arpeggios of motif 23 are ubiquitous.

121. (Op. 38, No. 8) Stille Liebe (Silent love)

Kerner – November 1840

If I could praise you in my songs, they would be endless, the singing would never be done.

But to my great grief I can only carry you, my love, silently in the shrine of my heart.

And this grief forced me to sing this little song; bitterly regretting that none of my songs has yet proved worthy of you.

Instead of bitter sorrow here is a sweet melancholy; instead of just one little song the music is all melody, itself the unattainable endless singing of which the verses speak. The result, if not outstanding for its relevance to the text, is outstanding among the Kerner songs for harmonic richness and melodic appeal.

NOTES. 1. A third verse is omitted (after bar 26).

2. The structure of the music is puzzling. Thus it is not easy to see why the chord of the first half of bar 23 should be altered from its counterpart in bar 11, while the corresponding harmony at bar 36 is ambiguous. An augmented fifth is added at the last note in bar 24, but not in bar 12 or 37. The semiquaver group in bar 17 is written as a sextolet in some editions though the intended effect seems rather that of a written-out turn, e.g.

And why do the semiquaver chords at bar 5 become long-drawn-out quavers at bars 44 and 45?

3. These questions may be helped by tracing the sources, conscious or other, of Schumann's inspiration. Thus the melody at bars 10–12 is akin to that at bars 5–7 of Beethoven's Op. 98, *An die ferne Geliebte*, a favourite source-book; while the piano interlude which follows in Beethoven has much in common with the piano prelude here.

4. There is a specific resemblance: Schumann's prelude chords are, note for note, the opening harmony of the Schubert masterpiece *Dass sie hier gewesen* (Op. 59, No. 2). There are other Schubert echoes, e.g. in the sequential treatment of the prelude's melody as in *An die Geliebte* or *An die Nachtigall*.

5. All these songs are in their different ways expressions of the sadness of separation from the loved one; the cumulative force of all this yearning nostalgia breaks into embellished chromatics in the style of Chopin, who might almost have written the postlude to this song. Even in the first few months of his marriage Schumann is still creating new forms from the emotional experience of separation from Clara.

6. The sad key change to the minor third above (M 25) is actually heard here

as a relationship via the flattened or minor third of the first key. There is the dreamy staccato of motif 32 in bar 6 (and therefore perhaps analogously in bars 44–45, though none is marked). At bar 11 are the affectionate dominants of motif 64 and the rising sixth of the singing motif 19 which together epitomize Schumann's song; the last four notes of the right hand speak of beauty (M 65). The yearning of motif 16 is ubiquitous.

122. (Op. 38, No. 9) Frage (A question)

Kerner – *c.* November 1840

Were it not for you, holy light of evening, or you, starbright night, or the finery of flowers, the richness of the budding grove, or the solemn glory of mountains, or birdsong out of high heaven, or the full-throated song of man – without these things what joy could the heart find in time of adversity?

NOTES. 1. The m/s is undated; but style, poet and order in Schumann's records confirm end-1840.

2. This song has the function of linking two others. Thus, it makes a diatonic contrast with their chromaticism, and its harmonies modulate from No. 8's E flat to No. 10's C major. Not many composers wrote songs as bridge-passages; and it is not surprising that this is the typical piano-piece, with added voice.

3. The final question is motif 45. The use of the dominant of the relative minor here, as in *Stirb, Lieb und Freud* and *Die Sennin*, seems to expect a discouraging answer: 'none, alas'; and see No. 202, Note 3.

123. (Op. 36, No. 10) Stille Tränen (Silent tears)

Kerner – November 1840

Just roused from sleep, you wander through the meadow; from east to west the sky arches, miraculously blue.

But while you were lying careless in untroubled slumber that same sky was weeping down tear after tear the whole night through.

So in the silent night many a man weeps out his sorrow; though in the morning you may think to look at him that his heart had always been gay.

Weeping at night is the burden of the poem, a secret sorrow; but Schumann seems to express waking ecstasy, a savoured joy. In its solemnity of sustained bass notes, its lush chromatics, its mezzo-staccato reverie, the music dreams but does not grieve. At most there is the longing of separation, a sumptuous vision of unattainable beauty.

NOTES. 1. The dark sustained bass notes are motif 29^{B}; the repeated chords are humility (M 38); the mezzo-staccato is dream (M 32). The idea of walking brings out motif 20 in the bass in bars 5–8 (at the word 'wandeln'). The augmented fifth of motif 12 and the dominants of motif 64 are ubiquitous. The trills in the bass and treble are elation, combined with the beauty motif 65 at bar 54 and in the postlude passim. It is no surprise to find the Clara-themes P[1] and Q[1], as in the Rückert songs and *Dichterliebe*, informing the postlude, with the yearning acciaccatura chord (M 16) as in *Frauenliebe*.

2. The postlude here as in No. 121 above has the mood and manner of Chopin.

3. The song was first printed in a supplement to Schumann's journal, the *Neue Zeitschrift für Musik*, in 1841.

124, 125. (Op. 35, Nos. 11 and 12)

Kerner – December 1840

124. Wer machte dich so krank? (Who made you so ill?)

Why have you been so ill? Who has done this to you? It was not any chill wind from the north, nor any starry night; not the shade of the trees, nor the heat of the sun; not sleeping or dreaming among the valley's flowers. It is mankind that has given me my death-wound. Nature healed me, but mankind gives me no peace.

125. Alte Laute (Old sounds)

Hear the bird sing on the flowering branch; cannot that deliver you, my heart, from your anxious dream? What do I hear? A voice from the past, the voice of a sorrowing lad who trusted the world and its pleasures. Those days are long past, there flowers no balm to heal me; and from this grievous dream only an angel will wake me.

The same melody is used for two different poems simply to echo a soft slow music with something even softer and slower; a linked sweetness long drawn out. But the two poems have nothing in common save that they are metrically analogous, and maudlin; and this effect, rather than any sense of finality, is what the music achieves.

NOTES. 1. The first poem has had its third verse excised to make it balance.

2. The music was designed for No. 124; the clashes on 'krank' and 'Tod' are expressive in that song, pointless in the next. So the changes in the second song are due to its words.

3. In this way we learn that Schumann scans more by *length* of syllable (e.g. compare the first vocal bar in each song), than by stress or sense. There is much evidence of this elsewhere in the songs, but few examples are so compelling.

4. As to motifs, we learn that 'Lust' with the acciaccatura to the dominant must express that word (M 16) in bar 18; and the change at 'bangen' in bar 24 is motivated by the distress of motif 13. The sad minor third key change is motif 35 in both songs.

126. (Op. 127, No. 1) Sängers Trost (A poet's consolation)

Kerner – December 1840

Even though there be no sweetheart to weep over my grave in time to come, yet the flowers will drop their gentle dew there.

Though no traveller linger there awhile on his journey, yet the moon will shine down there as she goes by.

And though in these meadows no living soul should think of me, yet the field will, and the silent grove.

Flowers, grove and meadow, stars and moonlight that I sang, they will not forget their singer.

The piano part presents the sweet singer of sad lute songs. The vocal melody pauses on the dominant; its three-fold repetition builds up a powerful tension of questioning and expectancy, discharged in a climax of piercing sweetness at 'Mondenlicht' against a background of soft mellow modulation to a flat key, whence a sustained high note shines out in a satisfyingly Schumannian reaction to the idea of a moonlit night. By way of coda the wistful melody is given a new turn of impassioned conviction; 'no, they will never forget me' it asserts, and the piano postlude reaffirms.

NOTES. 1. Kerner has 'Vorüberziehn' and 'dahin' in bars 13 and 17.

2. Why was this left unpublished until 1854? Perhaps Schumann found it derivative; there are echoes of other Kerner songs (compare e.g. the prelude here and in No. 118), of *Dichterliebe* and the piano-music.

3. The higher vocal line should be preferred in bars 28–30.

127. (Op. 142, No. 1) Trost im Gesang (Comfort in song)

Kerner – November 1840

The lone wanderer, deserted by moonlight as well as sunlight, sings a song through the darkness; and takes fresh heart.

With renewed courage he strides out on his way, which though empty of humankind is yet peopled with his bright songs.

It is night with me; my friends are far away; the last star of all has vanished from my sky.

Yet I go on my deserted path rejoicing; my songs go with me and brighten my way.

The poem's pedestrian metaphor deserves a similar setting. In the result the music is unconvincing; it conveys not so much a real comfort, as a resolve to march up and down and sing to show that it is not afraid.

NOTES. 1. Kerner has 'gehen' not 'ziehen' in bars 28 and 46; the repeats are Schumann's.

2. The manly motif 56 asserts courage in adversity; there is 'Glückes genug' (M 1) at bars 28 and 48, steadfast despite the gloom of the slow minims and the low semibreves suspended in bars 9–11, etc. (M 31/39), and walking (M 20) in the descending quavers of bar 6.

3. Perhaps the idea of brave walking in darkness, not to mention the vanishing of the sun or last star, put Schumann in mind of *Winterreise*; cf. bars 15–16 here with the last two bars of *Gefror'ne Tränen.* And simple though the idea of the poem is, it is not taken into account by Schumann, who puts his piano interlude between the first and second verse. Such considerations (see No. 126, note 2) may explain why he left the song unpublished.

4. Note the variation between bars 7 and 32, 8 and 33, 9 and 34.

Zwölf Gedichte (Twelve poems) aus Rückerts Liebesfrühling Op. 37

Rückert (not Heine) was Schumann's favourite source of texts. Lyrics from *Liebesfrühling* (Love's springtime) began and ended *Myrthen*, Op. 25; and that choice later seemed right to celebrate a marriage as well as a wedding.

In 1841 Schumann wrote to his publishers 'I should like to give my wife a surprise on her birthday (in mid-September) in the following way. We have written a number of Rückert songs together (sic) in the form of questions and answers (sic) and so on. I should like to see this collection in print by her birthday; would it be possible for you to have the volume ready by that time? I think these songs should arouse interest; they are kept light and simple throughout, and were written with much joy and love.'

The letter, like the music, expresses Schumann's love of romance in every sense. The success of *Myrthen* should have been repeatable in these new songs. He was as blissfully happy in marriage as in courtship; there is the same pattern of personal emotion, mystery, cyclic unity. But bliss is not inspiration. What should have been a rich tapestry of feeling becomes an edifying sampler; and even this is turned inward on to a private felicity, so that all we see is the dull underside of the weave.

Something has gone sadly wrong. Perhaps the new element of objectivity in Schumann's work was already somewhat at odds with poems of personal lyric feeling, as in some of the Kerner songs above. With Rückert's verse the duality is flagrant. Nos 7 and 12 of this opus are in fact duets (not considered here). No. 6 has the idea of duetting thrust upon it. The other songs seem to have a dual aspect of their own. Nos. 2, 4 and 11 (also omitted) are acknowledged to be by Clara Schumann; but they have an occasional master touch which is not hers. There is evidence that some, perhaps many, of Clara's songs and indeed much of her music in general had the benefit of Schumann's collaboration (see also No. 103, note 2). Conversely the Op. 37 songs attributed to Schumann himself do suggest that 'written together' was what he actually meant, in the sense that a primary musical idea by Clara was then developed by him. This conforms with his love of mystification, with his practice in many of the piano works which use a theme of hers (e.g. Op. 5, 6, 14), and with the musical evidence as discussed in the notes to each song. The secret collaboration in songwriting between Mendelssohn and his sister Fanny of which their friends the Schumanns could have been told in confidence is an obvious parallel and a possible source of the idea.

128. (Op. 37, No. 1) Der Himmel hat eine Träne geweint
Rückert – January 1841

Heaven wept a tear that thought to lose itself in the sea. But the mussel came and enclosed it, saying 'From now on you shall be my pearl. You need have no fear of the waves; I shall bear you calmly through them.'

Oh you my sorrow, you my joy, you teardrop from heaven in my heart. Grant, Heaven, that in purity of heart I may guard this purest of your drops.

Schumann was clearly in the mood to be impressed by a lyric climax where a mussel stands revealed (a solemn moment) as the Poet declaring his love; but his thick bland music makes the verse only a little more palatable.

NOTES. 1. Schumann repeats the last line.

2. It did not take his genius to write bars 1–5 and 15–18. The opening rhythm seems not to have his usual motivic sense of urgency (M 61); and his accentuation, though unimpressive, does not normally allot so many different note-values or stresses to the same syllable in the space of three bars as here on the word 'du' and 'mein' at bars 15–18. If these ideas are Clara's then the opening bars of other songs of this opus may be hers also, as a deliberate plan. It is interesting that bars 1–3 transposed a fifth higher make the opening piano part of the duet, Op. 37, No. 12, *So wahr die Sonne scheinet*, which is acknowledged as Clara's.

3. There are also typical Schumann touches, e.g. the key-change at bars 8 et seq., with its absurdly apt motivic sense of interpolation (M 47) at the very moment when the pearl is enclosed. The tenths at bars 19–20 and 25 suggest motif 57; the bass sings 'Clara' (her theme X) at bars 21–22, the poem's hidden and flawless pearl.

4. New material in the postlude suggests deliberate allusion or quotation in Schumann. Here is the melody of the then famous and still well-known love song *Caro mio ben*, attributed to Giuseppe Giordani (c. 1750–98) – a novel tribute to Clara.

5. Bar 21 reappears as bar 18 of *Auf dem Rhein* (q.v.) at the very moment where a treasure is enclosed, with exactly the same metaphorical sense as in this song.

6. Cf. Franz, Op. 48, No. 4.

129. (Op. 37, No. 3) O ihr Herren
Rückert – January 1841

You lords, oh you great rich lords, in your beautiful gardens have you then no need at all for a nightingale?

Here is one who has sought all through the world for a quiet corner; grant me but this, and I will repay you for it with my singing.

Compared with the independence and significance expressed in Goethe's poem on a similar theme (No. 176 q.v.) Rückert's verses here seem servile and trite. The square music of the opening section sounds as stiff and self-conscious as the poet's rhetorical question. But the nightingale's yearning for quietude elicits a more flexible lyric response, and the embowered singing suggested by the postlude is wholly delightful.

NOTES. 1. In this setting of run-on lines the internal rhymes of 'werten' and 'Gärten', 'stilles' and 'will es' are easily missed.

2. At bars 10–12 occurs a reminiscence of Mendelssohn's *Minnelied*, Op. 47,

No. 1, bars 10–14. The words of each song at this point are about birdsong in the shade.

3. The figuration of descending semiquavers that immediately follows the first mention of the nightingale in bar 8, and recurs in the postlude, is motif 21, perching.

4. The nightingale's brief solo in the postlude is, fittingly, a lovesong to Clara (her motif P).

130. (Op. 37, No. 5) Ich hab' in mich gesogen

Rückert – January 1841

I have drawn into myself the sweet spring which abides in me though vanished from the world. Here are the blue skies, the green fields; the scents and the flowers are here, the roses in bloom.

And here is my loved one close to me, longing for the bliss of springtime. She leans to listen, to hear in silent joy the springtide streams flowing in my heart.

And thence my songs rise and flow all about her in the full spate of a God-given springtime. And as she gazes in rapture her joy lights up all the world in a dream of spring.

Inner sweetness is stifled by too much earnestness in the music as in the poem. Yet there is at least congruence between words and setting. The music melts for the sweet sighs of love, flows in the streams of spring; and there is a well-timed reappearance of the first theme as spring returns triumphant.

NOTES. 1. Rückert has 'vollen' in bar 23.

2. Perhaps the opening bars with their prim sequences derive from an idea of Clara's. But their treatment is authentic enough. The staccato at bars 2 and 4 is typical (M 32).

3. Cf. Franz, Op. 50, No. 6. There is also a Schubert sketch for male voice quintet.

131. (Op. 37, No. 6) Liebste, was kann denn uns scheiden?

Rückert – January 1841

Dearest, what can part us? Can separation part us? No. Though we remain apart we are together in our hearts, I thine, thou mine for ever.

Dearest, what can part us? Can distance part us? No. Our love is not of this earth; we shall be united in heaven, I thine, thou mine, for ever.

Dearest, what can part us? Can sorrow or happiness part us? No. For better, for worse, our fates are linked together, I thine, thou mine, for ever.

Dearest, what can part us? Can the world's hatred and envy part us? No. Nothing can disturb the serenity of our love, we shall never be separated, I thine, thou mine, for ever.

NOTES. 1. The repetitions, and the idea of arranging the words as a notional duet, are Schumann's.

2. Again it did not take Schumann to write this. But the left hand at bars 7–9 makes his clear fingerprint (as in the piano piece *Aufschwung*, or the song *Lorelei*, bars 7–8, among other examples); and the tenths (M 57) are thematic enough, like the dominant question in bar 2 (M 43) and the rhetorical question in bar 6 (M 42).

132. (Op. 37, No. 8) Flügel! Flügel!

Rückert – January 1841

Wings, wings, to fly over hill and dale; wings, to set my heart floating on the dawn sunlight! Wings, to soar over the seas with the sunrise; wings, wings to soar through life, over death and the grave!

Wings such as my youth had, now flown away; wings like the illusion of happiness that deceived my heart! Wings, to fly after the days now fled; wings, to track down the joys now blown away in the wind!

Wings like nightingales, when the roses fade, to fly in search of them away from this land of mists! Wings, wings!

From this shore of exile with no ship in sight, oh for wings to bear me back to the homeland where my crown is shining. Oh for freedom, as the chrysalis splits to release the butterfly when the spirit of Nature moves! Often in silent midnights I feel myself wafted aloft by the power of dream to the gateway of the stars!

Yet the plumage resplendent at night falls from me by day in the morning breeze. The burning sun melts my pinions, Icarus plunges headlong into the sea; and in the roaring waves of sensual life the spirit is drowned.

This high-flown poem is very far from being as innocuous as the rest; in its way it has life, movement, even some significance. Schumann responds finely to this unexpected challenge. The opening page is uninspired and tentative. But from then on we recognize the composer. Wings! and immediately the piano scherzo theme gestures upwards; the music is poised for flight.

At 'von dem Verbannungsstrande' (from the shore of exile) the rhythm becomes strangely becalmed, a painted ocean of the musical imagination. The effort needed to get the song out of these doldrums, without a breath of help from the words, becomes all too audible. But in the last page the composer again has something to say. The scherzo movement returns, dark and serious, with a new emphasis, as if pointing a moral. In the last quatrain and in the postlude there is a great upsurge of regret, remorse and renunciation that sounds like a fragment of autobiography, a disjointed confession in music.

NOTES. 1. Bar 21 'die' not 'sie'; bar 26 'Schatt*e*' (preserving the rhyme); bar 42 'fliehn' not 'blühn' (which is senseless); in bars 46–48 both 'Flügel's and in bar 53 the second are Schumann's; bar 61 '*w*ann'; bar 68 'flüg*l*en'; bar 86 'über'*n*'.

2. Is the first page by Clara? Only in bar 18 does the music really take wing. The octaves reaching for freedom are motif 16: bars 49–52 are held back by motif 59. Bars 57–64 are a well-known recitative stereotype (note motif 48 at bar 61); the chords at bar 72 mysteriously refer to the main theme of No. 133 below. Plainly this is Schumann himself, if in a depressive phase.

3. Perhaps in response to the words, the music of the last page has a real sense of drive and drama in its piano writing. The postlude has impatient urging of motif 61, the repeated bid for freedom of motif 16, both held in check by the rectitude of motif 51, in the sad minor. One can only guess what all this is about. Perhaps there is subconscious reminiscence of the Beethoven song *Neue Liebe, neues Leben*, Op. 75, No. 2; compare e.g. bars 1–4 of that song with bars 80–84 here and bars 4–8 there with bars 93–96 here. That song is about being unable to forget a past love; the Rückert text here is taken from the section of his poems headed 'Estranged'. But the music is more devoted than ever; from the entry of Schumann's own authentic voice at bar 18, and again on the last page, the melody cries out 'Clara' (theme X) over and over again.

133. (Op. 37, No. 9) Rose, Meer und Sonne
Rückert – January 1841

Rose, sea and sun are an image of my beloved, who has filled all my life with her radiance.

All the outpoured sunlight, all the dew of the spring meadow, are blended and enclosed in the heart of the rose. All hues, all scents of the spring countryside, vie together to grace the rose.

Rose, sea and sun are an image of my beloved, who has filled all my life with her radiance.

All rivers run through the lands of earth only to pour out their yearning into the lap of the sea. All springs flow into the inexhaustible abyss and so complete a cycle all round the flowering world.

Rose, sea and sun are an image of my beloved, who has filled all my life with her radiance.

All the stars in the sky are the eyes of the night looking down in love, and dying in the morning's fragrance when the dawn awakens. All the flames of the world, all the scattered radiance of the sky, flow brightly together in the sun's wreath of rays.

Rose, sea and sun are an image of my loved one, who has filled all my life with her radiance.

The music too intends an outpouring of praise and adoration slowly gathering in intensity like a force of nature until the whole cosmos is consumed in a great welter of flame, fragrance and song. Perhaps a little of this effect is achieved. The accompaniment gradually builds up from a clear trickle of single notes, through a coloured cascade of thirds and fourths, to a flowering Niagara of triads. But the melody and harmony are so decorous, the rhythmic pattern so square cut and static, that the final picture is hardly more than a huge herbaceous border in tone. This, though somewhat short of the ideal, is still delightful; and we can feel and share the joy of the postlude's new theme as it contemplates the beauty made by its own tending.

NOTES. 1. Rückert has 'Alle Düft'' etc., in bar 20. The final repetition is Schumann's.

2. The main motif is that of the movement of nature, very appropriately (M 21); and the main vocal melody has the joyous arpeggio of motif 23. The numinous subdominant was only to be expected (M 50 in the second part of each section). At the end of the song is Schumann's mild equivalent for Rückert's lush eroticism; the affectionate dominants of motif 64 at bars 84–85 provide a climax to the voice part.

3. The falling fifths obscurely associated with roses (M 27) are at the bass in bars 14–16 etc. with the word 'Rose'.

4. In case bars 11–14, etc., left us in any doubt about the inspiration of this song, the postlude is instructed to dispel it; 'Clara' announces the left hand at bars 89–90 and 93–94 (Q^1), in its *Mondnacht* form

The whole postlude is comparable with that of *Dichterliebe*.

134. (Op. 37, No. 10) O Sonn', o Meer, o Rose (Oh sun, oh sea, oh rose!)

Rückert – January 1841

As when the sun rises in triumph the stars that stood in the sky turn pale and fade one after the other until all disappear in the greater light of the sun; so it was when I found you, my love. You came, and whatever my heart had loved before vanished in your light. Oh sun, oh sea, oh rose!

As when the sea opens its embrace to the rivers that ardently pour in until they find peace in its depths; so it was when I found you, my love. My wounded heart with all its longing found peace in you. Oh sun, oh sea, oh rose!

As when in spring a fresh green breaks out all around, and until the rose comes as the queen of summer there is dispute as to who should wear the crown; so it was when I found you, my love. But now the flowering crown of my whole life is yours.

The idea of deliberate thematic relationship between two successive songs of a cycle is another of Schumann's many original suggestions which later composers, notably Hugo Wolf, were to develop most rewardingly. But here something has gone wrong. Though the theme is the same, the treatment is depressingly dull in the first few bars. The interludes and the postludes transfuse fresh life into the song; but not in time to save it.

NOTES. 1. The concluding passage of each verse with typical textual repetitions, and the bold chromatics at bars 18–19, etc. (heard again conveying the idea of a heady perfume in the later song *Die Meerfee*) seem authentic enough. So do the interludes and postlude, borrowed from the previous song complete with the murmur of 'Clara' (theme Q^1) here in bars 23–24, etc. The insistence on these interludes is such that in the third verse it imposes on the voice part a two bars' silence between a word and its qualifying adverb – 'Königlich/eintretend'.

2. But what about bars 1–5 and 16–18? True, they have Schumann's own manly theme (M 56); true, they have what is perhaps an echo of the melody of Schubert's *Morgenlied* (its bar 13, bar 4 here) – in each song the sun rises in triumph in the opening bars. But the solemn presentation, as the main thematic material of a song, of the notes and chords of the major triad, seem too abject even for a depressed Schumann; and these bars may well have been, just as in No. 128, Clara's allotted contribution.

* * *

The following three songs of uncertain date may all have been composed in late 1840. Certainly they conform to that pattern; the music is apter for the dramatic (*Tragödie*) than for the lyric (*Auf dem Rhein*).

* * *

135. (Op. 64, No. 3) Tragödie (A tragedy)

Heine – 1841 or earlier

I

Run away with me and be my wife and find shelter in my arms. In far lands my heart shall be your fatherland and your home.

If we do not run away together I shall die of grief and you will be left lonely and alone; and though you stay in your own home, it will be like a foreign land.

[*Run away with me and be my wife and find shelter in my arms. In far lands my heart shall be your fatherland and your home.*]

II

A frost fell in the spring night; it fell on the delicate forget-me-nots; they are withered and sere.

A lad loved a girl; they fled from home at night; neither father nor mother knew.

They wandered afar; they found no luck, no happiness; they are dead and gone.

III

On their grave grows a linden-tree, where the birds and the night winds sing; and in its shade sit the miller-lad and his sweetheart.

The winds are so faint and fearful, the birds' song so sweet and sad, that the chattering lovers are suddenly silent and weep without knowing why.

Heine said he had heard the central lyric of this triptych sung as a folksong. He surrounds it with his own imaginative reconstruction of the drama. Schumann responds well. The bluff heartiness of the first song is made palatable by its very real vigour and excitement, together with a memorable melodic line. There is a dramatic plunge to the far side of E minor at 'entfliehn wir nicht' (if we do not run away) foretelling heartbreak, which gradually rallies to the major tonality again as the original music returns with a fine swing and sense of timing.

Halfway through the following piano postlude the music breaks off, and in this sombre mood the second lyric begins. Its brief prelude says that a sad story is about to be told. In what follows the words are matched with a sweetly regretful melody – perhaps Schumann's own nearest approach to folk-song – while the piano has lightly-touched accompanying chords. The effect, heightened by restraint, is most moving.

Then comes a curious anticlimax. Schumann freakishly arranges the last piece as a duet for tenor and mezzo-soprano. The purpose of this is wholly unclear; but its all too clear effect is to detract from the viability of the work as a whole. It seems justifiable to perform the second song separately.

NOTES. 1. The repetition in I is Schumann's; he also transposes the last two words of II. Alone among Schumann's Heine settings, this text is not to be found in *Buch der Lieder*. It had appeared in a ladies' journal (*Taschenbuch für Damen*) of 1821. Perhaps Clara had a copy; certainly she knew the poems – her setting of II above was her 1840 Christmas present to Robert. This may have led him to set the trilogy later; the first we hear of this work is an orchestral version in November 1841. But more likely he drew his text from the settings by Mendelssohn for a capella chorus, Op. 43, Nos. 2–4, published in 1838. His own music has evident affinity with his earlier Heine settings; an original piano version, dating from 1840, seems not unlikely.

2. There is another puzzle. The text of II was said by Heine to be a folk-song. It has however been attributed (e.g. in the *Oxford Book of German Verse*) to Anton von Zuccalmaglio (1803–69). He was, it is true, a prolific writer of what passed for folk-song. On the other hand he was a close friend of the Schumanns and a collaborator on the *Neue Zeitschrift*; and it seems incredible that there should be no record of his having claimed the poem if it were his.

3. In the postlude of I is an echo of the postlude to *Was soll ich sagen?* in the same key and no doubt with the same meaning. There is the impatience of motif 61 in I, *passim*; the dream staccato of motif 32, recitative style and the descending minor horn passages of motif 6 in II, prelude, etc.; and finally the doleful motif 8 sounds ominously in the last bar but two of III.

136. (No Opus No.) Soldatenlied (Soldier's song)

Hoffmann von Fallersleben – 1845 or earlier

A dappled horse, rifle at the ready, a wooden sword; that's all I need to be a soldier. As you can see, I can already march straight and keep step like a man. Bold and defiant I march out in the morning; but I come back at midday all peaceful and friendly. So I parade until late in the evening until sleep gives the order – Off to bed, quick march.

This piece was first published, as Schumann's, in an album of *Fifty new songs for children*, by H. v. F. (Mannheim 1845) with contributions from Mendelssohn and Spohr among others. Melody and accompaniment rank not far below Schumann's other pieces in this genre for piano solo (e.g. the popular *Soldatenmarsch* from the *Album für die Jugend*, Op. 68), and it is surprising that the song is almost unknown.

NOTES. 1. The text is in Hoffmann's poems of 1834 in the section *Childhood* under the rubric 'The way in which Sigismund played at being a soldier was sung as follows'. It is in the third person throughout, with 'Mein Bub' ' for 'ich bin'; there is no 'und' in bar 2 and 'zum' in bar 14 should be 'am'. It is interesting to know of this contact between poet and composer many years before they met in Düsseldorf, and at a time when Hoffmann's political activities were already attracting the attention of the Prussian authorities.

2. The authenticity of the song has been questioned; but there seems no real reason to doubt it. Schumann's characteristic manly motif 56 appears throughout, in suitably lightweight guise.

137. (Op. 51, No. 4) Auf dem Rhein (To the Rhine)

Immermann – 1846 or earlier

In a secret place in your depths lies buried the golden treasure, the hoard of the Nibelungs.

Your waves guard it until the day of judgement; no robber can ever force his way into your hiding-place.

In my heart too lies a treasure, as in the Rhine; there too it lies drowned deep till doomsday morning.

It seems odd that Schumann should have bothered with this uninspired setting of an unremarkable poem. Perhaps the Rhine symbolized the depths of his own feelings. One story has it that when he tried to drown himself in the Rhine at Düsseldorf during the first onset of his madness in 1854, he first threw in his wedding ring, feeling that this act had some deeply sacramental significance.

NOTES. 1. The idea of hidden treasure goes deep. Schumann repeats 'ewig'; hidden for all eternity. Bar 18 here is remarkably like bar 21 of *Der Himmel hat eine Träne*, also about hidden treasure. Again, the last bar here is oddly like the 'Dein Bildnis' idea found in *Süsser Freund* and *An mienem Herzen* in *Frauenliebe und-leben.*

2. One manuscript is dated 1846; but these allusions suggest that the song was begun in 1840, like the other four songs of Op. 51. There is some confirmation of this in the clear use of the Clara-theme X in bars 1–2 and 15–16.

3. The deep bass octaves at bar 14 for the deep secret places are motif 29. For other songs where the Rhine influence seems unduly strong see *Im Rhein, Sonntags am Rhein, Berg und Burgen* and *Auf einer Burg.*

4. The whole song seems to wish to pay tribute to Schubert's *Der Sieg*, with its words 'so rein und tief und klar' as the subconscious secret; compare for example bars 2–3 here with 10 there, or 15–16 with 13–14.

3 · DRESDEN 1847–50

Schumann's first and greatest period of song-writing culminated in the love-lyrics of Eichendorff and Heine, and then moved into a new objectivity. The attempts to recapture the lyric impulse resulted in the comparative failure of the Rückert songs. The acceptance of a new stage of development was fruitful; thence sprang the first two symphonies, the concerto, the quartets, and so on.

So the song-writing when it resumes in 1847 is in the more objective style. Furthermore, it resumes with the most successful of the themes with which that style began in 1840 – with character-sketches of women.

The Schumanns had moved to Dresden in 1844. It is interesting that the Dresden songs should begin with Mörike settings immediately after a visit from Robert Franz (whose many fine songs include several memorable Mörike settings) just as the Leipzig songs had begun with Shakespeare and Heine settings immediately after a visit from Mendelssohn (see pp. 32–33).

138. (Op. 64, No. 1) Die Soldatenbraut (The soldier's sweetheart)

Mörike – May 1847

Oh, if only the king knew how brave my dearest is, how bold! He'd lay down his life for the king, of course, and I'm sure he would for me too.

My dearest doesn't have any ribbons or stars yet, or crosses like the grand gentry; and they haven't made him a general yet either. I wish he were home on leave again just the same.

There are three stars shining bright over the church where we're to be married; the knot will be tied in pink ribbon; and he'll have his cross to bear at home.

[*Oh, if only the king knew how brave my dearest is, how bold! He'd lay down his life for the king, of course, and I'm sure he would for me too.*]

The spirit of this poem with its good-humoured and tender punning on

'Band' (=ribbon, and bond) and 'Hauskreuz' (=domestic trouble and strife, sc. wife) eludes verbal translation. Enthusiasts for Mörike may feel that this spirit has eluded Schumann's musical translation as well. But the song is a favourite, and not without reason. The girl's thoughts of her soldier lover are expressed agreeably enough in terms of an idealized military march, and are effectively rounded off by the repetition of the first verse, to the accompaniment of off-stage drumming. The guileless innocence of the music is engaging.

NOTES. 1. Schumann repeats the first verse.

2. The manly rhythm of motif 56 is heard throughout; at bar 32, etc., appears the drumming of *Der Soldat*.

3. The harmony is intermediate between the 1840 and the 1849 idioms, e.g. the increasingly chromatic use of the dominant seventh as in bars 9 and 10.

4. Schumann set the text again for women's voices, Op. 69, No. 4.

139. (Op. 64, No. 2) Das verlassene Mägdlein (The girl left lonely)

Mörike – May 1847

At cock crow, before the faint stars fade, I must stand at the hearth and light the fire.

The flames shine, the sparks fly; I watch them, sunk in sorrow.

Suddenly I know that I have been dreaming all night long of you, my faithless lover.

Then tear on tear falls. So my day dawns; would it were over.

Mörike's poem is one of the great lyrics of the world, and by far the finest poem that Schumann had ever set. Even in this arid year it strikes a spring of fresh music from him. Much of its force derives from the spiritual source of Bach, whose work Schumann had been studying in depth. A clear texture of three-part harmony is given slow minor expressiveness, with chromatic passing notes. The left hand, responding to a pulling undertow of an anguish past all bearing, sinks down a slow descent of two and a half octaves. Here is a new imagery of separation and grief, the death and burial of the heart. At the word 'Funken' (sparks) the tonality brightens briefly and flies upward to the highest note so far heard. For this moment the treble leaves its brooding; the right hand too lifts to its highest note yet, first with a thrusting discord, then cautiously hopeful. But now the inexorable descent begins all over again, reaching its nadir at the mention of night. This is acknowledged with a poignant discord as before. Then the wailing semitones clash over a long dominant pedal, tear on tear flowing, until the final chord lightens into the major to offer momentary consolation.

At least this is what Schumann's imagination told him, and what the imaginative listener can hear, as Hugo Wolf did, to his own delight and the world's enrichment. But for most hearers the beauty and intuitive perception will remain behind the music rather than part of it.

NOTES. 1. Schumann's 'schwinden' for 'verschwinden' and 'darein' for 'drein' also appear in Wolf's superlative setting, which is a subconscious recreation of Schumann's insight.

2. All the invention is contained in the first two bars. The second pair repeat this idea; the next extends it; the next echoes that extension. The rest is repetition, varied only by change of pitch. As a formal equivalent for the idea of obsession, the music is as original, as profound and as seminal as any ever writtten. But the moment of insight is too brief, the form too cramping, to be of real service to Mörike. The bisection of the second verse by a two-bar piano interlude, and the ending on a tierce de Picardie, are dolefully irrelevant.

3. Three-part harmony for a girl's grief is motif 34; the rising octave at bar 13 is the yearning of motif 16; the E flat chord in bar 12 may have the idea of light, a sonorous expression of watching the sparks fly upwards. The dark depths of the bass coincide with the word 'Nacht' (M 29B) and reappear at the fervent wish for another, perhaps a final, nightfall.

4. Again the harmonic idiom is in transition; the intense chromatic movement of e.g. bars 4 and 16 would have been quite foreign to the 1840 songs.

5. Cf. Franz, Op. 27, No. 4, Pfitzner, Op. 30, No. 2.

* * *

When songwriting again resumed in the spring of 1849, it was exactly as in 1847; the idea of people, of characters, was foremost in Schumann's mind. He had not long finished his opera *Genoveva* and was embarking on the music to Byron's *Manfred*. Meanwhile he hit on the novel idea of treating some of Geibel's translations from the Spanish in quasi-dramatic form, for one and two and four voices with piano accompaniment, under the title *Spanisches Liederspiel*, i.e. vaudeville or play with songs.

'I believe' he told his publisher optimistically, 'that these will be the songs which will become my best known; if so it will be due to the limpid and charming verses.'

This enthusiasm led to a second set, Op. 138, *Spanische Liebeslieder*, for the same voices but with piano duet accompaniment (an idea later gratefully accepted by Brahms in two superb sets of *Liebeslieder*), two of which were written (and the rest no doubt sketched) at about the same time.

Only the solo songs are considered here.

* * *

140. (Op. 74, No. 6) Melancholie (Melancholy)

Francisco Saa de Miranda (trans. Geibel) – March 1849

When, when will the day dawn that shall release my life from these bonds?

You my eyes, so dim with weeping, have seen only the pangs of unrequited love, have not beheld one solitary joy, have seen me given only wound on wound, grief on grief, and in a whole long life not one single happy hour. If only, if only it would come to pass that I behold the hour when I see no longer.

In the poem a single simple feeling is given florid and complex expression. So in the music. Already in the one-bar piano prelude a simple minor chord is produced with a rhetorical flourish; the word 'Leben' is protracted and decorated as if in commentary on life's length and futility. The whole song, with its solid bass line under vocal or treble leaps and arabesques gives an impression of strong supports carrying ornamental archways, as if Schumann were expressing the architecture of Moorish Spain. The result is not without grandeur.

NOTES. 1. Geibel has three 'wann denn's; and 'lös*e*t' in bar 9.

2. D minor is a melodramatic key in Schumann. The sorrow motif 8 is evident; the dominant question 43, disguised by suspensions, is at bars 5–6.

141. (Op. 74, No. 7) Geständnis (Confession)

Conde die Vimioso (trans. Geibel) – March 1849

I love you so, my love, that my heart does not even dare to cherish even one single wish.

For if I dared to wish I should begin to hope as well; and if I dared to hope I know I should anger you.

And so all alone I can only cry aloud for death to come, since my heart dares not cherish any other wish.

A strange middle-aged mixture of passion, caution and fustian. The effusive chords of the short prelude, the sighing strain with which the piano continues, the impassioned flow of vocal melody, are eloquent of a Schumann rejuvenated by the idea of devoted love. But after this first sweetness the inside tastes woody. The harmonic tension slackens, the accompaniment figure sags. True, this makes the first themes, as they return at 'Darum ruf ich' (so I cry aloud), sound the more impressive, even moving, by contrast. But then the music begins to posture again; and the peroration is all too deliberate and familiar.

NOTES. 1. The repetitions in bars 7–9, 18–19, and 27–33 are Schumann's.

2. The arpeggios in bars 2 and 3 have the joy of motif 23 (associated with motif 2). The vocal melody at 'also lieb ich euch' at bars 7–9 and 30–33 has the finality of motif 49, as an earnest of the conviction with which it was written and should be sung. The diminished sevenths at bar 12 express the poem's doubts (M 41).

3. All these are used in a fresh style not unlike the earliest songs. But some of the rest is ominously quirky mannerism. Thus, the musical material of bar 16 is no worse than uninspired, but its use to eke out the piano part at bars 30–31 is plainly synthetic. Similarly the sweetness of (say) bar 37 of *Er der Herrlichste* is to bar 28 here as sugar to saccharine (M 12).

142. (Op. 74 Annex) Der Contrabandiste (The Smuggler)

? (trans. Geibel) – March 1849

I am the smuggler; and well I know how to get treated with proper respect. I defy them all, I'm afraid of no-one; olé!

Who's for silk or tobacco? but my horse is tired; I must hurry, hurry, or the excisemen will catch me; then the sparks will fly! So gallop, dear horse, gallop, gallop.

Yes, I am the smuggler; and well I know how to get treated with proper respect, I defy them all, I'm afraid of no-one, olé! So gallop, good horse, etc.

Exit, pursued by coastguards, or so we imagine; but not before having provided the unique tableau of a comic song by Schumann.

NOTES. 1. Op. 74 had among its nine numbers only two for bass, neither a solo. It was perhaps to remedy this neglect that Schumann added the annex. The poem is not to be found in the sources used for all the other songs; and he may have asked Geibel to provide him with an extra lyric. It is hardly the kind of verse Schumann would have ever chosen for himself, though no doubt the repetitions are his.

2. Schumann's music derives directly from the text; but he is still unconcerned about individual words. Thus 'eile' (hurry) is spread over a leisurely minim in bars 33–34, while in the final galloping hurry of the coda this is almost the only word that Schumann fails to repeat.

3. The acciaccature express amusement (M 14).

143. (Op. 138, No. 2) Tief im Herzen

Camoens (trans. Geibel) – November 1849

Deep in my heart I bear my grief, unseen to outward view. I hide my dear grief well away from the world; it belongs to the inmost soul alone. As sparks of fire lie hidden in flint, so I bear my grief deep within.

Something in these verses – perhaps their affinity with the Harper lyrics from *Wilhelm Meister* composed in the same year? – prompted a suggestion of harp-playing in the spread chords of the accompaniment. The melodic invention is profuse. Many themes and fragmentary ideas compete for attention, leaving both the music and its hearers perhaps a little confused and dissatisfied. Yet the impression of gentle weariness created here can be most moving.

NOTES. 1. Schumann adds 'nur' in bar 25.

2. An effective unity could have used just the interlude melody in bars 5–7 and 10–12; or the harp-chords; or the song-like rising sixths (M 19) and sevenths; or the harmonic ideas at bars 7–9 and 17–18; or the rhythmic expansion from bars 19–20 through bars 20–24 and the postlude. Instead the music is mosaic; all pieces, no pattern.

3. Schumann rarely responds to poetic imagery unless it has some private meaning for him; contrast Wolf's vivid treatment of fire-in-flint in No. 23 of his *Spanish Songbook* with the curiously unmotivated harp-flourish here (bar 34 compared with bar 3).

4. The piano melody at bars 10–11 perhaps responds to the word 'Stille' in the preceding bar (M 26). There is the recitative motif 48 at bar 39.

5. This song, like Nos. 144 and 146 below, was not completed until November; but no doubt all three were sketched in April with the rest of the opus.

144. (Op. 138, No. 3) O wie lieblich ist das Mädchen

Gil Vicente (trans. Geibel) – November 1849

What a sweet girl she is; how beautiful and charming! Tell me, you bold seaman, whose home is the sea, whether the ship and its sails, whether the stars can be as beautiful?

What a sweet girl she is; how beautiful and charming! Tell me, you proud knight in shining armour, whether your charger and his harness, whether your battles can be as beautiful?

What a sweet girl she is, how beautiful and charming! Tell me, you shepherd boy watching over your sheep, whether your lambs, whether the meadows, whether the mountains can be as beautiful?

[*How sweet she is; how beautiful, how charming!*]

Schumann, with his predilection for the idea of movement and gesture, combines in his music the separate notions of each verse; nimble as a lamb, proud as a charger, gliding and lovely as a ship upon the sea. At the same time his voice sounds paternally affectionate; the graceful running semiquavers are halted as each address begins, and changed to the detached amusement of staccato quavers. If this is not Vicente's love-poem, it is within its own limits every whit as sure and masterly.

NOTES. 1. Geibel has 'voll *von* Anmut' in bars 8–9 and 36–37. All the repetitions are Schumann's.

2. There is a dainty stepping gait at bars 11–13, which remind us of *Der Sandmann*: a nobility of carriage in bars 7–8 (very like the nobility motif 51); the prelude is almost a march; the amorous dominants (M 64) are in bars 26–27, and the music yearns with the ringing high note and motif 16 in the bass at bar 40, echoed in the postlude at bar 48.

3. See No. 143, note 5.

145. (Op. 138, No. 5) Flutenreicher Ebro

Anon (trans. Geibel) – April 1849

Billowing river Ebro, with your banks all in flower, all you green meadows, you shades of the woodlands, ask my beloved as she rests among you whether in her happiness she thinks of me?

And you dewy pearls embroidering the green grass with bright colours in the light of dawn, ask my beloved, when she breathes the cool morning air, whether in her happiness she thinks of me?

You leafy poplars, you shining paths where my barefoot girl goes walking, when she meets you ask her, ask her whether in her happiness she thinks of me?

You swarming birds that greet the dawn with your fluted singing, ask my beloved, the flower of these shores, whether in her happiness she thinks of me?

We are to infer that she does not. But Schumann writes a song as gay as the lilt and lightness of the poem's description of nature, cheerfully unconcerned that these are contrasts, not comparisons. We may be glad that he did; for this brief but welcome return to his earlier manner has an added maturity of craftsmanship, and the result is a masterpiece of unsullied and radiant charm.

The accompaniment suggests not only the singer but the scene. The right-hand single notes sparkle with a delicate clarity that reflects the shine and glitter of waves, dew and wet leaves in sunlight; in the last verse the guitar itself begins to sing an impatient half-bar too early, heralding the birds as they herald the dawn.

NOTES. 1. Geibel has 'sticket' not 'schmückt' in bar 16. All the last-line repetitions are Schumann's.

2. Even the dominants of motif 64 have a youthful appearance (bars 9–10 etc.).

146. (Op. 138, No. 7) Weh, wie zornig ist das Mädchen

Gil Vicente (trans. Geibel) – November 1849

Alas, how angry she is. She walks the hills with her flocks; as beautiful as the flowers but as angry as the sea.

[*Alas, how angry she is, how angry.*]

As in No. 144 Schumann is not disposed to take the verses too seriously. The music pretends to be dismayed at the crossness of a little girl, with an amused tenderness proper to the father of three small daughters.

NOTES. 1. Instead of Geibel's 'wer mag mit ihr reden, wer?', Schumann has the colourless (and rhymeless) 'weh, wie zornig, weh, weh'. Geibel has 'als' before 'wie' in bar 16.

2. The acciaccature are still the laughter of motif 14; but in this context they are expressive of exaggerated sorrow, the idea of pretending to cry.

3. See No. 143, note 5.

147. (Op. 138, No. 8) Hoch, hoch sind die Berge

Pedro de Padilla (trans. Geibel) – April 1849

High, high are the mountains and steep are their paths; the water spurts from the springs and trickles down through the undergrowth. Oh mother, dear mother, it was there, there in the mountains with their proud peaks, that my dearest friend went one morning. I called him back with word and sign, I waved with all my might; but for all reply there was only the water spurting from the springs and trickling down through the undergrowth.

The words seem to remind Schumann of German folksong. So the fierce desolate tensions of the verse are slackened in this music to a mild regret, as if it all happened so long ago that the memory has mellowed into a major key. Yet this very transformation makes a mature blend of sweetness and melancholy. In the postlude the melody takes a final farewell by recalling the opening words; the rising phrase is now a lifted look, a gesture to the high mountains, a long hopeful pause, and then silence.

NOTES. 1. Geibel has 'schön' not 'lieb' in bar 12; the final repetitions are Schumann's.

2. Something of the same mood is found in *Sonntag*. Later Brahms made it very much his own, in songs like *Trennung*, Op. 97, No. 6, with an added element of true folksong simplicity which Schumann was never quite to achieve.

3. Note the unobtrusive lifting and quickening of the inserted triplets in bar 8 at the mention of the water spurting from the rocks. This expressive use later becomes a mannerism.

4. Expressive or not, it happens that in bars 27–29, where the words are literally 'I waved with all five fingers' the music for each hand uses all five fingers, the bass part doing so for the first and only time in the song.

Liederalbum für die Jugend (Song album for the young) Op. 79

The piano *Album for the Young* (1848) had been well received. At a period of song-writing the idea of this sequel was obvious; and it continues to fit into the pattern of character-study rather than direct self-expression. It was natural too for Schumann to make orderly arrangements of his work; and the natural order was that of increasing maturity. As he wrote to his publisher, 'I have selected poems appropriate to childhood, from the best poets (sic) and arranged them in order of difficulty. At the end comes Mignon, on the threshold of a more complex emotional life.'

He tried various ways of grouping the songs (and some duets, omitted here). At no time however did he attempt to distinguish between his own artistic expression (as in the masterpieces of this cycle, such as *Sonntag*, *Der Sandmann*, *Marienwürmchen*) and the sentiments he thought suitable for expression by or on behalf of children (*Frühlingbotschaft*, *Weihnachtslied*).

There is another sense in which the borders between the real and the unreal are becoming just a little blurred in Schumann's mind. In the previous year, 1848, a year of revolution throughout Europe, he had been writing works of great radical fervour; the *People's*

Spring, *Song of Freedom*, and so on. In this year, as he was at work on Op. 79, the revolution came to Dresden in reality. To escape conscription or worse he fled to the country and again immersed himself in the *Song Album for the Young*. As Clara wrote to a friend, 'Just when everyone thought he'd be breaking out into the most terrifying battle symphonies, there he is writing these dear peaceful little songs.' True, Schumann was no Wagner to fight at the barricades. Humility and dedication to his music were in the grain of the man; he would have to go on with the simple task in hand. Later he did write the *Four Marches* for piano, Op. 76, known to his own intimate circle as the 'barricade' marches, despite the rather tame music. It is true too that his work was to survive and the rebellion was to collapse. All the same there is some incongruity in his writing a song-book for children while his political ideals were being bloodily suppressed. His diary can be reconstructed thus:

29th April. 'Spring is here' [sketch for Op. 79, No. 24].
3rd May. The revolution is here.
5th May. Armed search; flight by rail; trouble everywhere. Finished 'Spring Song' for duet.
6th May. Nothing but terror.
10th May. In Dresden; all the signs of a terrible revolution.
13th May. *Song Album for the Young* completed.

148. (Op. 79, No. 1) Der Abendstern (The evening star)

Hoffmann von Fallersleben – April 1849

Dear star, you shine from afar, yet I love you with all my heart.
How dearly I love you; your shining eye is always watching over me.
So I look at you wherever you are; your friendly eye is always with me.
How you beckon to me in serene calm; oh dearest star, if only I were like you!

This modest beginning has the interest, for what it is worth, of being taken bar by bar down through a whole cycle of falling fifths; a star being gently wished down to earth by an imagined child.

NOTE. Falling fifths are here used as it were literally; the same idea (though in octaves rather than fifths) is found in *Mein schöner Stern.*

149. (Op. 79, No. 2) Schmetterling (Butterfly)

Hoffmann von Fallersleben – *c.* April 1849

Oh butterfly, don't fly away, why so hasty, here and there, far and near; I won't catch you, I won't hurt you. So stay with me all the time. If I were a flower I'd say to you 'Come here to me, I'll give you my heart, I love you so much'.

Even at this simple level Schumann cannot fail to organize his material. Delicate piano phrases move, settle and start again with the voice; canonic imitations imagine the attempt to intercept. Here is mastery and sensitivity too, lavished on a trifle.

NOTES. 1. Hoffmann's title was *Wie gut bin ich dir.*
2. The horn passages are motif 4; the canon a good example of motif 59. Perhaps it is the accents demanded by the canon that led to the time-signature 3/8; 6/8 seems more exact.

150. (Op. 79, No. 3) Frühlingsbotschaft (Spring's harbinger)

Hoffmann von Fallersleben – April 1849

Cuckoos call from the wood; let us sing and dance, it will soon be spring.
Cuckoos call; come to the woods and fields. Springtime, you come and join us too!
Cuckoos call, like brave heroes, and their deed is as good as their word. Winter is defeated and withdraws.

The author of *Deutschland über alles* introduces somewhat disquieting touches into his songs for children. Thus the butterfly above (like the ladybird in No. 160) needs reassuring that no harm will come to it; and the military metaphor here makes us think again about the text of *Soldatenlied*. However, Schumann has no qualms; indeed his music is more suggestive of a bugle-call than a cuckoo-call.

NOTES. 1. The repetitions are Schumann's.
2. The horn passages are again characteristic (M 4).

151. (Op. 79, No. 4) Frühlingsgruss (A greeting to spring)

Hoffmann von Fallersleben – April 1849

A thousand greetings, dear spring; welcome to our valley, dear spring; everywhere we greet you with singing and rejoicing.

Everyone is glad when you come, dear spring; meadow, wood and valley rejoice and are gay, dear spring; rejoicing greets you everywhere, lark and nightingale greet you.

So a thousandfold greeting, dear spring; stay long in our valley, dear spring; and stay long in our hearts, that all hearts may rejoice with ours.

This, like the poem, is a slightly more elaborate version of the same themes as in the previous song.

NOTES. 1. Schumann is still clinging to his bugle metaphor (bars 9–10) even when his poet manages without it.

2. The last three bars reappear in *Marienwürmchen*, with a great deal more vivacity and charm. Here they have the finality of motif 49.

152. (Op. 79, No. 5) Vom Schlaraffenland (Cloud cuckoo land)

Hoffmann von Fallersleben – April 1849

Come, let's all go off to the magic cloud cuckoo land, where all is joy and sorrow unknown. Living is easy, all is gladness, it's flowing with milk and honey, the very waterfalls are wine.

The trees are weighed down with cakes and buttered buns; figs and pineapples grow in the hedgerows; nobody has to work there, everything looks after itself. It's marvellous; how we'd love to live there.

All the streets and paths far and near are made of sugarplums and sweets and marzipan; all the bridges are stoutly constructed of pork crackling. It's marvellous; how we'd love to live there.

Yes, it must be a wonderful place to live and a marvellous life to lead. But somehow no-one ever seems to get there. Yes, and unless you had wings you couldn't even reach the gate; the entrance is barred by a huge mountain of plum jam.

The radical Hoffmann was as usual twisting the tail of the authorities by indulging in a little harmless social satire. To Schumann, however, despite his liberal sympathies, this was just a jolly song about eating and drinking, suitable for a child's song-book; and he makes it, in its way, a very fine one.

NOTE. A fifth verse is omitted. The repeats are Schumann's, as is the amendment of 'zechen' (carouse) to 'leben' in bar 8.

153. (Op. 79, No. 6) Sonntag (Sunday)

Hoffmann von Fallersleben – *c.* April 1849

Sunday has come, wearing a spray of blossom in his hat; his eyes are smiling and gentle, he is friendly to everyone.

He stands on the mountain, he walks through the valley, asking everyone to go along and pray with him together.

And just as young and old are all dressed in their best for Sunday so he makes meadows and valleys especially beautiful for them.

And just as he brings joy and peace to everyone, so you too should say, to everyone you meet, 'Good morning and God bless you.'

There is poetry here; and it calls out Schumann the composer from Schumann the paterfamilias. His music shines like a springtime Sunday recalled in vision from a country boyhood. The prelude has an unhurried ease. Soon the two-bar phrases are extended into four, a leisurely time; slow bells chime in the bass. The treble has an added sense of movement at 'er wandelt durch das Tal', as the day passes through the valley. Throughout the whole scene moves the Sunday melody, all innocence and calm.

NOTES. 1. The repetition is Schumann's.

2. Brahms must have loved this song; cf. his *Komm bald*, Op. 97, No. 5, bar 10 of which is bar 11 here (see No. 147, note 2).

3. The moving triplets at bar 17 are as in *Hoch, hoch sind die Berge*; the last bars of the postlude have the finality motif 49.

4. There are some puzzling features; thus it is not clear why the expression at bars 23–24 should differ from that at bars 5–6, or either from bars 39–40; or why the prelude should be altered in the postlude to a syncopation in dotted rhythm.

154, 155. (Op. 79, Nos. 7 and 8) Zigeunerliedchen (Gypsy ditties)

Anon: from the Spanish (trans. Geibel) – April/May 1849

154.

A gypsy lad went for a soldier; but he pocketed his bounty money and bolted, so he must hang tomorrow.

They took me out of my cell, they set me on a donkey, they scourged my shoulders till the blood ran on the road.

They took me out of my cell, they made me run for my life; quickly I went for my gun and got my shot in first.

155.

Each morning early when the daylight wakes me I wash my face in my own tears.

Where the mountains tower high on the horizon, there from my house and from its fine gardens they stole me away by night.

[*Each morning early when the daylight wakes me I wash my face in my own tears.*]

Here as in the Goethe song *Talismane*, Schumann compiles a song-text from separate quatrains. Again the results are successful and engaging. The first, for all its slenderness of material and strophic form, is full of fire and bitterness, while the second is moving in its melancholy and resignation.

NOTES (TO 154). 1. The text is three separate quatrains in Geibel.

2. There is kinship with other A minor songs of this Opus, e.g. *Die Waise*, *Der Sandmann* and *Käuzlein*.

NOTES (TO 155). 1. The text is a repeated Geibel quatrain sandwiching an unidentified one (possibly an interpolation of Schumann's own) which has the odd effect of suggesting that the speaker is not really a gypsy but a person of good family now in reduced circumstances – the Romantic myth typified. Perhaps Schumann's mind was already occupied with Mignon, whose story this is (see p. 212).

2. At bars 4–6 the thematic resemblance to Schubert might suggest that this is not just sad weeping (as in *Wasserflut* bars 19–20) but specifically a girl's (as in *Das Mädchen* bars 8–10).

156. (Op. 79, No. 9) Des Knaben Berglied (Song of the mountain lad)

Uhland – *c.* April 1849

I am the mountain shepherd lad, looking down on all the castles. My sunshine begins first and lasts the longest; I am the mountain lad, the shepherd of the hills.

The mountains belong to me; the storms may encircle them, but let the winds howl as they will from north and south, my singing is louder than theirs. I am the mountain lad, the shepherd of the hills.

Here I stand high in the blue sky with thunder and lightning at my feet; I know them, and I shout at them, leave my father's house in peace! I am the mountain lad, the shepherd of the hills.

And if ever the alarum bell sounds and there is fire on the mountains, why then I shall come down and join my band and swing my sword and sing my song – I, the mountain lad, the shepherd of the hills.

The first of Schumann's surprisingly few Uhland songs. He, like Hoffmann, and indeed like almost all Schumann's chosen poets, was a radical; and (like Nos. 152 and 168) this poem, innocuous though it now seems, once had quite revolutionary overtones. Perhaps these settings, like the four marches of Op. 76, were Schumann's modest contribution to the revolutionary movements of 1849.

NOTES. 1. Schumann adds 'vom Berg der Hirtenknab'' to each verse. A second verse is omitted.

2. Some political fervour, consciously or not, went into Schumann's music; hence the continuous trumpet calls and fanfares.

157. (Op. 79, No. 11) Käuzlein (Little owl)

Anon. (*Des Knaben Wunderhorn*) – *c.* April 1849

I, poor little owl, where shall I fly? I am so afraid alone in the night. That's because of that monster the great owl, the cause of great grief to me, [poor little owl.]

I'll fly off to another wood, to hear all the little birds sing. The nightingale's my favourite and she's very fond of me too, [poor little owl.]

The children believe I bring bad luck, they want to drive me away so that they won't hear my cry. I'm sorry if I'm a bird of ill-omen, but I can't help having a sad cry, can I, [poor little owl?]

The branch is withered that I planned to perch on, its leaves all faded and the nightingale gone. That's because of that great owl again; it always ruins all my happiness; [poor little owl.]

It seems hardy in the face of all this tribulation to urge that the poem is not wholly serious. But Schumann finds in it, if not humour, then a wry tenderness that is close kin to it; the result, a sympathetic soothing of ruffled feathers, makes a sweet song.

NOTES. 1. The one-line refrain is Schumann's.

2. The melancholy of the opening minor triad (M 7) harks back to the 1840 songs.

3. At bars 6–8 is the melody of *Zigeunerliedchen* No. 2 (155) at 'wenn mich weckt des Tages Licht'.

158. (Op. 79, No. 12) Hinaus ins Freie (Out in the open air)

Hoffmann von Fallersleben – *c.* April 1849

There's bloom in the valley, green on the mountains; how lovely it is in the open air! The springtime bids us dance to the sound of the shepherd's pipe. Who would not dance for the sake of the springtime who has driven away the long wicked winter? So come out into the open air, not to go home until we hear the evening bell.

An innocuous song with a certain rather stolid charm, due mainly to its affinities with the delightful *Marienwürmchen*, No. 160.

NOTES. 1. The repetitions are Schumann's. The device of repeating the end of a verse as the beginning of the next in order to provide extra material is characteristic of this opus, as in Nos 168 and 170.

2. The opening vocal melody is motif 23; the trill in the left hand in bar 12 may be a response to the word 'Weidenflöte'. Other features are puzzling. Thus, there seems no real constructional or expressive purpose in the dominant pedal at bars 9–12, or the restatement in the subdominant at bar 17 of what had already been said in the tonic at bar 13.

3. The relation with *Marienwürmchen* is in key and mood rather than detail; but bars 5–6 here may be compared with bars 3–4 there.

159. (Op. 79, No. 13) Der Sandmann (The sandman)

Kletke – *c.* April 1849

I wear little soft boots with little soft soles; I carry a sack; I slip quickly upstairs. I reach the bedroom as the children are saying their prayers, and I drop two grains of sand from my sack into their eyes. Then they sleep the whole night through in the care of God and all his angels.

I drop two grains of sand into their eyes, for good children ought to have sweet dreams. Now quick with sack and stick down the stairs again; I cannot afford to linger, there are many yet to be visited. And there they are, nodding off smiling into dreamland already; I hardly had to open my sack at all.

Again we hear Schumann's vivid imagination at work; or perhaps his memory. In the prelude the soft finicking steps of velvet slippers move upstairs in a dream pantomime. The music sings to itself; whistles; carries a sack so heavy with dreams that it slips and falls a tenth; moves on tiptoe for fear of disturbing the prayers; drops two grains of sand; lingers on as the children go down, gowned in long notes for sleeping;

surveys them full of tenderness and sadness too; and at last with a sudden resolve moves briskly off again.

NOTES. 1. 'Ihr Gebet' should read 'das Abendgebet'; 'heut noch' is inverted; the last couplet reads 'Nun seht, mein Säcklein öffnet' ich kaum/Da nickt ihr schon und lächelt im Träum.' The repetitions are Schumann's, in order to provide a second verse of equal length.

2. The dream-staccato (M 32) is in the left-hand prelude, the top notes of which also sketch in the walking theme (M 20) in the minor. The idea of the minor seconds is delicate or imperceptible movement as in *Die Spinnerin.*

160. (Op. 79, No. 14) Marienwürmchen (Ladybird)

Anon. (*Des Knaben Wunderhorn*) – *c.* April 1849

Ladybird, come and settle on my hand. There, you see, I won't hurt you at all, no harm will come to you, I just want to see your pretty wings, pretty wings my joy.

Ladybird, fly away home, your house is on fire, your children are gone, the wicked spider is spinning them in, your children are crying with fright.

Ladybird, fly off now to the children next door – you'll see, they won't hurt you either, no harm will come to you, they just want to see your pretty wings, and say hallo.

Another masterpiece, and a favourite one. Schumann's seventeen bars live in imagination through a whole series of tiny yet vivid experiences; clumsiness, reassuring tenderness, a premonition of delight, a sudden surge of pleasure, a dance of sheer joy. The child's folk-song becomes an epitome of life and feeling, so simply and sweetly that the mastery of the thing is hardly perceived.

NOTES. 1. Schumann seeks by repetition of 'nichts . . . zu Leide' et seq. to raise the words to the emotional level of his music. The directions 'ten . . . fp', and the marked mezzo-staccato, must be scrupulously observed.

2. The tenths at bars 12–13 are probably motivic here (M 57) (compare the similar passage in *Frühlingsgruss*); the rising sixth in bar 15 suggests singing (M 19) and the following semiquavers a dancing delight.

161. (Op. 79, No. 15) Die Waise (The orphan girl)

Hoffmann von Fallersleben – *c.* April 1849

Spring comes again and all is glad. I alone look downcast; there is no joy for me.

For what to me is all the glory and brightness of spring? If I twine flowers, it is for a funeral wreath.

Alas! there is no hand to lead me home to a father's house, no mother to hold out her arms to me.

O heaven, give me again what your love once gave. If I look down at the earth all I see is the tomb.

NOTES. 1. Schumann omits the fourth verse of five.

2. In the previous year the piano piece *Armes Waisenkind* (also in A minor) had true expression. This song is already perfunctory; and only two years later we find Schumann taking the orphan Elisabeth Kulmann very seriously (Nos. 228–234).

162. (Op. 79, No. 17) Weihnachtslied (Christmas carol)

Andersen (trans. ?) – *c.* April 1849

When the Christ-child was born who saved us from sin, he lay in his crib in the dark night with straw and hay for his bedding. Yet over the stable there shone a star, and the oxen kissed the feet of the Lord. Halleluia, child Jesus.

Be strong, my soul, no longer tired and ill, forget your gnawing cares. A child is born in the city of David, a comforter for all hearts. Oh let us go as pilgrims to that young child, and ourselves become children in mind and spirit. Halleluia, child Jesus.

NOTES. 1. Only three Schumann songs (cf. 218, 243) are overtly devotional; all sound contrived.

2. Bars 14–15 yield three new motifs; the rising thirds of motif 37, the IV–I Amen motif of choral singing (M 52) and the tremolando bass. These and the choice of lyric seem to indicate the beginning of a new tendency to religiosity.

163. (Op. 79, No. 18) Die wandelnde Glocke (The bell that walked)

Goethe – *c.* April 1849

Once there was a child who would not go to church; and every Sunday he always found a way of escaping into the fields.

But one Sunday his mother said, 'You hear that bell ringing? This time it's an order; and if you don't obey it'll come and fetch you.'

The boy thinks – 'How can it? Bells hang in belfries.' And he's off into the fields like a shot, as if he were running out of school.

The bell has stopped ringing now; mother must have been fibbing. Then, suddenly, what a fright! the bell comes waddling along behind him, with incredible speed. The poor child, terrified, runs and runs as if in a nightmare, afraid that the bell will cover him up.

But he gets away and with an adroit spurt he sprints through meadow, field and wood back to church, back to chapel. Now every Sunday and church festival he remembers the fright he got, and he's off to church at the first stroke, without waiting for a personal invitation.

The poem is full of affectionate indulgence. But Schumann is at first rather square and schoolmasterly about it, as if it really were a cautionary tale. The tolling in the piano prelude and occasionally in the first three verses is all too predictable. Then his imagination like the child's is seized by the idea of the pursuing bell. The sudden clangour in the piano at the moment when it suddenly appears just behind ('doch welch ein Schrecken hinterher'), and the following idea of the grotesque wobbling movement (at 'die Glocke kommt gewackelt') are given equivalents so compelling that the song comes to life; and becomes, within the limits imposed by its miniature framework, a spirited and effective ballad.

NOTES. 1. Schumann thrice departs from Goethe's text; once for his tune's sake ('eilt es' inverted at bars 46–47), once through inadvertence ('und' for 'zur' in bar 49) and once perhaps to make Goethe more poetical ('rennt' for 'kommt' in bar 39).

2. Cf. Loewe, Op. 20, No. 3.

164. (Op. 79, No. 20) Frühlings Ankunft (Spring's arrival)

Hoffmann von Fallersleben – April/May 1840

After these last dull days how bright the fields are. The tattered clouds fly away with the world's sorrows. Seed and bud struggle towards the light, and many a flower blossoms in silence up towards heaven. Yes, even the oak and the vines are green again. So let that be a sign to you, my heart; be gay and brave!

For this assertive lyric Schumann finds a diffident music. Its pensive flow of even semiquavers tells of a gentle stirring in nature, and of the hope that this brings. But it is no more than a hope; the latent harmonies are tense and wary.

NOTES. 1. Hoffmann repeats 'Herz'; but Schumann has no room for this in his bar 26.

2. The differences between bars 1–2, 11–12 and 21–22 are instructive. The tied left-hand crotchets in bars 1–2 say that 'trüb' is being interpreted to mean

long and dull days; the bass at bars 11–12 gives the sense of extra effort in striving towards the light; and at bars 21–22 the oaks have chords with deep roots in the bass (M. 29).

3. In the last bar is motif 21, perhaps suggested by the reference to oak and vine.

165. (Op. 79, No. 22) Kinderwacht (Vigil)

Anon. – *c.* April 1849

When good children go to sleep two angels guard them, cover them up, tuck them in, watch lovingly over them.

But when good children get up, their two angels go to sleep; for then God himself keeps watch.

Under the conventional piety of this music there is a lively and tender imagination responding to the first verse. The piano echoes sleepily 'schlafen gehn'; introduces two angels separately; makes smoothing and soothing gestures; and finally looks back indulgently and as it were blows the light out.

NOTE. Bars 4–6 have the canon of motif 59 with the tenths of motif 57, and a very pretty picture they make. Bars 7–8 are again a new idea with an obvious effect of a soothing downward gesture, no doubt related to motif 26 of silence. The affectionate dominants of motif 64 are apt at 'liebendes', and the finality motif 49 adds an agreeable finishing touch.

166. (Op. 79, No. 23) Des Sennen Abschied (The alpine herdsman's farewell)

Schiller – *c.* April 1849

Farewell, you meadows, you sunny pastures. I must leave you now, the summer is over.

We shall be coming back to the mountains when the cuckoo calls, when songs awaken, when the earth is clothed anew in flowers, when the springs flow again in the sweet Maytime, the sweet – [*Farewell, you meadows, you sunny pastures, I must leave you now; the summer is over.*]

The piano bass has the drone of the herdsman's bagpipe, the treble the wavering melody of its chanter reed, while the voice part evokes an Alpine folksong. At 'im lieblichen Mai, im lieblichen –' the voice is suddenly and unexpectedly cut off – as if by a gust of wind on a high hill?

NOTES. 1. 'Im lieblichen' in bars 38–39, and the last six words, are Schumann's repeats in a text from the opening of *William Tell.* The scene is the Swiss Alps. The herdsman there is singing from the mountain; his tune is said to be a variation of the nostalgic *Ranz des Vaches,* the melody sung or played on the alphorn to call the cattle home.

2. The 'Senne' of this song and his 'Sennin' in No. 215 spend the summer in the mountains herding the cows sent there by the farmers of the nearby valleys.

3. Even Schumann's ingenuity would have been severely taxed by producing an alphorn sound from his piano accompaniment; and he seems to have settled for the herdsman's bagpipe or Dudelsack.

4. The lifting arpeggio at the end of the song is motif 21.

5. Cf. Liszt (two versions).

167. (Op. 79, No. 24) Er ist's (Spring is here)

Mörike – *c.* April 1849

Spring lets his blue ribbons flutter through the air again. Sweet familiar scents drift over the countryside, full of promise; violets are already dreaming of their time to come. Listen; the soft sound of a distant harp! It must be you, Spring; it is you I have heard.

Mörike-lovers may consider this song a witless travesty of a beautiful poem. However, the music is undeniably charming and effective. Schumann's treatment of the verse suggests that the stolid kindergarten solemnity of the earlier spring songs has grown into the dancing pulse of a girl's first love-song.

NOTES. 1. This interpretation would explain the excited repetitions of the text. But the omission of 'von fern' before 'ein' in bar 19, and 'leiser' after it is inexplicable.

2. The falling fifths of the melody have floral associations (M 27). The melody itself at bars 5–6 is that of 'unten fängt's schon an zu *blühn*' from *Frühlingsnacht*; there is the waving foliage of motif 21 in the postlude. Perhaps the personification of spring also made some impression; there is the key of A major, and the harp music has the kingly or noble motif 51, in bars 20–21. But the main thematic material seems to be an equivalent for the idea of fluttering (see No. 181, note 3); perhaps the mind's eye saw Mörike's blue ribbons literally.

3. If so, something of the same idea may have conveyed itself to Hugo Wolf, whose own setting has similar though less extensive repetitions. Another setting worth comparing is Franz, Op. 27, No. 2.

168. (Op. 79, No. 26) Des Buben Schützenlied (The boy's hunting song)

Schiller – May 1849

Over hill and dale with bow and arrow goes the hunter in the light of dawn.

As the eagle is lord of the winds, so the free huntsman is lord of his own realm.

All is his dominion, sky and land, bird and beast, as far as his arrow can reach.

The manuscript has a laconic marginal note '3rd May (Revolution in Dresden)'. Schumann had some sympathy with the aims of the rising; no doubt his reading of *William Tell*, the story of a struggle against tyranny, was topical. To judge from the expressive quality of his contemporary music however (e.g. this song, No. 156, and the four marches, Op. 76, known to Schumann's intimates as the 'barricade' marches) his heart was not in it.

NOTES. 1. This is sung by William Tell's son in Act 3 Scene 1 of Schiller's play. 'Im' in bar 4 should be 'am'. The repetitions are Schumann's.

2. The motifs are stock-in-trade; e.g. joyous manliness, motifs 23 and 56, in the outdoor key of B flat major.

169. (Op. 79, No. 27) Schneeglöckchen (Snowdrop)

Rückert – *c.* April 1849

The snow that only yesterday was falling in little flakes from the sky has been cast as a bell, and hangs now from a delicate stem.

A bell of snow ringing in the silent woods; what can it mean? Oh come quickly; it is ringing a summons to springtime.

So awake from your dreams, bud, blossom and flower; come now into the shrine of spring.

The appealing verse charmed Schumann into a melody worthy of the 1840 songs, while the accompaniment is vivid and sonorous with Rückert's imagery. This cool, bright music is set melting and chiming with all the prettiness of a flower that is both snow and bell, and yet goes far beyond mere prettiness; it is the apotheosis of salon art.

NOTES. 1. Rückert has 'O Liebchen komm geschwind! dir läutet's' (bars 13–15) and four more verses. See also No. 172, note 1.

2. The odd notation in bars 1–5 is authentic, as in the first edition.

3. E flat major and the high keyboard register suggest brightness; the

chromatics in bar 6 elsewhere (e.g. *Mondnacht*) stand for the melting and blending effects of twilight. Each is very neatly adapted to the idea of the cool melting process needed for the casting of snowbells; the bell notes are then heard in the sudden descent into the bass in bars 8–9.

170. (Op 79, No. 28) Lied Lynceus des Thürmers (Song of Lynceus the lynx-eyed, keeper of the watch tower)

Goethe – *c.* May 1849

I am a born look-out, a devoted watchman, pledged to the service of my tower; and all I see delights me.

I look far and near, and I see the moon and the stars, the forest and the deer.

And in all things I see eternal grace; all is delight in my eyes, and my eyes are a delight to me.

Come what may, these are fortunate eyes that have seen so many things and all of them so beautiful.

In 1849 Schumann is still a fine songwriter, but no longer a great one; and he is still using poetry for his own purposes. It is not surprising then that we should find him in this collection of songs sometimes immortalizing minor verse (No. 153) and sometimes treating great poetry rather cavalierly (No. 167). Here is another example of the latter.

NOTES. 1. 'Was' should read 'wie' in bars 11, 13 and 15. Goethe's text is *Faust* II/V 1. 288–303. Schumann uses lines 1–12 with repeats for his first verse, and 5–16 with repeats for his second. In the result the same superlative words are set twice to two quite different but quite undistinguished tunes just to pad out the song's form, as in 166 above.

2. Again as in 166 there are the same stock motifs used with the same perfunctory expression; joy (M 23), and manliness (M 56) in the great outdoors of B flat major, as if Goethe's Lynceus were an elder son of Schiller's William Tell.

171. (Op. 79, No. 29, also Op. 98a, No. 1) Mignon (Kennst du das Land?)

Goethe – June 1849

Do you know the land where the lemon trees blossom, where oranges glow golden among dark leaves? A soft wind breathes from the blue sky; the quiet myrtle grows there and the tall laurel. Do you know that land? Would that I might go there with you, my love.

Do you know the pillared house? Its rooms shine and gleam. Its marble statues stand and look at me as if to say 'What have they done to you, poor child?' Do you know that house? Would that I might go there with you, my protector.

Do you know the mountain and its cloud-wrapped path? The mules pick their way in the mist, the ancient brood of dragons still dwells in the caves, the rock falls sheer and over it the river. Do you know that mountain? There lies our path; oh father, there let us go!

In Goethe's *Wilhelm Meister* the Italian girl Mignon was abducted by vagabonds and brought into Germany, a beaten and half-starved waif forced to dance and sing in a troupe of entertainers. In this lyric she remembers the beauty of a southern homeland, the splendour of her home, and the mountain paths over which she was brought by her captors.

As always, Schumann adapts the poems to his own expressive ends, here a child's song-book. Despite its charm the result is incongruous in its inadequacy, relying too much on the composer's instruction 'with enhanced expression in the second and third verses'.

NOTES. 1. All the repeats at the end of each verse are Schumann's.

2. The lemon-tree and the laurel each receive the accolade of a leafy arpeggio (M 21) at bars 7 and 16. Schumann follows Beethoven in breaking out into triplets at the mention of the soft breeze in bar 10 et seq.

3. Cf. Beethoven, Op. 75, No. 1; Schubert; Liszt (two versions); Wolf.

Minnespiel (Love songs) aus Rückerts Liebesfrühling, Op. 101

After the Dresden revolution came a wonderful summer, as memorably recorded in Schumann's diary as that peerless springtime in Leipzig in 1840.

Then his mood was at one with the season. But the Dresden aftermath was a depressive phase, a time of dark strange thoughts in the bright daytime. Before the shadow fell he had time to write yet another work for vocal ensemble and piano, again with the help of

Rückert's *Liebesfrühling* (*Love's springtime*). As before the personal love-song lyric is treated quasi-dramatically.

Only the four solo songs are considered here. In the middle of them a dramatic change seems to have occurred in Schumann's song-writing. Three are sweet, not to say fulsome, with chromatic relaxation; one is sharp, not to say acrid, with chromatic tension. For the first time, there are ominous signs not only in the man but in the music.

172. (Op. 101, No. 1) (for tenor) Meine Töne still und heiter

Rückert – June 1849

My soft joyous singing rises up to her window; oh that I might follow it there! Sweet songs, lay your sorrow on her heart, since she will not suffer me to be there.

The beloved has silently opened her window and leaned out where I could see her; and she greeted me with her serene gaze, she strewed over me roses, sheer roses.

She smiles with lips and cheeks, and the world blooms like a flowering rosebush; she smiles down roses and then closes the window again, with a secret smile.

She smiles in her room, bright as a rose. But alas I may not be with her. If only I could be with her in her room for a year! She must surely have smiled it full of roses.

Schumann again takes two separate poems, out of sequence, and sets them as one song. The first's tonic G major is treated as an emphatic dominant introducing three more verses in C major. Key and rhythm alike seem a little colourless and unyielding for the rosy plush of Rückert's hyperboles, but the result is likeable enough, especially the gracious melody that begins the second part of the song.

NOTES. 1. All the repetitions are Schumann's. The second poem ('The beloved . . . etc.') was printed in the almanac *Moosrosen* for 1826 (of which Schumann seems to have possessed a copy, since it was the source of No. 169, written a month or so earlier). This may well have provided the impetus that sent him back to *Liebesfrühling*, which had not been called upon for a song-text for nine years.

2. At this time, as we know from diary entries, Schumann was in the depressive phase. Here we can see its eerily inhibiting effect; bars 10–15 are quoted, no doubt unconsciously, from bars 9–14 of *Er ist's* (showing incidentally that the songs are still conceived as piano pieces).

3. However, the music is in other respects as original and seminal as ever.

Thus the texture of the first song could serve the forthright Brahms for the expression of bibulous jollity, as in *Unüberwindlich*, Op. 72, No. 5, and with only slight adaptations is equally at home in the more rarefied atmosphere of Fauré's *Chanson d'amour*, Op. 27, No. 1.

4. The amorous dominants (M 64) of the postlude indicate a happy ending; the first appearance of the word 'Rosen' at bar 51 is greeted with the falling fifth (M 27) in voice and piano; the flattened sixth of motif 8 anticipates the word 'Schmerz'.

173. (Op. 101, No. 2) (for soprano) Liebster, deine Worte stehlen

Rückert – June 1849

Dearest, your words steal the heart from my breast; oh how can I hide from you my joy, my sorrow!

Dearest, your music raises me to new heights of exaltation; let us soar together from the earth to join the chorus of blessed spirits!

Dearest, your lute strings draw me in a trance through the skies; let me embrace you so that I do not fall, dazzled by this radiance!

Dearest, your songs wreathe a glory round my brow; how can I thank you for the riches wherewith you garland me!

Schumann has the odd idea of linking this song to the last by the same chord, using the first line of this poem as recitative introduction. Other eccentricities follow. Thus, the poet intends a pleasingly regular metrical pattern: 'Dearest; your words, your music, your strings, your songs', etc. But each time this pattern recurs it is set, with maddening inconsistency, to a different rhythm and melody.

NOTES. 1. All the repetitions are Schumann's. 'Ranken' in bar 28 should read 'wanken'.

2. Amid such a welter of variants it is a relief to note the unity in bars 4–7 and 36–39.

3. The dominant at bar 8 may show that this is for Schumann a real question (M 43) despite the poet's exclamation mark.

4. The confusion may even make the song end in the wrong place. There would be more finality if the voice part were prolonged by an extra bar, postponing 'umlaubt' to bars 41–42 where it fits if anything rather better. Perhaps it is that word which suggests the arpeggio of motif 21A in the postlude.

174. (Op. 101, No. 4) (for tenor) Mein schöner Stern!

Rückert – June 1849

My lovely star! I implore you not to let your serene radiance be dimmed by the dark clouds in me; rather help my darkness to shine with your light.

My lovely star! I beseech you not to sink down to earth because you see me here; rather lift me up to heaven, my lovely star, where you already are!

The verses sound many a responsive chord in Schumann, who reveals his own inmost thoughts in this sensitive and vulnerable music.

His diary entry for his 39th birthday, 8th June 1849, just a few days after these songs were written, has the simple but infinitely sad and heartfelt entry 'Mein 39 Geburtstag. Die gute Clara und meine Melancholie'. There are other references to folly and hypochondria during the same period; his wife's love sustained him in these dark days. The poem's emotion is one that he was personally able to experience. Only on that condition, as we have seen, did his song-writing ever take fire; and the result here is a beacon among the otherwise unilluminating songs of *Minnespiel*.

NOTES. 1. The text, already as apt as it could be to the composer's mood, is left unchanged.

2. The left-hand octaves' symbolism articulates the song, giving the sense of separation (the falling octave) and yearning (the rising one as at bars 10, 17, etc.: M 16).

3. The pattern of repeated chords with bass octaves conveys a sense of solemnity (M 30). The unobtrusive canon as the voice is echoed by the left-hand melody from bar 3 is no doubt expressive (M 59), the affectionate dominants are evident throughout (M 64); the allusion to the subdominant in the postlude (as in M 50) was only to be expected from both the theme and the image of the verse. Perhaps there are motifs 48 (recitative) and 61 (impatience) at bars 14 (32) and 15 (33) respectively.

175. (Op. 101, No. 6) (for contralto or soprano) O Freund, mein Schirm, mein Schutz!

Rückert – June 1849

Oh friend, my shelter, my protection! Oh friend, my jewel, my pearl! My pride, my comfort, my courage! My bastion, oh my shield! In time of strife I take refuge with you. When the world seeks to hem me in I fly to you; when it threatens me with bitterness I cry my need to you. You will not send me away without a word of comfort; you are, and will remain, my haven. I make light of the woes of the world, so long as I can lay myself and my burden of sorrow to rest on your heart. Whatever you do to me, oh world, I shall rest for ever in silent peace here on my friend's heart.

By way of complete contrast, here is nothing for Schumann to express. Instead, the fustian text, with its quaint overtones of Biblical imagery done into botched verse, seems to put him in mind of the church cantatas of Bach. But he also modernizes the musical language, giving it a new insistence and angularity to match Rückert's short lines in rhymed triplets. The result must have sounded very singular in 1849 and is still without parallel in Schumann's work.

NOTES. 1. Schumann adds 'mich' in bar 12 and the repeats in bars 13–14, 28–29, 41–43.

2. Note the finality motif 49 in the voice at bars 2–5 and 29–33.

Lieder und Gesänge (Songs and ballads) aus Goethe's Wilhelm Meister, Op. 98a

Goethe's novel *Wilhelm Meister* is especially memorable for the lyrics sung by the mysterious Harper and Mignon. Neither knows that she is his child by his own sister. This is the sin that has sent him wandering crazed through the world far from his native Italy. His harp-songs are heavy with guilt and despair. Mignon's songs are full of secrecy, grief and yearning for love and homeland. The sheer magnificence of Goethe's poetry gives all these emotions a universal quality that speaks for mankind.

Op. 79 had ended with Mignon, 'on the threshold of adult life'. This may well have suggested the idea of further *Wilhelm Meister* settings. At this time Schumann was also working on his *Scenes from Faust*. A typical diary entry says 'Mem: collect all these Goethe pieces into one volume'.

Cosmic drama in literature and in history are in Schumann's mind; he might have thought of both *Faust* and the abortive Dresden revolution as his country's greatest tragedy. Perhaps it is in response to these ideas that his music is so chromatically overwrought and tense. But the tragic state seems to be more his own. Certainly the weird angularity of the song just finished, No. 175 above, was not wholly motivated by the words. It is difficult to see how this new music, sometimes poised, sometimes veering from frenzy to stupor, is related to Goethe's muse; and all too sadly easy to see how it is related to Schumann's own psyche.

For almost the first time there is a suggestion that piano-music is not the primary conception: the larger canvas demands quasi-orchestral effects. Similarly, for the purpose of larger dramatic expression the diatonic harmony of 1840 is broken down into the new expressive syllabary of rising or falling tones and semitones. These poignant or tragic expressions provide unifying motto themes, which can be schematized thus (in C minor or G minor).

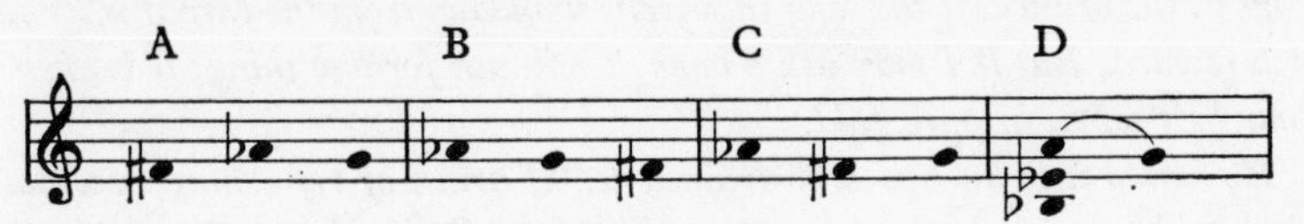

The notes are usually conceived as melody, thus

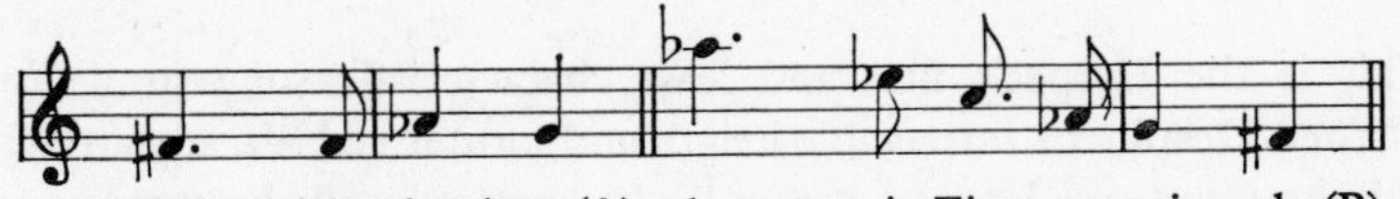

heiss mich schweigen (A) brennt mein Ein - ge-wei - de (B)

or as a melodic outline thus

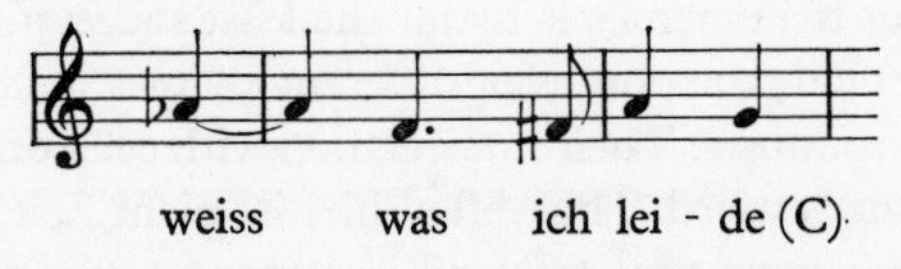

but they also appear as harmony, e.g. motto C might be flat supertonic, dominant seventh, tonic, in G minor. Motto D is typically a suspension over a major chord, the dissonance of the first note producing a characteristically poignant effect.

176. (Op. 98a, No. 2) Ballade des Harfners (The Harper's Ballad)

Goethe – June 1849

'Who is that I hear singing outside my gate and upon the bridge? Let him be brought to sing before us here!' So spoke the king; out ran the page and returned, and the king cried, 'Let the old man enter!'

'Greetings, noble lords, and greetings fair ladies, as many and as shining

as the stars! Who could name you all? In this hall full of splendour and magnificence I must close my eyes; this is no time to gaze in surprised delight.'

The minstrel closed his eyes and sang full-throated. The knights looked on boldly, the ladies looked demurely down into their laps. The king, pleased with the song, commanded a chain of gold to be brought to honour him for his performance.

'Give this golden chain not to me but to your knights, before whose fierce looks and valour the lances of your foes splinter; or give it to the chancellor you have, to add a golden burden to his other burdens. I sing, as the bird sings in the branches; the song that wells unbidden from the throat is its own rich reward. But if I may ask a boon, I will ask for one thing; a beaker of your best wine, in pure gold.'

He raised it to his lips and drained it. 'O drink of refreshing sweetness! A blessed house indeed where this is but a small gift. In your good fortune think of me and thank God for your blessings as warmly as I thank you for this wine.'

This is the Harper's first and least characteristic song in *Wilhelm Meister*. Despite its intractable length and form it had already attracted Schubert and was later to attract Wolf. No doubt all three composers sincerely responded to Goethe's allegory of the artist in society, and its central thesis that song is its own reward. None of these settings is outstanding, but Schumann's is by far the least successful. His musical ideas are in turmoil; the dozens of different themes include six for the basic idea of harp music. Their interrelation with each other is obscure; with the words it is weird. Thus, after 'hier ist nicht Zeit, sich staunend zu ergötzen' (this is no time to stand and gaze, etc.) a piano interlude stands and gazes, for four bars of dreamy melody. Again, at 'ich singe wie der Vogel singt' (I sing as the bird sings) the voice changes from effortless singing to a laborious arioso half-remembered from ten years earlier. In such ways the song's many fine moments are all lost in a welter of irrelevance and confusion.

NOTES. 1. Schumann is using a text (apparently the Paris edition of 1840) which is obviously inferior to the readily available standard version; for example it seems absurdly bathetic for the Harper solemnly to request that his wine be brought 'in reinem Glase' rather than 'in purem Golde'. In that text Schumann inserts 'seinen' to fill up bar 77, and repeats 'das Lied' and 'reichlich'.

2. In so far as Schumann's motifs can be authenticated the following catalogue will show both their inventiveness and their irrelevance:

(*a*) The harper's preluding strains have the kingly motif 50. The king himself appears in stately chords, at bars 8 and 10. But later (bar 20, etc.) the harper, not to be outdone, calmly appropriates the royal minims.

(*b*) The page scampers off (bars 13, etc.) to a motif curiously suggestive of the appearance of the hand in *Belsatzar*.

(*c*) The further suggestion of the nobility motif 50 in bars 20–24 seems relevant; but not the doleful bass line (M 8) in bars 27–30 or the canon (M 59) in bars 30–32.

(*d*) The descending phrase heard briefly in bar 26 is very like the four-note phrase in bars 57–58; each follows a reference to 'fair ladies'.

(*e*) The quaver groups in bars 33 and 35 ominously foreshadow the slack writing of 1850. There is an even worse moment at bars 116–117.

(*f*) The lovely but irrelevant melody at bars 39–43 mentioned in the commentary above is never heard again. The bass in these bars has motif 61 which in other contexts means impatience.

(*g*) The melody at bars 53–55 means finality elsewhere (M 49) and it is true that the Harper's setpiece song ends hereabouts.

(*h*) The rising semitones in both hands at 65–67 are essentially motif 11 for distress. They contrast with the 'dream' of motif 32 at the mention of gold, with an almost covetous effect, again as in *Belsatzar*.

(*i*) The illustrative chords at 'splittern' in bar 73 use the Goethe motto D.

(*j*) The melody already mentioned in the commentary at 'Ich singe wie der Vogel', etc., also begins *Intermezzo*; perhaps there is a vague association with the ideas of singing and flying, as in that song.

(*k*) In bars 89–90, 100–102, and 106–107, is a flowing music of gratification at the gift of wine, the pleasure motif 10.

(*l*) Even in the postlude Schumann is still inventing recklessly. After a novel form of the harp-motif (including the dominants of motif 64, perhaps suggested by the preceding warm thanks) the original motif of the prelude ('the Harper') exits to its own accompaniment ('the Harp') standing together for the final flourishing chords of farewell.

3. Cf. Schubert; Wolf.

177. (Op. 98a, No. 3) Nur wer die Sehnsucht kennt

Goethe – June 1849

Only those who have known hopeless love can fathom grief like mine. Alone and sundered from all joy I scan the skies to the south, for he who knows and loves me is far away. My senses reel, my inmost being burns.

Only those who have known hopeless love can fathom grief like mine.

Goethe's fine lyric is unified by one set of rhymes throughout. Schumann too has a unifying idea, the falling tone or semitone, at whatever pitch, tempo or timbre. From this fluid medium the music is drawn in a great wave of pain and lamentation, gathering from the depths of a bass octave and cresting in a despairing cry on the word 'brennt' (burns). This climax is raised high above the rest of the song by a quicker movement, a wide-ranging vocal phrase, a sudden high note, where voice and piano split violently in opposite directions, and an especially expressive harmony. The wave is then to break and to recede. At its lowest ebb it moans an echo of the same harmony. Now the movement is much slower, the vocal line lower, the melody a monotone, the voice and piano in unison; a spent force.

The idea has a certain majesty. But in order to realize it Schumann has to repeat nearly all the poem, which is not long enough for his purposes, and this is managed with curious ineptitude. As the wave recedes it takes with it much of the sense of Goethe's beautiful lyric, like flotsam. Worse still, the musical quality is at a low ebb all the time.

NOTES. 1. The poem finishes at bar 21. Schumann's further selection fills another sixteen bars. The text he was using has 'schwindet' at bar 15, but of course 'schwindelt' should be sung.

2. The falling tone or semitone is ubiquitous. Each of the double rhymes stresses this idea in bars 4, 7 (26), 11 (30), 14 (33) and 21 (37). There are many other examples, some obvious, as in the semitonal descent of the left hand in bars 4–7; and some less so, as in the implied melody A♭, G, B♭, A, in the top notes right-hand bars 2–4. As part of the tonal structure there is this interval between the low Gs at the beginning and the end and the top A♭ halfway through.

3. The crest and trough of the wave (bars 16–17 and 35–37) need expressive interpretation. Each has similar harmony (flat supertonic, dominant, tonic): each is a motto theme (B and C). The falling tone at e.g. 'Seite' is motto D.

4. There are the usual editorial problems; thus, why should bars 24–26 differ from bars 5–7, either in the vocal rhythm or the mordent?

5. Cf. Schubert's six settings, Beethoven's four, and many others including Loewe, Medtner, Tschaikovsky, and Wolf.

178. (Op. 98a, No. 4) Wer nie sein Brod mit Thränen ass
Goethe – July 1849

The man who has never eaten his daily bread with tears, nor spent the sorrowful nights weeping on his bed – he knows you not, you heavenly powers!

You lead us into life, you let the poor man become guilty, then you abandon him to torment; for all guilt is punished here on earth.

A counterpoise to the previous song. Here the thematic unit is the rising not the falling tone or semitone, giving the suggestion of firmness, even defiance. As before, this structure cannot bear the emotional weight with which it is charged. The treading bass, the well-known triplet accompaniment rhythm, the obsessive harmony, the unmotivated introduction of prodigious harp-flourishes, as if the instrument had suddenly been remembered; all these things create an agony of frustration for the listener who can hear both the nobility and originality of the conception and the confusion and banality of its execution.

NOTES. 1. Schumann repeats the last line.

2. The accompaniment figure throughout is a variant of the pain motif 11.

3. There is motto C at bars 10–11 and 27–28; and motto D on the word 'Erden' in bar 29.

4. At bars 13–14 is an expression found again in the Lenau song *Da liegt der Feinde*, where it suggests immobility. Perhaps the heavenly powers are being imagined in the music; they are apostrophized by the emphatic 'Ihr' in bars 15 and 18.

5. Cf. Liszt (two settings); Schubert (three settings); Wolf.

179. (Op. 98a, No. 5) Heiss mich nicht reden
Goethe – June 1849

Bid me not speak, bid me be silent, for I am sworn to secrecy. I should willingly show you my whole heart, but Fate has willed it otherwise. In its due time the sun returns to dispel the dark night, making it yield to brightness; the solid rock cleaves, freely releasing its hidden springs.

We all seek a friend's embrace to sob out our grief; but my lips are closed by a vow, and only a god can unlock them [*only a god; bid me not speak, bid me be silent; my lips are closed by a vow, and only a god can unlock them*].

Perhaps the intense inward secrecy of these lines makes them unsuitable for musical expression. Even Wolf is more successful in the metaphor of releasing the secret than at the idea of keeping it. Schumann's music seems in a perpetual desperate need to blurt it out. Loud dramatic chords begin the song; it seems that some portentous utterance is imminent. But no; 'Heiss mich nicht reden', which comes as something of a surprise. The piano interlude plucks at the sleeve for attention. But still the secret must be kept; and the effort is painful. 'Geheimnis' (secret), and later 'schweigen' (be silent), are accompanied by moans from the piano; so is 'der harte Fels' (the solid rock), an image of silence. Meanwhile the idea of divulging the secret has given real pleasure to the music. 'Ich möchte dir' (I should like to) sings the voice; and the piano goes on contentedly singing this strain before and during the following pronouncement about how fate has willed it otherwise. There is a clear untrammelled major tonality for the first time at 'Zur rechten Zeit', etc., (In due time) with impatience in the rhythm, as if to bring that time nearer. The piano treble rises in delight with the sun; there is a flowing A major melody as the springs pour out their troubles. So the song proceeds, a new strange idea at every turn. It culminates in a funereal E flat minor, portentous bass octaves, and a grinding dissonance; as if the need for confession were forcing a wordless cry from beyond the grave. This eerie vision dissolves as the voice repeats wonderingly, as well it might, the opening and the closing words of the poem.

This disjointed and wilful music must be among the strangest examples ever offered of an art that is essentially unitary, intimate and responsive to language.

NOTES. 1. The music might have derived from a personal if eccentric interpretation of Goethe. But all the evidence of all Schumann's songs is to the contrary. In this Opus for example the verbal repetitions are flatly insensitive; and those here in bars 12–14, 45–46, and especially in 54–60, with their suggestion of a handy synopsis of the poem for latecomers or the inattentive, are among the worst. The impression is overwhelming that this song is about some tragic secret of Schumann's own.

2. At the same time the music is certainly expressive of some idea derived from the poem. Here is an attempt to describe the creative process:

(*a*) We know, first, that Schumann was experiencing tragedy and drama in his life and his other music. So he treats this most intimate of all German lyrics in terms of a sombre dramatic scena, for soprano and orchestra.

(*b*) Against this background bars 1–4 are a dramatic prelude of accented C minor chords. Just as in Beethoven's *Sonata Pathétique* (or Schumann's own *Wichtige Begebenheit*) this means a solemn pronouncement.

(*c*) At bar 4 is the falling tone of motto D, at bar 6 the falling semitone of motif 8; the secret is identified with sorrow.

(*d*) At bars 7–9 is motto B, for Goethean tragedy; again the enforced silence is equated with sorrow.

(*e*) The words 'ich möchte dir', etc., are stressed first with a grupetto (which elsewhere has the sense of yielding or melting), and then by the imitation of their melody in the piano in bars 9–10 and again at bars 11–12.

(*f*) The words 'heiss mich nicht reden', etc., are repeated, with motto A; another double expression of sorrow in silence.

(*g*) On the other hand any hint of releasing the secret is greeted with a joyous musical response. Thus at the following mention of the sun's dispelling the dark night the tonality brightens into the major. With this goes the urgency of motif 61 in the new syncopated rhythm at bars 16 and bars 18–21. The piano looks up hopefully for signs of sunrise at bars 22–23.

(*h*) But now at bars 24–25 the music darkens tragically again, in motto A; apparently at the thought of the unyielding rock.

(*i*) However, the rock has secret springs and all is well; so by the very next bar the music is flowing again, this time sleek with the humility of motif 38, perhaps because of Goethe's metaphor.

(*j*) Now the urgency is again stressed at bars 31–35; the need to confide is dominant. This passage is near speech, as the recitative of motif 48 confirms.

(*k*) Then humility returns, for solemn submission to the vow and the God that exacts it; and this deity is identified by Schumann's secret mind as Death himself, in a strangely unexpected E flat minor. That same thought is again stressed by the ominous repetition of 'nur ein Gott!', to the motto B for tragedy.

(*l*) At this climactic moment the music is clearly orchestral, indeed operatic, in conception. The composer's mind sees the darkened stage, the lone figure in anguish; over a sustained A flat on cellos and basses the horn-chords strain upwards distraught. The idea of divulging the secret heard in bars 22–23 reappears in the worried diminished sevenths of motif 42. There follows a grinding dissonance. The music cries aloud, on the point of death, 'shall I tell? I must; oh, I cannot' in a purple climax of high melodrama.

(*m*) Now the mental turmoil subsides exhausted; the music's spirit is broken. A few mumbled words are recalled from the previous excitement (complete with motto A and the recitative motif 48) and all is over.

3. Cf. Schubert; Wolf.

180. (Op. 98a, No. 6) Wer sich der Einsamkeit ergibt

Goethe – July 1849

He who surrenders to solitude is all too soon alone. Others live and love and leave him to his pain. Then leave me too with my anguish. And if I can once know true solitude – still I am not alone.

For as a lover softly steals to see if his beloved is alone, so pain and anguish steal softly after me in my loneliness, by night and by day. But if I can once find true solitude in the grave, there I shall be left alone.

The harp music has a melancholy dignity, with expressive vocal melody. As the insistence of pain and anguish are compared with the attentions of a lover ('Es schleicht ein Liebender') the music is first finely tender, then sharply anguished, while keeping the same texture of repeated triplet quavers to show that grief too can be cherished. But for the rest the confusion and contrivance are all too evident.

NOTES. 1. The blunder of repeating 'Pein' in bar 38 (so printed ever since the first edition) instead of Goethe's stressed 'Qual' should of course be corrected.

2. The confusion is most noticeable in the tonality; thus the first notes have

needless accidentals. The contrivance is apparent in the mechanical repetitions of Motto A at bars 22–25.

3. Motifs occur when there is feeling in the music. In bar 26 the left-hand thirds have the quietude of motif 37; the right hand in this bar is the pleased motif 10. The sombre E flat minor arrives very pat on the word 'Nacht' in bar 34.

4. Cf. Schubert; Wolf.

181. (Op. 98a, No. 7) Singet nicht in Trauertönen

Goethe – *c.* June 1849

Do not sing in mournful tones of the loneliness of night; no, fair ladies, it is made for companionship.

How can you like the daytime, that interrupter of joys? It is useful as a distraction but for nothing else.

But when at night there is sweet uncertain lamplight and intimate exchange of loving and jesting from lip to lip; when fleet-footed Cupid will often tarry awhile to play, in exchange for some small gift; when the nightingale sings its song for lovers that sounds to others like pain and lament: then with how gay and excited a heart you hear the twelve solemn strokes of midnight announcing peace and security.

So remember this during the long daytime, dear heart; each day brings its worries, each night its pleasures.

Here Schumann is doubly relaxed. The light verse relieves him for a while of the crushing responsibility of matching some of the greatest poems of his country's greatest poet. Better still, the main subject of the verse appeals to him. We hear the music being captivated by the charms of the vivacious young soubrette Philine from *Wilhelm Meister*. The prelude is all gaiety and grace, changing in the accompaniment to a pizzicato guitar serenade; and the vocal melody is straight from the heart of Schumann's, or anyone's, lost youth. This memorable strain brings out counter-melodies from the piano, until all the music is alive with singing.

But then the light fails. Goethe speaks of night; but as the bringer of jollity. The music seems duller than required. It does little to mitigate our impatience for the return of the opening melody. This is delayed so long that when it does come it seems to have lost much of its first sparkle. And the rest, it must be admitted, is banal, except the pleasantly playful postlude.

NOTES. 1. Schumann omits the second verse; presumably because it was less apt to his opening melody, with its joyous arpeggio (M 23).

2. The song is undated. The main theme is April music. But by the last page there are crude repetitions and raw thematic material; the middle section even seems to suffer from an attack of depression, as the motto theme A (bars 21–22) reveals. Perhaps the song was finished amid the June melancholia which suited the Mignon songs.

3. Schmunnn's penchant for vivacious young women was expressed in *Die Kartenlegerin*, also in the light E flat major. The semiquaver movement here seems more expressively precise. It has been noted in *Er ist's*, with the main image of 'flattern', and recurs in *Ins Freie*, as a direct and no doubt unconscious quotation, at the word 'flattert'. Perhaps this is a musical equivalent for the idea of feminine prettiness, derived from an imaginary picture of the play of ribbons.

4. Cf. Wolf.

182. (Op. 98a, No. 8) An die Türen will ich schleichen
Goethe – July 1849

I shall creep from door to door, I shall stand quiet and docile. Christian hands will give me food, and I shall go on my way.

Whoever sees my figure before him will count his blessings and shed a tear for me, while I wonder why he weeps.

Here, perhaps because the words had some deep personal significance for him, Schumann comes closer than anywhere else in the Goethe songs to a truly lucid and moving speech.

Among the slow creeping progress of the minims in the brief prelude, the staccato notes tap like a blind man's stick. The semiquaver figure sidles and pleads. The vocal melody is guileless and sad. Its opening notes recur in the piano part, first after 'stehn' and then in a more extended interlude after 'gehn', as it were standing unobtrusively at the door and then going away again. In between there is a moment of rare beauty. By 'Fromme Hand wird Nahrung reichen' Goethe meant perhaps no more than a gift of food. But Schumann has quiet arpeggios; not the grandiose harp-chords that so tyrannize the other Harper songs, but different gestures of other hands; soothing gestures, as an old man is fed and comforted like a child.

Now the music falters, as for the first time it has to express the feelings of others. There is not only a properly charitable piety but even a hint of complacency in the square-cut chords that follow. But the main theme returns with enhanced effect as the music once again becomes the old minstrel. Now the melody is first firm, then uncertain, a little confused in its harmony – where are they taking me? why are they weeping? — ending once more on the soothing arpeggios. In the final chord the music is no longer sad but friendly and docile in the tonic major – the only time that this chord has been struck in the whole song. And suddenly this smiling sound is the saddest moment in the whole doleful sequence of the *Wilhelm Meister* songs.

NOTES. 1. The repeat from 24 on is Schumann's.

2. Motto A is in bars 24–26 and motto D in bar 10. Each is used with more feeling and less rhetoric than elsewhere. The 'wandeln' motif 20 is used in a novel form in the semiquaver groups; the canon of motif 59 appears with perplexed harmony (M 41) very aptly at 'scheinen' in bar 16.

3. Compare Wolf and Schubert, Op 12, No. 3; for them as for Schumann this was the most inspiring of all the Harper lyrics.

183. (Op. 98a, No. 9) So lasst mich scheinen

Goethe – June 1849

Let me seem to be an angel until I become one. Let me go on wearing my white dress. I am passing from this fair earth down to my long home.

There I shall rest in silence for a while until my eyes open renewed. Then I shall leave behind this pure raiment, girdle and garland. For those heavenly forms make no question of man or woman, and no clothes, no folds trammel the body risen.

True, I lived without worldly cares; but I knew deep sorrow. I grew old with grief before my time; now let me be made for ever young again!

The child Mignon was dressed as an angel, white-robed and golden winged, for her part in a children's charade. When the time comes for her to change her costume, she sings this song, to a zither accompaniment. In the lyric and in its whole context there is deep tragic feeling; Mignon is to die young. But Schumann's setting seems to reflect only his own mental state. The two-bar prelude is a vague gesture, a halting observation.

This rhythm is heard again in the third bar and the fifth, and then vanishes, apparently forgotten. This brief confusion typifies the whole song. Ideas gleam and fade; nothing coheres. Thus, there are seemingly endless shifts of rhythm; hardly any two bars are even analogous. In the voice part there is no longer even a rudimentary sense of scansion; in the music as a whole not a flicker of life, despite the palpably intense effort of creation.

NOTES. 1. Schumann repeats the last four words to make a climax – with a senseless stress on 'auf'.

2. The weary appoggiature of the vocal line take precedence over the manifest sense of the words, e.g. at bars 7 ('*Kleid* nicht aus') and 12 ('*feste* Haus'). This is the typical Goethe word-setting exactly as in *Nur wer die Sehnsucht kennt*; there are other obvious echoes of that song.

3. Motto A is at bars 3–4; C in the bass at 22–23; and D at 'rein' in 18.

4. The sense of the prelude remains a mystery. Another puzzle is the snatch of piano melody at bars 30–31.

5. Even the typical Schumann motifs sound distraught. The key of E flat is obtruded at the idea of sudden light in bar 15, etc.; a hint of the finality motif 49 seems to appear at bar 35, left hand, and again at the end of the post-lude; there is the rhetorical perplexity of motif 42 in the diminished seventh at 'doch'. A clearer example is the shape of the 'Stille' motif 26 in the bars 12–14 where that word occurs.

Drei Gesänge (Three ballads) Op. 95, to words by Byron

We have seen that in the Goethe songs of late June and July 1849 the music seemed unreasonably excited and portentous, conformably with Schumann's own mood at the time. But the pendulum was already swinging. By the end of November the diary again notes the onset of melancholia, impelled perhaps by rumours of cholera; after which Schumann was 'suddenly ill'.

The Byron songs of December are as depressive as the Goethe songs were manic; the product of a mind torpid in its idea of more harp songs, slack in its choice of verses, pedantic in its alterations, dull in its setting. These songs have as their only comment the sad one that they may contain further evidence of deterioration.

184. (Op. No. 95, No. 1) Die Tochter Jephta's (Jephtha's daughter)

Byron (trans. Körner) – December 1849

Since our Country, our God – Oh, my Sire!
Demand that thy daughter expire;
Since thy triumph was bought by thy vow –
Strike the bosom that's bared for thee now!

And the voice of my mourning is o'er,
And the mountains behold me no more;
If the hand that I love lay me low,
There cannot be pain in the blow!

And of this, oh, my Father! be sure –
That the blood of thy child is as pure
As the blessing I beg ere it flow,
And the last thought that soothes me below.

Though the virgins of Salem lament,
Be the judge and the hero unbent!
I have won the great battle for thee,
And my Father and Country are free!

When this blood of thy giving hath gush'd,
When voice that thou lovest is hush'd,
Let my memory still be thy pride,
And forget not I smiled as I died.

NOTES. 1. Körner has '. . . dein Gelübde den Feinden gab Schmerz/Hier entoblösst ist's, durchbohre mein Herz'' at bars 6–10 and 'sei gedenk mein . . .' at bars 51–52.

2. At 'die Stimme verhallt' bars 48–49 is a jaded example of the 'going away' motif 45.

3. The odd choice of melody notes a seventh apart in bars 10 and 18 (the C should be sung) confirms that the 1849 song-writing is still based on the piano piece.

185. (Op. 95, No. 2) An den Mond (To the moon)

Byron (trans. Körner) – December 1849

Sun of the sleepless! melancholy star!
Whose tearful beams glow tremulously far,

That show'st the darkness thou canst not dispel,
How like thou art to joy remembered well!
So gleams the past, the light of other days,
Which shines, but warms not with its powerless rays;
A night-beam Sorrow watcheth to behold,
Distinct, but distant – clear – but, oh how cold!

NOTES. 1. The repetitions in bars 19–22 and 40–43 are Schumann's. There are extensive changes from Körner's text, which has 'glüht zitternd fern' at bars 10–11, 'wie die Erinnerung seliger Tage gleicht' (which at least rhymes) at bars 15–19, etc; 'So glänzt, Vergangenheit! ihr fernes Licht' at bars 26–29; and 'doch wärmt sein matter Schimmer nicht/Der wache Gram schaut eines Sterns Gestalt/Sichtbar doch ferne; hell, doch ach! wie kalt,' on the last page.

2. Even the harp music is remembered from the Harper's ballad (prelude and postlude here, cf. bar 123 there with two of the same chords).

3. This poem was also set by Mendelssohn and Wolf, each in a different translation. The former setting may have been known to Schumann; the phrases he substituted for the second and third passages mentioned above seem to be borrowed from its (anonymous) translation.

186. (Op. 95, No. 3) Dem Helden (To the hero)

Byron (trans. Körner) – December 1849

Thy days are done, thy fame begun;
Thy country's strains record
The triumphs of her chosen Son,
The slaughters of his sword!
The deeds he did, the fields he won,
The freedom he restored!

Though thou art fall'n, while we are free
Thou shalt not taste of death!
The generous blood that flowed from thee
Disdain'd to sink beneath:
Within our veins its currents be,
Thy spirit on our breath.

Thy name, our charging hosts along,
Shall be the battle word!
Thy fall, the theme of choral song
From virgin voices pour'd!
To weep would do thy glory wrong;
Thou shalt not be deplored.

NOTES. 1. Körner has 'der Volkgesang' at bars 3–4; 'edlich und so treu' at bar 19; 'fliess' ' in bar 23; 'begiebt's' not 'rüstet's' in bar 29; 'klagen' not 'künden's' in bar 32; and 'Die Trän' entweihete dein Maal/Wir weinen nicht um dich.' in the last lines.

2. There are certain stirrings of expression here, e.g. motif 53 in the accented bass notes at bar 8, for the strongly-wielded sword, and the vigorous octaves at bar 9 which clearly stand for 'Taten' in that bar; but their relevance ends with the first verse.

* * *

In 1849 Schumann's music was first hyperactive to the point of turmoil, in the Goethe songs; and then, in the Byron songs, inert to the point of torpor.

When in April 1850 the song-writing is resumed we can hear at once that the music is whole and wholesome, as before. Yet at the same time it seems curiously innocuous and genteel, as if some spirit or virtue had gone out of it.

The work lacks character in every sense. From now on returns the element of pure lyric self-expression that had hardly been heard since 1840. And with the mature Schumann this seems spurious, despite the modest charm and success of some of the results.

* * *

187. (Op. 51, No. 5) Liebeslied (Lovesong)

Goethe – *c.* April 1850 (? 1840)

I am anxious to tell you all my heart. I heard that this too is your heart's desire. Yet how sadly the world looks at me.

In my mind only my friend dwells, no one else, no trace of any enmity. A plan dawns upon me like sunrise.

I shall from now on devote my whole life to his love. I think of him and my heart bleeds.

I have no strength but to love him in silence. How will it all end? I yearn to embrace him and cannot.

Words and accompaniment have a certain wan charm; the interchanged melodies of voice and piano suggest another *Nussbaum*, if a barren one. But the song, uniquely in the Lied literature, is a private communication in a code to which the music offers no key.

NOTES. 1. Goethe's text, from which Schumann omits 'von heut an' after 'liebe' in bar 25, is found under the heading 'Codes' among the explanatory notes attached to the *Westöstlicher Diwan*. It illustrates how lovers can communicate in a private code, by page and line reference to a mutually agreed text (here, notionally, the poems of Hafis). The words are of course gibberish, and hopelessly unsuitable as a song text; but they well illustrate Schumann's attitude to song-writing, and his obsessive love of mystification.

2. Op. 51 was published in 1850. There is no other evidence of date. However, it seems likely that Schumann sketched this song for the private pleasure of himself and Clara (they had once exchanged letters in code[1]), when setting other *Diwan* lyrics in 1840, and revised it in a barren period. Occasional patches have the aridity of 1850, e.g. the dull semiquavers in the second half of bar 9, and the clumsy triplets in bars 35–36 as in the 'von der Neun' songs (May 1850). At bars 19–20 there is affinity with *Aufträge* (April 1850).

3. But there are also indications of 1840 as the original date of the music, and Schumann's love for Clara as its unsurprising secret. Her theme P is in the opening vocal line, and P/P¹ (the same melodic sequence as in *Und wüssten's die Blumen* and *Frühlingsnacht*) in the right hand at bars 13–16. The hovering around B minor in A major is also characteristic (bars 4–5, 12–13). The latter is shared with *Jasminenstrauch*; so are the puzzled descending diminished sevenths (M 41) here at bar 41. There is motif 64 in the amorous dominants at bars 33–35, and the finality of motif 49 at the repeated last words.

188. (Op. 77, No. 5) Aufträge (Messages)
Ch. L'Egru – April 1850

Not so swift, little wave, wait a while; I have a message for my sweetheart. As you glide past her give her my love; say I would have come with you and boldly begged a kiss, but you were too impatient to be away.

Not so fast, light-winged dove, wait a while; I have a message for my sweetheart. Give her my love and say I would have flown with you over stream and hill and boldly begged a kiss, but you were too impatient to be away.

But you, slow old moon, I must urge you on. You know what I want you to do – peep through the window-pane and give her my love; – and say that I would have ridden through the sky with you and boldly begged a kiss, but that I was too impatient to be with her.

At first hearing, and indeed at repeated hearings, this is a song of the utmost charm, with its irrepressible demisemiquavers rippling and

[1] See *Musical Times*, December, 1966.

fluttering their response to the idea of waves and wings, just as in *Dichterliebe*. It seems a fitting companion to Schubert's *Liebesbotschaft*, where similar music responds to a similar theme. But sooner or later it will pall just a little. What seems to be a spring of ebullient invention is after all hardly more than a threefold repetition of music which though full of its own special grace is, like the verse, rather too hectic and florid for what it has to say.

NOTE. The demisemiquavers are motif 21[A] throughout; in the opening bars is the 'wandeln' motif 20; and at the end of each verse the sadness of absence has the flattened sixth of motif 8.

189. (Op. 83, No. 1) Resignation

Buddeus – April 1850

I must love you with all my soul, all my heart, passionately, past all concealing. How can this be? How can I know that I love you?

My heart beats higher when you smile; it quivers in pain when you go, it quivers and burns in silent love, and tears brim in my eyes.

I shall never hold you in my arms, your eye will never brighten for me; the silent force of longing will never draw you to my side.

Is my love then without hope? It is; but not without comfort. The future is unknown. But even if we must part for ever there is a reunion Beyond.

Here is the new and disturbing voice of the 1850 Schumann; the bland vagueness of its harmonic language is only too fitting a match for the sickly drivel of the verse.

NOTES. 1. No doubt the repetitions are Schumann's. Julius Buddeus was also responsible for the text of *Die Meerfee*.

2. This new harmonic style is well adapted to motivic writing. The diminished sevenths in bars 4 and 5 suit the rhetorical questions, as again in bar 33 (M 42). The octave drop in the semiquavers at bars 18–19 parallels the idea of renunciation and negation; and may be compared with the rising octaves at bar 7 for 'höher' at the idea of affirmation. The three-part harmony at bar 26 may be quasi-motivic (M 34); note also the inversion of the theme at this point.

3. In conformity with the new Goethe-style of wordsetting each disyllable is persistently placed on two falling tones or semitones, as e.g. in *Nur wer die Sehnsucht kennt*.

190. (Op. 83, No. 2) Die Blume der Ergebung (The flower of resignation)

Rückert – April 1850 (? 1840)

I am the flower in the garden, and must wait in silence to see when and in what guise you come to me.

If you come as a ray of sunlight I shall silently open my heart to you and bask in the warmth of your gaze.

If you come as dew and rain then I shall preserve your blessing in my chalice for ever.

If you pass gently over me in the breeze I shall bow before you, saying: I am yours alone.

I am the flower in the garden, and must wait in silence to see when and in what guise you come to me.

The piano prelude says in its quiet A major that there is a springtime stillness and expectancy about the day, with scarcely a breath of wind in the air. Over the gently nodding semiquavers flowers one of Schumann's most colourful melodies.

The whole music is intent on the notion that the promised vision will surely come; the postlude, secure in this knowledge, is the very flower of patience and quietude.

The music has its roots in 1840; but the harmonic climate of 1850 was unpropitious, and it has now withered into a pressed flower in a rarely-opened album. Still, it is among the most endearing and enduring keepsakes of Schumann's last period.

NOTES. 1. The final repetitions are Schumann's.

2. The springtime A major, the stirring of the piano part (M 21^A), the variation of vocal melody at the third beat in bars 36 and 38 (cf. *Lied der Suleika*), the sweet augmented fifth (M 12), the falling fifth for flowers (M 27) (prelude and postlude and at the word 'Garten') and the joy motif 2 at bars 10–11, are all very typical 1840. Note too the sense of certainty conveyed by the pedal bass at bars 9–12 and in the postlude (M 29): the latter is combined with the silence motif 26.

3. Typical 1850, on the other hand, are the chromatics of the prelude and the needless variations which mar the unity of the song. Thus the triplets at bar 27 are puzzling; the patterns of semiquavers at bar 18 and bars 22–23 seem to derive from the just completed *Resignation* (bars 7 and 9); there are obvious analogies with *Ihre Stimme*.

4. Cf. Loewe, Op. 62 (II), No. 6.

191. (Op. 83, No. 3) Der Einsiedler (The hermit)

Eichendorff – April 1850

Come, silent night, comforter of the world; how gently you come down from the mountains. The winds are all asleep; just one sailor, tired of wandering, sings his evening song across the sea, praising God in the harbour.

The years pass by like the clouds and leave me standing here alone, forgotten by the world; and then you came so wonderfully to me as I sat here lost in thought in the shadow of the woods.

Oh silent night, comforter of the world, the day has left me so tired, the wide sea is already darkling; now let me rest from pleasures and desires until the sunrise of eternity comes dazzling through the silent forest.

A fine poem, and one that should have made a suitably eloquent and moving farewell to Eichendorff; yet the music hardly achieves more than a certain tired facility. There is one gleam of past mastery, as the sailor sings 'sein Abendlied' (his evening song). Schumann feels at one with that mood: to rest from labour and to sing one last song of praise before nightfall. But the effort is too much; the music resumes its muffler of thick commonplace chorale and turns homeward with a jaded piety that dulls the memory of that living voice.

NOTES. 1. Note the persistent gloom of the falling tone and semitone at bars 3, 7, 11, 13 (M 8).

2. Motif 52 falls very pat at 'Abendlied'. This expression for song, with its faint suggestion of religiosity, has now wholly replaced motif 19. The 'Amen' association is even clearer in the last bar, where the tremolo expresses generalized reverence and awe, much as in *Weihnachtslied*. The rising thirds in bars 8–9 are motif 37.

192. (Op. 87) Der Handschuh (The glove)

Schiller – *c.* April 1850 (? begun 1840)

Watching the lions' arena, waiting for the fighting to begin, sat King Francis, surrounded by the lords of his realm; and with him on the high balcony to left and to right sat the ladies, a lovely garland. At his sign the gate opens, and with measured tread a lion paces in, looks soundlessly around with a long yawn, shakes his mane, stretches his limbs and lies down.

At another sign from the king, a second door quickly opens, and from it a tiger comes leaping out with a wild bound. As it sees the lion it gives a loud roar, lashes its tail in a menacing arc, and lolls out its tongue. Then it stealthily circles the lion, snarling with rage; and then lies down by the lion's side, growling.

Once again at the king's sign the double gates open, to disgorge two leopards together. They make a murderous rush at the tiger, which slashes at them with its cruel claws. The lion rises with a great roar. Then there is silence. Once more the great cruel cats, hot for slaughter, crouch down in a ring.

Then from the edge of the balcony a glove falls from a fair hand, right between the tiger and the lion. And Lady Kunigunde turns mockingly to Sir Delorges – 'Sir Knight; if you in truth love me as passionately as you always declare, why then, you may pick up my glove for me.'

And the knight runs quickly down into the fearful arena and with a bold hand removes the glove from between the two savage beasts. The other knights and the noble ladies watch in amazement and terror as he calmly brings back the glove. Then the whole company bursts out in praise of his bravery; but Lady Kunigunde receives him with tender melting glances that presage great bliss in store for him.

And he hurls the glove in her face with 'I desire no thanks from you, lady' – and leaves her from that moment on.

This long poem is admirably matched by Schumann; indeed it is hard to think of a better setting of a Schiller ballad in the whole literature of the Lied.

The first scene presents the assembled nobility; the second makes great imaginative play with the sight and sound of the great cats, as the piano part settles down, leaps, stretches and roars. Then the music presents the ladies on the balcony as the glove falls at 'es fällt von des Altans Rand'. These gracious strains are interrupted by splendidly ominous octaves at 'zwischen den Tiger und den Leu'n' and then resumes gracefully as before; not only presenting the scene graphically but also perhaps making the point that the felinity is not confined to the arena.

NOTES. 1. Schiller has 'der *weite* Zwinger' at bar 15.

2. Op. 87 was published in 1851. There is no entry for this song in the Compositionsbuch. 1850 seems to have the authority of Wasielewski, Schumann's first biographer; but he is often unreliable. A letter of Schumann's of 16th February 1840 implies that he had been writing more than one long ballad. Only one (*Belsatzar*) is known from that period. This may well be another. The poem is among the very few Schumann mentions in his letters, as early as 1834. Most

of the music is typical of 1840. There are many affinities with songs of that year, e.g. the lion-music of *Die Löwenbraut*. Only the last page, with its quirky harmony, suggests a later date. Finally the music as a whole seems too lively and inventive to have been within the grasp of the Schumann of 1850. This may well be an early work, revised, not necessarily to its advantage, in 1850. Cf. also *Liebeslied*.

3. The nobility motif 51 is at its aptest here, for the king and his nobles (bars 5–6, 7–8), for the king of the beasts (bar 64), and again for the gentry at bars 97 and 98. A rising motif for the opening of the gate is obvious enough at bar 15, and for the opening of the lady's eyes and heart at bars 103 and 107.

4. The second and third pages are preoccupied with the recitative motif 48, for obvious reasons. This progression gives a sudden leap at bars 33–34. There is more leaping at bar 55, which may be related to motif 15 of laughter; this also occurs in its own right at the syllable 'spott' in bar 75.

Sechs Gesänge (Six ballads) Op. 89 and other 'von der Neun' settings

By May 1850 Schumann's mind and music are in perceptible decline. Both return to a weak and sickly subjectivism. He believes the turgid claptrap of 'Wielfried von der Neun'[1] to be 'very musical poetry'; his own music for them is mainly stereotype from earlier and better songs.

But even in decline Schumann is still sporadically original. In some of these settings the inward and the elated moods of the previous year mingle and blur together in the new chromatic style. In the absence of diatonic tensions and contrasts a new principle of organization is needed; Schumann accordingly invents and applies the principle of thematic change, later adapted so superbly by Wolf. But it is here applied to banal music for a trivial purpose.

It is as if Schumann's hand had acquired a new cunning and his mind had lost an old one.

[1] i.e. of the Nine (Muses); a typically pretentious pseudonym of the time.

193. (Op. 89, No. 1) Es stürmet am Abendhimmel
'von der Neun' – May 1850

There are storms in the evening sky; the sunlight trembles. On high a lonely cloud speaks to the sun of joy and love. The cloud, driven by the storm, stretches its arms out wide; it glows crimson with love, it sues amid the roaring of the storm. Then its sweetheart, the sun, departs; the cloud in its turn is snatched away by the storm. The crimson has now quite vanished; the horizon is black and ominous.

NOTES. 1. Thematic change as a principle of construction arguably begins with this song. A rising semitone is associated with the idea of storm as tragic fate (a). Semitones lour and loom over every bar. In the prelude the bass growls ominously; thunder (b). Octaves sidle up ingratiatingly in semitones; a plea (c). Then they come storming up; a great wind (d). Part of that idea is turned into tremolando chords; sighs of love (e). Then suddenly the theme is blown together in diminution (f), blown out in augmentation (g), and blown apart in disconnected fragments (h), but survives for an off-stage moan (i) before a final reappearance in emphatic octaves (j) to pronounce doom on life and love in the postlude.

The music's treatment is as ingenious as its material is banal.

2. The wind-effect is motif 22 throughout.

194. (Op 89, No. 2) Heimliches Verschwinden (Secret departure)

'von der Neun' – May 1850

At night, in an unknown hour, sweet spring leaves the meadow, giving a farewell kiss to whatever is quietly in bloom, and then vanishing without trace.

All around the flowers are aglow in a bright blush at his kisses, but delicately ashamed that butterflies cannot be restrained from hanging on their lips.

Yet the people outside say that spring is past; and summer's tyranny begins to make itself felt in sultry days. And we think with regret of this secret departure; it always makes us sad that the springtime never said goodbye.

In the same way we grieve when our first love leaves us without saying goodbye; we should bear the worst calmly if only she had first said a word of farewell.

NOTES. 1. A major is Schumann's sunny spring or summer key; the accompaniment is the decoration of motif 21 as in *Am leuchtenden Sommermorgen*, of which this song sounds in places like a jaded echo.

2. There is wistful regret in the music as in *Erinnerung* from the *Album für die Jugend* of two years earlier. The melodic curves coincide at bars 1–2 there and 5–6 here; while each piece has the 'departure' motif 45 there at bars 3–4 and here at 31–32, aptly illustrating the word 'floh'.

3. The dominants of motif 64 are very apt to 'Küssen prangen' at bars 10–11, so are the clinging tenths (M 57) at bars 14–15, and the recitative motif 48 following the word 'sagen' in bars 21–23. The dominant of motif 43 gives this last phrase the added sense of a question, 'Can spring really have gone?'

195. (Op. 89, No. 3) Herbstlied (Autumn song)

'von der Neun' – May 1850

Through the firs and the lime trees the crimson sunset weaves; and my heart is overcome by regret that I shall soon be in autumn too.

But no; I seem to hear songs and tidings of comfort from the forest, consoling for the dying of the sunlight.

True, the sun is down and dead, and its light powerless. But the splendour of the colours in the treetops speaks of a heaven afar.

NOTES. 1. The repeats on the last page are probably Schumann's.

2. Note the construction, imitated from 193 dated the previous day. Again the music has a banal left-hand leitmotif spread over the centre of two bars to symbolize the prevailing mood, here the gently-falling mood of autumn.

3. The tremolandi throughout are motif 22. The arpeggios at bar 16 are 'joy in nature' (M 21) as in No. 198. The 'weakness' of motif 54 occurs at 'ohne Macht' (powerless) at bars 30–31.

196. (Op. 89, No. 4) Abschied vom Walde (Farewell to the woods)

'von der Neun' – May 1850

Now the traveller with heart and voice takes his leave of the dying forest. 'How quickly you became dear to me; how you sang your songs to me without cease.

And I surely understood your speech and your songs, and will often sing them to myself henceforth in grief and regret.

But now, oh forest, have done with your sighing and roaring; I would not exchange everything for the melodies of Autumn.'

NOTES. 1. 'Glückes genug' (M 1) is in the vocal line at bars 7–8; 'Lieb' leads to the dominants (M 64) at bars 6–8; 'sorrow' occurs unlooked for in bar 10 (M 8). The impatient rhythm of motif 61 occurs throughout, as if the singer's real intention is to get away from the woods at all costs. The music is suddenly quite petulant at 'Doch nun', etc.

2. Perhaps the vague idea of melancholy weeping in the woods stirs a memory of *Hör ich das Liedchen klingen*. The melody at bars 25–28 is that of 'da löst sich auf in Tränen' from that song. Here and elsewhere the chord of E flat minor seems to be emphasized – perhaps because of 'sterbenden' (dying) in the first verse?

197. (Op. 89, No. 5) Ins Freie (Into the open)

'von der Neun' – May 1850

I feel constraint everywhere I go; my heart beats aloud, and what it beats are songs. From the forbidding encirclement of gloomy walls I fly afar, brisk and gay; there I shall breathe freely and know joy again.

Then from the freed heart there flutters a desire for vanished pleasure and hoped-for joys; the winds carry it off heavenward, the grasses offer up prayers for it as they bow their heads in the sunshine.

[*I feel constraint everywhere I go; my heart beats aloud, and what it beats are songs. From the forbidding encirclement of gloomy walls I fly afar, brisk and gay; there I shall breathe freely and know joy again.*]

NOTES. 1. No doubt the repetition is Schumann's.

2. All the music is stereotype; the horn passages (M 4), the key of B flat, the joyous arpeggios (M 23) at bars 6 and 13, the late song motif 52 at 'Lieder',

impatience (M 61) at bars 10–12, etc., nobility (M 51) in the final cadence, and manliness (M 56), throughout, with the general model of the Kerner *Wanderlied* well to the fore. At the same time Schumann's memory is again playing him queer tricks, with an unconscious quotation from *Singet nicht* (bars 7–8 there, bars 22–23 here).

198. (Op. 89, No. 6) Röselein, Röselein (Little rose)

'von der Neun' – May 1850

Rose, little rose, why must you bear thorns? Thus musing, I once fell asleep by a shady brook, and in my dreams I saw, standing in golden sunshine, a thornless rose. And I plucked and kissed it; a thornless rose!

Then I awoke and looked around. I knew I had seen one; where was it? All around, near and far in the sunshine stood roses, all with thorns!

And the brook laughed at me 'Leave your dreaming; you may be sure that all roses have thorns.'

NOTES. 1. No doubt the final repetition is Schumann's.

2. This song about roses doubly stresses the falling fifth of motif 27 by repeating it in the voice part alone in the opening bars. There follows the dominant question 43 at bar 4, with the motif of springtime joy (M 21) at bar 6 (and again at bars 23 and 32 and in the postlude). A comparison of bar 8 with bar 34 suggests that the latter has been altered, deliberately or not, to express the idea 'Träumen' with the staccato of motif 32. Bars 20–21 are remembered from bars 12–13 of *Herbstlied*; finality (M 49) is in the close at bars 39–40. The postlude has love-duetting voices as in *Intermezzo*, for no clear reason.

3. The interesting change at bar 11 to the chord of G sharp major sounds arbitrary until one recalls the clear association in Schumann between the key of A flat and the word 'Golden'.

4. The key change at bar 22 is a good example of the 'tragic' modulation to the key a minor third above, with the underlying idea of the relative minor joining the two (M 25) as well as the idea of interpolation (M 47).

199. (Op. 96, No. 4) Gesungen! (Singing)

'von der Neun' – July 1850

When you hear the rain hammering the trees, the branches snapping in the stress of the storm, then you hear too in the woods the sweet prayerful throats of birds commending themselves to God's love.

When you see the torches of strife flame in the land, when you hear wickedness challenging the righteous to combat, then sing with the whole heart's strength and let peaceful song tame the wild cries of madness.

NOTES. 1. There is pathos in the radical Schumann's tame acceptance of this fatuous notion of meeting trouble by snuggling down and warbling; and there is pathos too in the inept reference to stifling incipient madness.

2. But in the music there is little save an ominous automatism. The feeble wind in semiquaver tremolandi throughout (M 22) recalls *Herbstlied*, No. 195 supra; the minor seconds in bar 4 (M 8) recall *Resignation* No. 189. These jaded echoes are in turn the source of even feebler material such as Op. 104, No. 5.

3. Note the curious trick of composing in several minor keys at once, as in the Goethe songs.

4. Motif 64 occurs in bars 13–14 at the mention of 'Liebe'.

200. (Op. 96, No. 5) Himmel und Erde (Heaven and Earth)

'von der Neun' – July 1850

How boldly the treetops strive up to the light on high! How the white mountaintops soar among the clouds of Heaven! How in May the flowers of the field blend with the blue of the sky! How the autumn glow of the woods merges into the light of dawn!

So you are united, Heaven, with mother Earth; and I shall bear my earthly bonds with joy, being bound for Heaven.

NOTES. 1. The melody at bars 7–9 is a Brahmsian turn of phrase, also heard in *Ihre Stimme*; the vocal melody at bar 19 is also from that song.

2. The middle section in B major is a derivative of *Frühlingsnacht*, complete with descending scale passages in the right hand.

3. The change in the pattern of the accompaniment rhythm at bar 14 seems unmotivated. The accompaniment itself is remembered from *Wer sich der Einsamkeit* at bars 33–34.

4. The manly motif 56 already implied in the earlier music arrives on the second beat of the bar at 18, 20, 22, 24, etc. together with the upward leap (M 16) of the flattened seventh (M 50). There are the calm thirds in the right hand at bars 16–17 (M 37) and a recognizable finality motif 49 in the last few bars for the voice.

* * *

From now on Schumann has two quite distinct styles, corresponding to the duality already noted in the 1849 songs, and possibly to the manic and depressive components of a personality which had reached a stage of dissociation. There is the hectic chromaticism of the Goethe songs, heard again in the 'von der Neun' songs just discussed, and in some of the Lenau songs to come. This stands for heightened emotion, especially sorrow and love. There is also the bland and insipid diatonic style, which stands for cheerful or domestic feelings. Each style, whether polychrome or monochrome, is lacklustre, as if the once bright colours had run or faded.

* * *

201. (Op. 96, No. 1) Nachtlied (Song in the night)

Goethe – July 1850

Peace lies over all the hills; in all the treetops there is scarcely a stir. The birds are hushed in the wood; just wait a while, soon you too will be at rest.

From this great poem Schubert drew a marvellous music of stillness and wisdom. Schumann renounces all pretensions to the cosmic and writes instead the music of ordinary human relaxation and placidity; which though a very long way from Goethe is not negligible.

NOTES. 1. Goethe's title is *Wanderers Nachtlied.* He has 'Vögelein' in bar 16 and no repetition at the end.

2. The triplet thirds in contrary motion convey the idea of calm (M 36) and have perhaps in Schumann's mind the shape of his stillness motif (M 26). Calmness has two more equivalents; the tied semibreves in the last line (M 35), and the rising thirds at the end (M 37).

3. Schubert's setting of these words (also in an Op. 96) seems not to have influenced Schumann; but his *Meeresstille*, Op. 3, No. 2, also to words by Goethe and also about a great calm, may have done.

4. Cf. also Liszt (two versions); Wolf.

202. (Op. 96, No. 2) Schneeglöckchen (Snowdrop)

Anon. – July 1850

The sun looked at the earth; a gentle breeze blew; and suddenly there stood a snowdrop, a strange pale child. And suddenly it was time for old King Winter to depart, amid tumult and pomp. Swift as arrows the clouds sped away to the dark north. The ice broke, the snowflake melted, the storms went howling by; and amid all this turmoil there stood the snowdrop with bowed head alone.

Now come, little white sister, how long are you going to stand there? King Winter has announced the end of his reign, it is time for us to go home. All his subjects on earth that wear his white livery are now to make ready and depart in haste.

But the snowdrop looked at itself and trembled and thought half in dream

'If indeed these are Winter's robes, why are they hemmed in green? Surely it cannot be the rough hand of Winter which wove that tender green therein; and if I do not belong to him, what then am I? whence and whither do I fare, where is my homeland?'

A poem remarkable mainly for its ineptitude takes possession of Schumann's mind; and there it mirrors for us an indwelling dark confusion.

All begins well enough. The peaceful A flat mood, the pathetic chord on 'Schneeglöckchen' amid the gentle quaver movement, speak with a certain wan eloquence of a lone flower swung by the wind. But then the sense dies away. Schumann finds that his flimsy music is caught out in a storm, and hastily dresses it up in big octaves and expressive chords. But when the storm arrives the music is still so ill-protected that it veers with every impulse, pursuing a distracted course among suggestions of melting, darkness, gusts of wind and a bowed head. Even stranger aberrations follow. The tonality brightens into the remote A major; key, rhythm and texture alike are given a febrile gaiety. The words are about the departure of winter; the music insists on the arrival of spring. The glee with which Schumann proposes to frogmarch the winter away is wholly incongruous; and it contrasts oddly with the return on the last page to the original snowdrop music, now with unaccountable variants and decorations, and drooping in an all too pathetic recitative. Perhaps for Schumann the snowdrop's predicament was painfully like his own; already claimed by some other more ominous realm, yet allowed to remain for a while.

NOTES. 1. No doubt the poem is best left anonymous, though its turgid pretentiousness might suggest the Julius Buddeus of *Resignation* and *Die Meerfee*. The repetition at bars 76–80 is likely to be Schumann's.

2. After ten years the Schumann song is still a piano solo with vocal accompaniment, as in this striking example.

3. The work bristles with such stereotypes as the recitative motif 48 from bar 19 et seq. Some, such as the pressing octaves introduced at 'eilen' in bar 25–26 are not inept, while the floating arpeggios in the piano with floral falling fifths (M 27) in the voice are even attractive. But such curiosities as the sliding gruppetto in bar 35 for the ice melting (as also perhaps in No. 179, q.v.); the fatal key of E flat minor for the dark north and the storms that drive there (perhaps a subconscious association with death); the dull little gust in octaves at bar 39; the illustration of the head bowed in both hands at bars 40–43; the sweetly Schubertian interpolation complete with dominant question (M 43) at bars 51–52; the stock Schumann melody (Ex. B on p. 2) in the right hand at bars 54–55; the dread drums of *Husarenabzug* at bars 62–63, 66–67; the flourish and fanfare of heraldic trumpets at 'Liverei' at bars 67–71; the bustling chords

typifying the final departure; all these things, and others, repeat the melancholy message that the creative mind of a great composer is here heard in decline.

4. Even this pales beside the fantastic last page, where the composer's whole life work in song is peered at through a mist of blank confusion. Bars 92–93 and 94–95 here are a version of bars 22–23 from *Er der Herrlichste*; the next two are the piano accompaniment of *Mein Herz ist schwer*, itself related to bar 16 of *Mit Myrthen und Rosen*; the next two are based on bar 10 of *Sehnsucht nach der Waldgegend*, not to mention *Frage*; and the final questioning – again motif 43 – recalls *Stirb Lieb und Freud* and *Die Sennin.*

203. (Op. 96, No. 3) Ihre Stimme (Her voice)

Platen – July 1850

Let me read the truth deep within you; do not conceal from me what magic being speaks from your voice.

So many words reach our ears to no purpose; they are forgotten even before they die away.

But your tones can reach my ear even from afar; I delight to hear them, I never forget their least murmur.

Then I tremble, kindled with sudden fire; my heart and your voice understand each other only too well.

Platen was a far better poet than Schumann's selection suggests. But this sonorous verbiage assorts well with its smooth tune and bland accompaniment of broken chords. Indeed, it maintains the pattern of true feeling tempered by conventional responses that was to sustain the drawing-room ballad for nearly a hundred years. For a time the young Schumann returns: there is sweetness in the melody, strength in the firm octaves and sudden high note at 'Zauberwesen' (magic being) with a suggestion of faint-heard whispers on a wind in voice and piano at 'von ferne/ dein Ton' (from afar your tones). But in its essence this is the music of comfortable middle age, a shade too poised and mellifluous to convince for long; and the calculated coda, all deprecating cough and modest bow, is finally alienating.

NOTES. 1. Platen has 'behorch' ' not 'belausch' in bars 19–20; the repetition is Schumann's.

2. The recurrent melody, once fresh in *Im wunderschönen Monat Mai* sounds jaded here; the coda, bars 32–36, once slender and charming in *Volksliedchen* sounds flabby and tiresome.

3. But the song has an attractively mature quality which may have appealed to Brahms; the melodic line in bars 7–8 is a fingerprint of his.

204. (Op. 77, No. 2) Mein Garten (My garden)

Hoffmann von Fallersleben – July 1850 (? begun 1840)

Violets, rosemary, mimosa, lilies, daisies and roses all flower here in my garden.

Every flower that can be woven into a lover's garland is here; only the flower of happiness is nowhere to be found.

And though here on earth it may be hidden and hard to find, yet, dear heart, there is some consolation in having sought for it so long.

The agreeably variegated show of the first verse withers into a dry allegory. Schumann provided music which would be almost as dull, were it not for the interest of its tonal confusion. The first verse, ostensibly cheerful, is set lugubriously in the minor. So is the following assurance. But at the central emphasis on a happiness hard to find, the music goes contentedly into the major.

NOTES. 1. The basic idea is that of a piano piece vaguely melancholy and compounded of Clara-themes ingeniously hidden and hard to find (though X is clear enough, even as an inner voice, in bars 32 and 34). There is evident affinity with Chopin's G minor nocturne Op. 37, No. 1, published in Leipzig in June 1840. The poem was published in 1834 (where it reads 'Tausendschön und Rosen' in bars 7–8 and 'gemüht' at the last word). The quotation of Schumann's favourite *An die ferne Geliebte* melody at 'ob sie heimisch ist heinieden' is probably deliberate. All these points suggest 1840 or earlier as the date.

2. On the other hand July 1850 is the date in Schumann's own composition-list; his 1840 word setting though not exemplary did not usually wear the harmony back to front as here; all the other Hoffmann settings date from 1845 on; and some of the harmonic touches, such as the insistence on the diminished seventh and the progression at bars 26–27, confirm a later date. The inference is that this is a piano piece from 1840 or earlier, perhaps part of some Chopin variations, refurbished to make a song in a barren period – perhaps in association with No. 206 below.

3. At least the use of the nobility motif 51 in the minor at bar 12 and in the major in the postlude is in conformity with the self-congratulatory words.

205. (Op. 77, No. 3) Geisternähe (Near in spirit)

Halm – July 1850

What is this blowing gently around my brow like a soft spring wind? What plays around my cheeks like the sweet scent of roses?

It is your dear thought that finds and comforts me; it is your silent yearning that laves my brow.

And what is it that troubles my sense like the sound of harps? It is my own name that softly escapes your lips.

I feel your presence; it is your longing, your soul drawing me from afar back to your heart.

The poem is the eighth and last of a cycle of so-called wedding songs written on the occasion of the marriage of the poet's beloved to another man. This theme moved Schumann profoundly throughout his creative life; and here his music is a direct reaction to the words. Thus the opening semiquavers are the idea of the wafting of gentle breezes; the simple tonic-dominant cadence in A major at 'laue Frühlingsluft' has strayed in from Schumann's own springtime; harp music comes into the accompaniment at 'Harfenklänge'; and so on. So direct a contact with verse might once have been electrifying; now it elicits little more than a sporadic twitch from a once great song-writer. In the coda the ballad-style banality finally wins.

NOTES. 1. This is the final example of the 'unhappy wedding' theme.

2. The harping at bar 19 is tedious, like the stereotyped coda. Other reflexes are the dominant question 43 at bar 10, the 'Demut' motif 38 at bar 12, etc., and the springtime A major. In the alternative vocal notes at bars 35–36 it seems better to follow the piano line as usual, avoiding the over-dramatic higher notes. Not least interesting is the disappearing motif 45 at 'von deinen Lippen irrt', where the name escapes her.

206. (Op. 77, No. 4) Stiller Vorwurf (Silent reproach)

Wolff[1] – *c.* July 1850 (? begun 1840)

In lonely hours my sorrow wells up; my old wounds reopen. Oh let them bleed; they do not hurt so badly now as when first you made them.

Whether you are repenting the pain you cost me, or whether you are heedless and merry with others, what can that matter to me now?

Whatever you are doing, the pain is over; I cannot chide you, I can only forgive you.

The memory of Schumann's separation from Clara was a bitter hurt to him for years after. But though the music wells from this same rich source as some of his finest work it is not from the same depth; there is no vitality to help the maudlin lyrics.

NOTES. 1. Wolff was the biographer of Carl Banck who was for a time Schumann's rival for Clara. No doubt the repetition is the composer's.

---

[1] According to Paula and Walter Rehberg, *Robert Schumann* (1951).

2. Op. 77 was published in 1851. But this song is directly addressed to Clara and may well therefore, because of the sense of the words, date from 1840 or earlier. The left hand begins with the Clara-theme X in its clearest form; that theme recurs and is then heard again in the treble line in bars 5–7. The same thought underlines the piano right hand at bar 21, 'was auch du beginnest'; and at the reconciliation of the closing words there is the Clara theme in the Q^1 form associated with reconciliation in *Dichterliebe*. However, the harmony has an occasional 1850-ish touch, e.g. in bars 14–15, suggesting revision in that year, perhaps at the same time as No. 204 above to which it is close kin (compare bars 4, 14, 23 here with bars 16–17 there).

3. Note the manly rhythm (M 56) and noble harmony (M 51) appearing in the doleful minor in the postlude; the tragic hero epitomized. The recitative chords of motif 48 and the dominant question (M 43) occur at bars 19–20. The sorrowful semitones of motif 8 are in evidence throughout, and are given the special sense of *wounding* in the appoggiatura phrase associated with that word in bars 4 and 5.

4. The song's construction as piano music with added words is clear from a comparison of bars 1–4 with 11–14.

207. (Op. 125, No. 1) Die Meerfee (The sea-fairy)

Buddeus – July 1850

The bright sound of silver bells comes ringing through the air from the sea; girls' voices sing softly around. In her frail coach of pearl the fairy rides by, as the melody rises and falls, borne along by the sea breeze.

Bright sparks burn around her in a gay dance; a fragrance like roses is wafted down from mast to keel. The boy on board sees it all as if in a dream; but then the foaming waves carry the apparition away.

The intention is a mystic metamorphosis of sound, sight, and scent; the achievement is all blur and tinkle. Into a Mendelssohnian fairyland, all bells and sea breeze, wafts a heady Chopinesque sensuality, all musk and pot-pourri, in dreaming and languishing chromatics at 'und der Knabe sieht es' (and the boy sees it). So this music hints at its own profound underlying knowledge of the duality of love. But any creative spark is smothered by the smooth inanities of the verse, and Schumann's own matching mood.

NOTES. 1. The prettifications, e.g. the semiquaver figures at bars 7–8, etc., and the fragrant chord on 'Düfte', bar 24, are dull echoes of *Die Blume der Ergebung* and *Er ist's*. The lush sensual chromatics at bars 28–33 have an expressive quality unique in Schumann.

2. The dream staccato of motif 32 is useful for this vision; there is a vague suggestion of the nobility motif 51 as the fairy drifts off in the postlude; cf. *Der Gärtner*.

208. (Op. 125, No. 2) Husarenabzug (The hussars march off)

Candidus – July 1850

What's coming out of the dark gate in the distance? – not a swarm of gnats? Hark! snatches of bugle-tunes are born aloft on the breeze. Make way now for the handsome hussars; milkmaids to one side, close in to the parapet of the bridge. Brave lads go trooping gaily off to the wars.

See, friends, how the stallion cavorts, how the captain hoists his fat paunch. Let us be gay and not think of the white stone where the loved one's little foot rested as she stood with her friend by the well.

Suppose that a gust of wind should blow by the spring, making its smooth flow whirl about in spray? Never mind, darling; your hussar will chop that wind-god's chubby cheeks for him!

The musical ideas, though jaded, are perhaps tolerable enough for one verse of this appalling poem; but they are already inept by the second, and the stolid repetitions of the drum and tucket effects soon become deadly.

NOTES. 1. The song derives from *Ins Freie*, sharing its outdoor key of B flat, its ostensibly joyful arpeggio (M 23) (bars 35–37 here, bar 6 there) and its dull imperfect cadence followed by a flatward turn in the harmony (bars 11–18 here, and 7–10 there). It also offers drums passim and trumpets at bar 10 etc., with the full swell of a brass band at bars 22–25 and the vigour of motif 53, here flabby (bar 38, etc.).

2. This is fortunately Schumann's only Candidus song. But Brahms inherited either Schumann's copy of the poems or his taste for them, and set several to music.

209. (Op. 125, No. 4) Frühlingslied (Spring song)

Braun – July 1850

The corn is springing, the birds singing, spring is here; the streams sparkle, the young fish are swimming. Everywhere is the sound of rejoicing; delight fills each heart, each blade of grass.

The bee hums, the hornet drones, the spider spins her webs, sits in ambush and peers out, dreaming of her prey. Gnats fly into the web before they can think; as they wonder how it could have happened they are already caught.

There are many nets, my child, hung round you in springtime; first you gaze and trust, then you are trapped.

NOTES. 1. There are agreeable reminders of earlier Schumann, e.g. the rural music of the Dudelsack's open fifths in the first bar, and the springtime key of A major, though the joy of motif 21 sounds lacklustre.

2. The strophic repetition entails such anomalies as the separation of subject from verb by two crotchet rests ('liegt . . . es') in verse 4.

210. (Op. 125, No. 5) Frühlingslust (The joy of spring)
Heyse – July 1850

Now the roses are in bloom, now love spreads its nets; poor frail fluttering butterfly, how can you hope to escape?

If I had been caught in this young time of roses, I should die of sorrow, even though love were the prison.

I was not made for sorrow and yearning; my path lies through the blossoming woods, my airy songs fly up to the treetops.

For once Schumann has found some verses with a certain lilt and dexterity; so the music has its own bloom and innocence under the artifice of over-elaborate harmony and over-ornate piano writing.

NOTES. 1. Heyse has 'seh*n*en' in bar 21 and 'lu*f*t'gen' in bar 26.

2. The innocence and ardour clearly impressed Brahms; compare for instance the thirds between voice and piano in bars 13–16 here with the thirds in his Op. 52, No. 5.

3. Note the dominants of motif 64 and the joyous arpeggios of motif 21.

211. (Op. 127, No. 4) Mein altes Ross (My old steed)
Strachwitz – July 1850

Old steed, old companion, you look at me and neigh; but I have lost heart, we shall never ride out together again. You shake your head and whinny; I believe you are dreaming, old friend, of how we once flew over the mountain ridge, the old well-loved path.

A creaking gate; you stamping before it, your bridle flecked with foam; a rustling dress, a white hand patting your glossy neck. The gravel flies like dust . . . sleep well, sweet dreams, and back again in the blue night, storming back over the dewy ridge in the moonlight.

I ride with slack bridle, a dream in my heart, the farewell kiss on my lips; drumming hoofbeats, a quail's call, and in the distance the sound of the river running.

One last look back at the sleeping house of my love. My dear old friend, how sad that all is over now. My friend, that path we knew is hidden under snow; the gate walled up, the loved one lost, and my heart broken.

The young Count Moritz of Strachwitz, rich in estates and promise, died at twenty-five in 1847. Thoughts of that lost youth, and of Schumann's own, converge in a stronger current of music than any other of the 1850 songs.

The opening strains are Schubertian in their guilelessness and their response to the words. The first page is all resignation. Then as the recollection becomes livelier a rider's memory dominates the song. Hooves stamp after 'du scharrest davor'; the rhythm relaxes to a standstill for the meeting and greeting, and tightens again to an insistent jerking of dotted quavers for the imagined riding home. After 'ein letzter Blick zurück' (a last look back) the harmony halts on a dominant; and now the hoofbeats change imperceptibly into a knell tolling for a young love and a young life.

NOTES. 1. The poem has 'meine Seele', not 'deine Sehne' in bars 6–7.

2. Motifs are the question 43 at bar 6, 'going away' 45 at bars 18–19, and the manliness rhythm 56 passim.

Sechs Gedichte (Six poems to words by Lenau) und Requiem, Op. 90

Some of these Lenau songs (e.g. 212, 215) and their arrangement by keys suggest the 1840 style; indeed, these may have been earlier sketches now refurbished, since all the poems had been published by 1838. But for the most part Schumann responds in his typical 1850 chromatic style.

212. (Op. 90, No. 1) Lied eines Schmiedes (Blacksmith's song)

Lenau – August 1850

There, horse, you'll soon be shod; then off you go, brisk and good, and come back again one day.

Carry your master always true to the guiding star that shines bright over his road.

And as you go with each step carry your rider nearer heaven.

And now you're shod, so off you go; and be sure to come back again one day.

Shorn of the dramatic irony given by its context in Lenau's *Faust* the poem has the very qualities of Schumann himself. There is firm strength in the accented strokes of hammer on anvil, and earnest tenderness in the unaffected hymn-like simplicity of melody and harmony. In this innocent music thoughts and actions are one. The rhythm is not only the shoeing but the comfortable jog-trot of a well-shod hoof; the harmony is not only the peace of a contented mind but a well-wishing, each stroke a blessing.

NOTE. This unusually happy conjunction of music and verse is likely to be coincidental, judging from the rest of Op. 90. Schumann omits the third verse and repeats the last line of the others. In the last verse 'beschlage' should read 'beschlage*n*'; here the direction 'piano' may perhaps be meant to suggest that it is to be sung in a farewell reverie as the imagined horse trots off shod.

213. (Op. 90, No. 2) Meine Rose (My rose)

Lenau – August 1850

To the precious jewel of springtime, to the rose, my joy, already drooping and pale from the heat of the sun, I bring a beaker of water from the deep well.

And so to you, rose, of my heart, drooping and pale with sorrow, I would silently pour my soul out at your feet as I pour water for this flower – even though you might not then revive like the rose.

[*To the precious jewel of springtime, to the rose, my joy, already drooping and pale from the heat of the sun, I bring a beaker of water from the deep well.*]

The sense of the poem is replaced by a dazed rich grandeur, a velvet music of sated love and dark roses. The drooping melodies in voice and piano merge and sigh over rich supporting harmonies that fall away flatwards on to deep bass notes at the mention of the dark well. But elsewhere there is blandness, indeed blankness. The beauty of the music is still a cut flower wilting on the stem, even though this makes its giving in homage all the more poignant.

NOTES. 1. The repetition of the first verse distorts both the syntax (by stressing what is merely a subordinate clause) and the sense (by ending more optimistically than Lenau intended). The addition of 'dunklem' in bar 13 to eke out the melodic line, and of 'freudig' in bar 33 completes the destruction.

2. Yet this pot-pourri may express Lenau in a Schumannian sense; it is redolent of 1840 flower-music. The idea of roses is associated with a falling fifth (M 27); and Clara-melodies covering a falling fifth (see p. 23) come singing into Schumann's mind to make the first six bars of *Meine Rose*, thus

Ex. 1

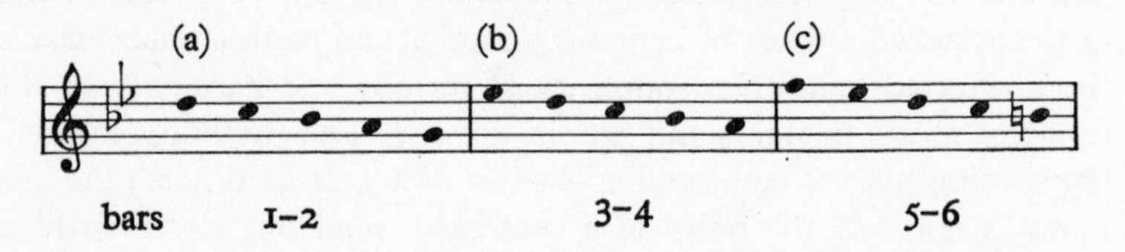

The first of these phrases is found in *Der Hidalgo*, where it leads up to a passage about dark roses falling (Ex. 2). Earlier in the same song is a bass progression (Ex. 3) containing the sweetness of the augmented fifth (M 12).

These elements compose *Meine Rose*, bars 1–2, thus

It happens also that the sequence (a) and (b) of Ex. 1 above is found in two other 1840 songs about love and flowering, as the opening melodic line of both; *Frühlingsnacht* (piano part) and *Und wüsstens die Blumen* (voice). Further, (c) and its continuation correspond closely with the opening melodic line of *Intermezzo*, where it is clearly a Clara-theme (P[1]).

So it may not be coincidence that at the imagined transition from wilting to reviving there is heard a theme first drooping then rising

bars 30–31 31–32

3. The key change of the second verse is the mediant interpolation of motif 47; the added bass notes are motif 29. The recitative passage naturally has motif 48.

4. The variants may be motivic; e.g. the diminished seventh chord at bar 18 anticipates 'Schmerzen' in the next bar, while the corresponding chord in bar 5 is a dominant seventh, perhaps anticipating 'Freude'.

214. (Op. 90, No. 3) Kommen und Scheiden (Meeting and parting)

Lenau – August 1850

Each time we met, the sight of her seemed as dear as the first green in the woods.

Her words reached my heart as sweetly as spring's first song in the trees.

When she waved goodbye it was as though the last dream of my youth was taking leave of me.

The sense of the poem wavers and blurs into a rich confusion just as in the previous song; but here the musical outline is beginning to fade too, and what might have been a most beautiful song is vague and inarticulate.

NOTES. 1. This time a *rhyme* is omitted; Lenau has 'im Hain' after 'Lied' in bar 16.

2. Again this is piano-music, but no more than a confused background to murmured words. Bar 3 gets lost when the music is repeated; Lenau's words disappear in the dream staccato (M 32) at bar 16; the chords in bars 7 and 23 are bizarre. The final oddity is the notation of the postlude, which changes the look of the music without changing its sound. The intention might be to contrive a tonal as well as a poetic link between this song and the next (cf. Nos. 75 and 122).

3. The piano part has increasing leaps (the sixth at bar 6 becomes an octave at bar 13) in a version of motif 16 also found in *Ich kann's nicht fassen*. The diminished sevenths in arpeggio in bars 18 and 20 have the sad perplexity of motif 41.

215. (Op. 90, No. 4) Die Sennin (The cowgirl)

Lenau – August 1850

Once more sing your call down into the valley so that the bright echoing speech of the mountains wakes at your clear voice.

Hark how your song has reached the heart of the high hills, that now respeak it each to each.

But all things pass, and one day you and your song will depart for ever, when love has claimed you or death takes you.

And the grey hills will stand deserted, looking down sad and speechless remembering you and your songs.

The music has beauty and clarity, which fade and blur as soon as the original idea is spent. But on the last page the tolling fifths in the bass, the wistful questioning of the harmony, well match the pathetic fallacy of the high hills hushed in memory of a lost song.

NOTES. 1. The clear harmonies of the first ten bars suggest an earlier Schumann; the poem was published (in the *Deutscher Musenalmanach*) as early as 1836. That version moreover has Schumann's 'Sennin' in the second verse (bar 13) while later texts have 'Mädchen'.

2. The opening recalls, not surprisingly, *Des Sennen Abschied* of the previous year.

3. The responses in bars 21 et seq. are mechanical; thus the broken chord triplets of bar 24, etc., lean heavily on bars 13–14 of *Heimliches Verschwinden* of a few months before.

4. The sudden sforzando bass note at bar 14 is a striking example of motif 29^{B}, here used to express the rooted strength of mountains; the final dominant harmony on the last page (i.e. the dominant of the relative minor) has the questioning of motif 43 and suggests an extension of motif 45 (departure).

216. (Op. 90, No. 5) Einsamkeit (Solitude)

Lenau – August 1850

A wild tangle of dark fir-trees; the ceaseless lament of the fountain; heart, this is a fitting scene for your painful renunciation.

One sombre bird alone in the branches sings your sorrow; and your questioning receives for answer only the silence of the woods.

Though the silence of the woods remains unbroken, cease not your lament; the spirit of love listens and understands.

Heart, your secret weeping is not lost in vain among the moss; God understands your love, your deep hopeless love.

The music too renounces all, and dwells in tangled thickets of sound. The spiky falling quavers suggest the trickle of a poisoned spring through thorn-bush. The tonality moves into the major for the consolation of soft moss and sweet water; but Schumann has no inspiration to express the healing spirit of love, and the chromatic taint of hopelessness persists to the end.

NOTE. There is motif 45 at the word 'geht', denying the offered consolation. The whole song is composed of the grief and renunciation of motif 11, here in the deadly context of E flat minor.

217. (Op. 90, No. 6) Der schwere Abend (The sultry evening)

Lenau – August 1850

The dark clouds hung so oppressive and heavy; we were walking sadly in the garden together.

So sultry and silent, so overcast and starless was the night, so like our love, fit only for tears.

And when I had to go and bade you goodnight I found it in my anguished heart to wish us both dead.

A song as oppressive as the night it describes. But the congruence with Lenau seems coincidental, as if the death-wish were Schumann's own rather than the poem's; and inside this lifeless music all expression lies stifled.

NOTES. 1. The song is a piano piece deriving from the 1840 *Ich hab' im Traum geweinet* which has the same recurring rhythm in almost the same chords, in Schumann's funereal E flat minor and the same doleful use of the nobility motif 51, here at 41–43. The construction is confused; thus when the music is repeated an extra bar (21) creeps in unnoticed.

2. Cf. Franz, Op. 37, No. 4.

218. (Op. 90, No. 7) Requiem

Latin text (in Follen, trans Anon.) – August 1850

Rest now from your painful striving, from your passionate burning love; he whose desire was for reunion in Heaven has passed beyond, into his Saviour's dwelling. Even in the tomb a bright star shines on the righteous man; and to him shall appear a true star in the night, his Lord in the glory of Heaven.

Intercede for him, holy souls; let not your comfort fail him, holy spirit.

Hark, psalms of triumph resound, solemn tones among which sings the beautiful harp of the angels.

[*Rest now from your painful striving, from your passionate burning love; he whose desire was for reunion in Heaven has passed beyond, into his Saviour's dwelling. Even in the tomb a bright star shines on the righteous man; and to him shall appear a true star in the night, his Lord in the glory of Heaven.*]

This song was added to Op. 90 partly as an offering to the departed Lenau, partly perhaps to soften the harshness elsewhere in the verses. Both purposes converge in its sleek religious flow; both wear an aspect of falsity, which the music does little to redeem.

NOTES. 1. Schumann told his publisher that he had added the Requiem in the mistaken belief that Lenau was already dead; and then discovered that Lenau was in fact dying – 'as if I were tolling a passing knell all unawares'. However this may be, the relevance of Heloïse's lament for Abelard with chorus of monks is not very clear. The scansion suggests that the German text had 'drein' not 'darein' (an alteration made elsewhere by Schumann, cf. No. 139, note 1) and did not repeat 'erschaut' in bars 25–26. The Latin text as given by Adolf Follen has nine verses, of which only the following three are used here.

Monales: Requiescat a labore
doloroso at amore!
unionem coelitum
flagitavit
jam intravit
salvatoris adytum.

In obscura tumbae cella
Alma micat justo stella
instar ipse siderum
refulgebit
dum videbit
in fulgore dominum.

Sanctae animae, favete!
consolare paraclete!
audin? sonat gaudia!
cantilena
et amoena
angelorum cythara.

2. Some motifs are apt enough; there is 'silence' (M 26) in the piano prelude; and happiness (M 1) which is relevant (if tame) for the bliss of 'erschaut in Himmelspracht' in bars 26–28.

3. Others however are puzzling. Thus the perpetual harping of the accompaniment presumably flows from the mention of angelic harps in bar 44; but

the thought is obscure. Its texture contains inexplicable patches such as the *Einsamkeit* formula of motif 11 in bar 8 (where the poem says 'selig' and the music says the opposite) and the *Herbstlied* accompaniment formula (bar 32 of that song) throughout.

4 · DÜSSELDORF 1851–52

With the move to Düsseldorf in September 1850 came some improvement in Schumann's health and spirits. For a time his choice of theme, and even his music, recuperates. The following songs for example are almost all character-studies of men and women as in the Leipzig or Dresden days; a princess, a servant-girl, a tragic heroine, a bandit, a soldier. But neither the characters nor the songs really come to life.

219. (Op. 107, No. 1) Herzeleid (Heartache)

Ulrich – January 1851

The willows trail their weary branches, and the waters drift sadly by. The poor whitefaced wretch stared blindly down in a dream. And she let fall a wreath of everlasting flowers, already heavy with tears, while the waves whispered in soft warning – 'Ophelia, Ophelia!'

At least the verses move Schumann into music. But his response is all too apt; stupefied, and only on the brink of achievement. The pity is that from the whole wealth of German poetry he has chosen two dull quatrains about madness and death by drowning, not long before his own breakdown and attempted suicide from the Rhine bridge at Düsseldorf.

NOTES 1. The motif 21 that Schumann used for both foliage and water is apt for a weeping willow; it sounds throughout the song as M 24. There is the hint of a distinction between the two ideas by marking the former staccato (bars 1–6), the latter legato (the rest of the song). There is some aptness too in its final apotheosis low in the left hand in the postlude for the idea of a watery grave (M 29A).

2. Brahms's *Intermezzo*, Op. 119, No. 1 might be interpreted as a successful recreation of the mood Schumann had in mind here.

220. (Op. 107, No. 2) Die Fensterscheibe (The window-pane)

Ulrich – January 1851

As I was cleaning the windows for the festival, so that they would catch the sunlight, polishing and thinking of many things, he *went by, head in air.*

And I was so taken aback that I smashed the pane, and the blood ran out red over my hand.

And though my hand may bleed and hurt badly, yet you did look up at me – when you heard the glass breaking. And I looked into your eyes, for the first time for many a long day.

But when my heart broke you never gave me so much as a glance; it broke in silence.

For once a tolerable poem; but there is the uncomfortable feeling that – as in the Lenau songs Op. 117 – Schumann is reacting to the blood and pain rather than the feeling and the imagery as such. Even then his reactions are slow and numb. The splintering glass and heart sound as glum little dissonances among colourful but irreparable fragments of music. The sad day has come when Schumann is surpassed even by a second order poet.

NOTES. 1. Ulrich has 'dass ich gleich in die Scheiben brach hinein' in bars 15–16.

2. Schumann has now no reaction to obvious verbal points. The text has a capital for 'Er', though even without this the sense of '*He*, my lover' would be obvious enough. Schumann elides this on a semiquaver; his emphasis says that whoever it was, he went by *proudly*. The contrast between 'leis' and 'laut' is also completely missed.

3. The curious treatment of 'stolz' suggests that there was some association for Schumann between pride and a six-four chord on B major. This same chord later does duty for blood; perhaps through some subconscious connexion with the colour red. Similarly, the long note on 'über' in bars 19–20 may express numb shock as blood wells out.

4. At the last words the piano has the typical three-part harmony of motif 34 for ladies in distress.

5. The resemblances to *Der Gärtner* are evident; no doubt that song had just been written and Schumann in a more barren mood was subconsciously re-composing it along with other echoes of past work.

221. (Op. 125, No. 3) Jung Volkers Lied (Jung Volker's song)

Mörike – January 1851

She who carried me in her womb, and rocked me in the cradle, was a handsome saucy sun-tanned lass who couldn't stand men.

She just joked and laughed aloud and left her suitors flat; 'I'd rather be the wind's bride than any man's.'

The wind, hearing this, came and took her as a lover; that's how I was conceived, her cheerful child.

NOTES. 1. The outlaw Jung Volker appears in Mörike's novel *Maler Nolten*. Singers might now restore the bowdlerized text. The first line ends 'trug im Mutterleib' which is also needed for the rhyme; the last line is 'in ihren Schoos empfangen'. 'Froh' in bar 14 should read 'frech' and 'als' in bar 31 'denn'.

2. Verbal points are freely misrepresented, as usual in this last period. Thus Mörike's symbol of passion ('Windesbraut' = gust of wind) is not even a stiff breeze; in bars 29–36 is the limp semiquaver figuration of motif 22.

3. Note the 'laughter' motif 15 in the prelude, in bar 24 (at the word 'lachte') and in the postlude – the last laugh. The opening melody is borrowed from – of all things – *Mondnacht*, at 'die Erde still geküsst, etc.' and is not only in the same notes and key but even has (bar 45) the added decoration. Perhaps the word 'Ehe' was a subconscious link, cf. No. 53, note 2.

222. (Op. 107, No. 3) Der Gärtner (The gardener)
Mörike – January 1851

On her favourite steed, as white as snow, the most beautiful of princesses is riding down the avenue.

On the path where her steed so delicately prances, the sand of my strewing gleams like gold.

You rose-coloured bonnet nodding up and down, throw down just one plume for me, in secret; and if you would like a flower in exchange, then take a thousand for one, take them all.

Mörike's radiant poem brightens Schumann, making his music shine more easily than usual in these dark days, and giving the result a lasting lustre; but the high gloss cannot hide the flaws. The picture is painted in D major. The princess is depicted in the alert little chordal figures of the prelude, the capricious steed in the curvetting rhythm that follows. The eloquent and tender melodies with their sad overtones do much to re-create the mood of adoring love. But the designing hand falters, and the music is heard as mosaic, with some of its bright inlays fragmentary or false.

NOTES. 1. Schumann intends a unifying rhythm (as in Wolf's setting). But his music has intention tremor; and instead we hear a fantastic proliferation of slightly different rhythms. The piano part alone exemplifies *more than two dozen* ways of filling up a bar of two-four time, including such aberrations as

which are all but impossible to make clear.

2. The princess motifs

are elegantly composed of the nobility motif 51. They combine most effectively with capriciously dancing rhythms and wistful harmonies, e.g. for the image of the riding princess at 'du rosenfarbs Hütlein', complete with the falling fifth redolent of roses (M 27).

3. The diminished sevenths at the end suggest questioning irresolution, 'will she, won't she?' (M 42), until in the final chords she rides past and away. There is fine invention here, which clearly influenced Wolf in his setting; but the material wears badly in such patches as the peroration at 'Nimm tausend für Eine', with its destructive repetitions.

223. (Op. 107, No. 6) Abendlied (Evening song)

Kinkel – January 1851

All is still; so hushed is the evening that you can hear the footfalls of passing angels.

All around, night darkens and deepens; now cast away your sickness, my heart, and your despair.

Now the stars arise in majesty in the encircling sky; the golden chariot of time passes on its assured way.

And your way through the night shall be safely guided too, so now cast away your sickness, my heart, and your despair.

Again a fine inspiration is lost. The prelude is all serenity in its calm triplet rhythm. But this is disturbed as the voice enters, because of the need to fit in the vocal melody. Such artifice vitiates the song; the chromatically altered chords sound merely affected, the relaxed rhythm merely limp.

NOTES. 1. The middle two verses of the poem are omitted. Kinkel has 'Thale' not 'Tiefe' in bar 12. Schumann responds to his own misreading; the bass notes at 'Tiefe' and in the following bar are the clearest possible examples of motif $29^{A/B}$.

2. The first edition has *acciaccature* not appoggiature in the voice part at bars 11 and 26.

3. At bars 19–20 are the calm rising consecutive thirds of motif 37. The prelude's triplets also mean nocturnal peace to Schumann (M 36) (as in *Nachtlied*). The idea of angels invests these triplets with the nobility motif 51.

4. Of the alternative vocal lines at bars 16 and 31, the higher piano line is preferable.

Vier Husarenlieder (Four hussar songs) Op. 117

224. (Op. 117, No. 1) Der Husar, trara

Lenau[1] – March 1851

Hurrah for the hussar! What is danger to him? his sweetheart, and at her sign he leaps to her side.

Hurrah for the hussar! What is danger to him? his wine; let it flow, let his sabre drink it deep, drink blood.

Hurrah for the hussar! What is danger to him? his song, his favourite song; let it sing him to sleep.

The ostensible mood is one of bluff assurance. But the music, like the verse, bristles with short sharp phrases like sabres arranged in a compulsive pattern, and hectically overemphasized by repetition.

Nevertheless this is an effective song; perhaps too effective for comfort.

NOTES. 1. The basic motto theme announced as a prelude occurs in one form or other nine times in the first verse, and hence twenty-seven times in the song's two pages.

2. In bars 9–10 the higher notes, as the piano's melodic line, are more in the spirit of Schumann's song-writing.

225. (Op. 117, No. 2) Der leidige Frieden

Lenau – March 1851

Hateful peace had lasted too long, and we had parted company, my trusty sword and I. While I savoured the cellar's wines you hung rusted on the wall. I sampled the vintages one by one; meanwhile the blood dried upon you. But at last hot war flared, my sword, and your moment had come. I scoured

[1] Another Lenau song of this period, *Frühlingsgrüsse*, was left unpublished: see *Musical Quarterly*, January 1942.

your blade bright again; I let you whistle your deadly song; then to your loud work in the reek of powder, your joy and mine. Drink now of this new wine, my thirsty blade, drink deep from heart to heart. While you savoured the red blood, my tongue was speechless with joy.

The music begins with a memory of the battle song just heard. But it is stiff and rusted in its rhythm. Voice and piano share a brutal insistence; the piano's echo in the higher octave suggests an exasperated cry of frustration. At the mention of wine the tonality mellows into the major, only to give place to motionless menacing octaves and unisons at the thought of the rusted sword hanging alone. By the last verse the music's muscle is restored: the movement is more ponderous and more active, with a terrifying image of crazed sabre strokes swinging wildly to left and right, ending in agonized discords in the postlude.

NOTES. 1. Lenau has 'gab' in bar 31. The strange antithesis of his last verse contrasts 'du' and 'mir'; a point completely missed in the music. But elsewhere the verse makes a very powerful impression on the composer; wholly Wolfian for example is the way in which the word 'hingst' hangs motionless across the bar line.

2. Note how the rising minor horn passage of discontent (M 5) is transformed in the last verse to the glee of its major counterpart (M 4). The falling phrase at bars 3–4 is also at bars 7–8 of the previous song.

226. (Op. 117, No. 3) Den grünen Zeigern

Lenau – March 1851

The green bushes of the inn-signs, the red cheeks of the girls, the merry sound of the fiddle; these I used to follow from carouse to carouse, for as long as I can remember.

But now I wear the green bush as the plume on my shako; the red cheeks I slash on the enemy with a right good will; and for music all around I have the roar of the cannon.

[*The green bushes of the inn-signs, the red cheeks of the girls, the merry sound of the fiddle; these I used to follow from carouse to carouse for as long as I can remember.*]

The poem is less obviously crazed than the others, and the song has zest and drive.

In the repeated first verse there is a striding bass line to emphasize the nature and durability of the conversion from irresponsible youth to proper manhood. At the end the bugle's summons is heard and obeyed.

NOTES. 1. Schumann's repetition of the first verse damages the sense of the words, as in the earlier Lenau song *Meine Rose.*

2. Bar 22 here has the E flat octaves of bars 12–13 in the previous song.

227. (Op. 117, No. 4) Da liegt der Feinde

Lenau – March 1851

There lies the enemy's troop, in its blood-red blood. How sharp he hews, how deep, the brisk hussar!

There they lie, aha! so pale and red; their souls still trembling, hush, on his helmet's plume, there they lie dead.

And again the trumpets call; he wipes his wet sword on the horse's mane, and remounts his charger with the blood-red hooves.

The prelude sadly surveys the battlefield with its ominous falling figures; mourning and warning. The voice strikes in with the same dark solemnity. This music pays its respects to the defeated dead in Lenau's first two lines. In the next two the living victor is heard; at first martial and alert, then returning in cold clanging octaves to survey the battlefield. This pattern is repeated, as usual in this cycle, less aptly for the second verse. Finally elation triumphs, with a ringing of bugles and hoofbeats, riding off in unbridled zest for more killing. At last the bugle-calls sound out high in the major key; and the dying echoes with their suggestion of universal mortality lend a touch of humanity to Lenau's dark poem.

NOTES. 1. For the bleak shrouded effect of the opening measures compare *Winterzeit* II, Op. 68, No. 39; and see No. 178, Note 4.

2. The manly motif 56 throughout suggests that the song is wrongly barred, with real stress at the present half-bar.

3. The final galloping off recalls the giant's striding home in *Es leuchtet meine Liebe.*

4. Is this the subconscious source of Duparc's *Le Manoir de Rosamonde*, also concerned with shed blood and a pursuit on horseback? Each song has repeated octaves, a dotted triplet rhythm, a rising motif in the bass, and falling semitones (bar 14 here, bars 13–14 in Duparc).

Sieben Lieder (Seven songs to words by Elisabeth Kulmann) Op. 104

Elizabeth Kulmann died at seventeen in 1825, by which time her prodigious facility for rhymed verse had produced some 100,000 lines, which went through several editions. Schumann's choice of poems (including the four duet settings of Op. 103) suggests that he had read through them all. In retrospect it is hard to say which is more daunting, the thinness of the gruel or the immensity of the ladle. More disconcerting still is the alacrity with which Schumann laps it all up, gravely commending its flavour. The girl who died young was for him, like Mignon, a tragic figure, and his sympathy is touching. But one cannot balk the fact that his comments on each poem, still loyally preserved in the Breitkopf and Härtel edition, are both fulsome and obtuse; nor the painful evidence they offer of a mind in deterioration.

228–234. (Op. 104, Nos. 1–7)

Kulmann – May 1851

228. (Op. 104, No. 1) Mond, meiner Seele Liebling

Moon, my soul's beloved, why do you look so pale today? Is it perchance that one of your children is unwell? Or perhaps your consort the sun came home ailing and you have come out of your dwelling to weep out your sorrow here?

Oh, good moon, just such a sorry fate has befallen me. My mother is lying indoors ill with only me to care for her. Sleep has just come and closed her eyes for a little while, and I have left her asleep to seek fresh courage for my heart.

So let your sight, oh moon, be a comfort to me, to show that I do not suffer alone; you are one of the rulers of the world and yet you cannot be always happy.

NOTES. 1. The text used has 'siehst du' in bar 3.
2. There is the dominant question (M 43) at 'unpass' in bar 8.

229. (Op. 104, No. 2) Viel Glück zur Reise, Schwalben!

The best of luck on your journey, swallows, now hastening in a long skein to the fair warm southlands in bold gay flight.

I should love to go with you one day to see the thousand marvels that every realm has to show.

But I should always return, however fair those lands were, however rich in wonders, and come back to our own dear fatherland.

NOTES. 1. The final repetitions are Schumann's.

2. The demisemiquaver wings flutter in the out-of-doors B flat.

230. (Op. 104, No. 3) Du nennst mich armes Mädchen

Poor girl, you call me; you are wrong, I am not poor. If only you would take the trouble, just out of curiosity, to rouse from sleep one morning and see my lowly cottage when the lordly sun rises in the dawn sky; its roof is pure gold. Or come in the evening when the sun is sinking into the sea and see my one window, how brightly it shines in topaz jewels.

[*Poor girl, you call me; you are wrong, I am not poor.*]

NOTES. 1. Schumann repeats the first line to help explain the point.

2. The intention is the plain expression of naïve thoughts. All the more disturbing, then, is the total incoherence of the rhythms in the piano part, which make a dozen different patterns in two dozen bars (see also No. 222, note 1). Even the opening words 'du nennst mich' have a pointlessly different scansion on repetition.

231. (Op. 104, No. 4) Der Zeisig (The Finch)

It is maytime, child; cast aside your books, come outside, and sing a song with me. And let it be a song contest; and let anyone who likes decide which of us sang better.

NOTES. 1. The final repetition is Schumann's.

2. The slightly more robust verses suggest stronger equivalents – canon for the two vying voices, and B flat for outdoors. The song is quite acceptable at its level; in Op. 79 it might have made more of a name for itself.

232. (Op. 104, No. 5) Reich mir die Hand, o Wolke

Reach me your hand, cloud; lift me up to you. There stand my brothers, at the open gate of heaven; there they are, though in life I never saw them, and our father in the midst of them. They look down on me and beckon me to their side. Reach me your hand, cloud, lift me up quickly.

NOTES. 1. The semiquavers are motif 22.

2. The song recomposes the futile Op. 96, No. 4 (No. 199 above).

233. (Op. 104, No. 6) Die letzten Blumen starben

The last flowers have died; the rose, fair queen of the summer moon, went to her rest long ago. You, gracious dahlia, no longer lift your head; even my tall poplar is stripped of leaves. And I, who am neither tall poplar nor sweet slender rose, why should I not perish, if even roses fade?

NOTES. 1. 'Sah', not 'seh' in bar 9, second verse.

2. This recomposes the hopeless Op. 104, No. 1 above, a shadow's shadow.

3. The rose still has a falling fifth (M 27).

234. (Op. 104, No. 7) Gekämpft hat meine Barke

My bark has striven with the angry sea. But now I see the horizon clear; the sea's rage abates. I cannot avoid you, oh death not of my choosing. But the end of my suffering will be the beginning of my mother's grief. Oh sad-hearted mother, let not sorrow oppress you too sore. Death's sea sunders us for only a few moments. Once I arrive there I shall never quit that shore; I shall be for ever turned earthwards, helping others to land.

NOTES. 1. The insistent rhythm is also a feature of No. 175.

2. The surprising anticipation at bar 4 expresses the word 'erzürnt'.

235. (Op. 107, No. 4) Die Spinnerin (At the Spinning-wheel)

Heyse – *c.* August 1851

Each of the village girls sits in her room, happy at her spinning-wheel. Each has her sweetheart; how briskly the wheels turn!

Each is spinning her wedding dress to please her true lover; before long there'll be wedding bells.

But no friend comes to talk with me; I sit in sad despair, and my hands falter.

And the tears silently run down over my cheeks. What need is there for me to go on with my spinning? I cannot tell.

NOTES. 1. The date is conjectural. Op. 107 was published in 1852.

2. Schumann repeats 'nicht lange'. The poem with only a few revisions inspired Brahms to his masterly Op. 107, No. 5.

3. See No. 159, Note 2.

236. (Op. 107, No. 5) Im Wald (In the wood)

Müller – August 1851

All alone I go into the wood. Oh see two butterflies flying and fluttering in the sky; when they rest they are cradled in the fragrance of a flower; and I am so alone, so full of care.

All alone I go into the wood. Oh see two birds frightened from their warm nest but still singing, chasing and playing high in the boughs; and I am so alone, so full of care.

All alone I go into the wood. Oh see two deer coming to the green hillside together, and as they see me they fly far off over hill and dale together, leaving me alone, so full of care.

NOTES. 1. The text appears not to have been printed in Schumann's lifetime; no doubt it was a private communication. The published version has 'fliehen' for 'entfliehn' and repeats the 'ich' in the refrain, variants which seem more likely to be Schumann's than Müller's. The poem's undemanding meaning is ignored by the music; e.g. the stressed 'mich' in bar 36 is elided on a quaver triplet.

2. Cf. Franz, Op. 12, No. 3.

237. (Op. 119, No. 1) Die Hütte (The cottage)

Pfarrius – September 1851

In the woods in the green countryside where treetop looks over treetop, there in the quiet meadow valley I have built myself a cottage.

It stands sheltered from storms under the lee of the grey mossy cliff. Giant trees tower around it in friendly protection; the rose blooms at the window, the green vine climbs to the roof, and with a confiding murmur the meadow brook flows nearby.

In a fortunate hour I found the site in the wood in this far valley, and now I have built this cosy cottage there. How fresh and alive it looks among the leaves when the dawn smiles at it; how dreamily it fades into the valley when the evening breezes blow around it. At noon a tree shades it with its branches; at night the elves dance there and softly sing.

In the woods, in the green countryside with trees all around, there in communion with Nature I have built myself a cottage.

NOTES. 1. It is sad to find the virile motif 56 in this reduced state, passim.

2. The accents that stand well enough for the strength of the storm and the towering trees in bars 15 and 19 are inept for the smiling dawn and the evening breeze later on.

238. (Op. 119, No. 2) Warnung (Warning)

Pfarrius – September 1851

The day is declining that offered light and freedom; be silent, little bird, you are singing yourself into death.

The night winds stir, the leaves tremble in fear; your song betrays you to your enemies that listen therein.

The burning eyes of the screech-owl glower their menace through the branches; be silent, little bird, you are singing yourself into death.

NOTES. 1. Voice and piano are so independent as to seem disjointed; thus the voice part would read more naturally if rebarred at the present half-bar.

2. The descending line of the prelude that dominates the song is an equivalent (M 24) for the decline of daylight into darkness and death.

3. B minor is associated with the idea of enmity.

239. (Op. 119, No. 3) Der Bräutigam und die Birke (The bridegroom and the birchtree)

Pfarrius – September 1851

Birch tree, birch tree, beauty of the woods, I am getting married and there are many things I need; what will you give me?

'I'll give you a green bough to carry at the wedding.'

I like that green bough very well; what else will you give me?

'I'll give you a birch that will come in handy for your children.'

I like that slender birch very well; what else will you give me?

'I'll give you a strong broom for your young wife to sweep with.'

I like that strong broom wery well; what else will you give me?'

'I'll give you a whipstock that you can swing over a team of horses.'

I like that whipstock very well; what else will you give me?

'It's also possible to make wine from me by letting my sap run.'

I like that birch-sap very well; what else will you give me?'

'I've given you all I have now; all I have left is my very life.'

Then, birch-tree, your life must be a burden to you. I'm getting married, and I still need a lot of things; so you can come with me and heat the room!

Poem and music have a certain unpretentious cheerfulness that makes the song worth an occasional hearing.

NOTES. 1. One verse is omitted: Pfarrius has no 'noch' in 29.

2. Again the artifice of construction is plain; the voice part would be more naturally barred at the present half-bar.

3. Note the dominant questioning of motif 43 in different forms at bars 4, 9, 14, 19, 23, 27.

240. (Op. 139, No. 4) Provenzalisches Lied (Provençal song)

Uhland – January 1852

The song of the troubadours first flowered in the valleys of Provence. It was the child of springtime and courtly love, sweet intimate companions. So it was born blossom-bright and sweet-voiced like its father the springtime; from its mother came its loving heart, full of deep yearning.

Blessed valleys of Provence, you were always full of bloom, but your richest flower is the radiance of the troubadours' song. Those bold knights in their finery, what a noble order of minstrels; those most fortunate ladies, how beautifully their praises were sung.

High and stately minstrelsy; now to be portrayed in scenes from those days of chivalry and the troubadours.

Des Sängers Fluch (The minstrel's curse) was arranged by one Richard Pohl from various texts by Uhland and set by Schumann as Op. 139 for soli, chorus, and orchestra, dedicated to Brahms. The two songs given here have harp accompaniments; they are the last flowers of Schumann's genius as a song-writer, and they make a good end.

The first song is simple and beautiful until the most disastrous of all Schumann's perorations, where the rhetorical flourishes are pompous and futile. Some ground is recovered in the postlude where the delectable main theme is again heard, and for its sake the song is well worth not one but many hearings.

NOTES. 1. Down to 'worden' in bar 52 the lovely text is the first and fourth verses of a long poem, *Rudello* (except that Uhland has 'holder, inniger Genossen' in bars 11–12 and 'war' not 'ist' in bar 37). Then follows the last of four verses of a quite different poem freely altered to provide a libretto. It is sad to think that Schumann connived at this tasteless outrage; and it is only poetic justice that his music degenerates into windy pomposity at that very moment.

2. Note the nobility motif 51, very apt to the verses, in the postlude and implicit throughout.

241. (Op. 139, No. 7) Ballade (Ballad)

Uhland – January 1852

In the high hall sat King Sifrid. 'Now, ye harpers, who can sing me the finest ballad?' And a young man stepped briskly forward, a harp in his hand, a sword at his side.

'I know three songs. The first you have long forgotten; it was you who treacherously stabbed and killed my brother; I say again, you killed my brother.

The next song is one I made in a dark night of storms; you must fight with me single-handed to the death; I say again, fight to the death.'

Then he stood his harp by the table and swiftly drew his sword; and they fought long, with wild cries, until the king fell in the high hall.

'Now I sing the third song, and the best, that I shall never tire of singing; King Sifrid lies dead in his red blood; I say again, dead in his red blood.'

The words have the sombre power that makes Uhland so great a master of the ballad; the cutting edge of a vivid story strikes home with the weight of centuries. And into this realm Schumann follows; with an effort, true, but with strength and dignity and therefore with impressive effect.

NOTES. 1. Schumann omits 'wohl' after 'Harfe' in bar 32 and inserts 'sie' after 'und' in bar 35. Uhland also has the archaic 'seim' for 'seinem' in the last line.

2. Note the nobility motif 51 in the last two bars (and in 3–5) and the impressive use of bare octaves for the idea of death and doom – cf. Brahms e.g. in the *Vier ernste Gesänge*.

3. Note the bold key-change as the youth speaks for the first time; each verse thereafter returns with increasing assurance to the home tonic as the story moves to its inexorable end.

Gedichte der Königin Maria Stuart (Poems of Mary, Queen of Scots)

242–246. (Op. 135, Nos. 1–5)

Attrib. Mary, Queen of Scots (trans. Vincke) – December 1852

242. Abschied von Frankreich (Farewell to France)

I am going away, away; farewell to you, my happy France, where I found the dearest homeland of all, you the nurse of my childhood. Farewell dear country, farewell my past; the ship bears me far away from happiness. Yet only a part of me is leaving; one part will be for ever yours, my happy land, and by it you can keep me always in memory.

243. Nach der Geburt ihres Sohnes (After the birth of her son)

Lord Jesus Christ whom they crowned with thorns, protect this new born child. And, if it be Thy will, let his race long rule in this realm. And let everything done in his name be to Thy fame and praise and honour for ever, amen.

244. An die Königin Elisabeth (To Queen Elizabeth)

One thought alone dominates my mind, holding it in joy and sorrow, so that I hear the voices of hope and fear as I lie awake at night.

And if my heart chooses this missive as messenger, and announces my desire to see you, yet, dear sister, a new fear seizes me, because it lacks the power to prove its sincerity.

I see the boat in the harbour almost hidden and held back by the storm and the force of the waves, and the serene face of heaven darkened by night. So I too am beset by fears and cares; not fear of you, my sister, but the force of fate often hurls down the sail in which we put our trust.

245. Abschied von der Welt (Farewell to the World)

What is the use of the time still left to me? My heart is already dead to earthly desires; my spirit is sundered from all save sorrow; only the happiness of death remains now for me.

Cease your envy, my enemies, my heart is turned away from the honours of great rank, excess of sorrow will destroy me – soon hatred and dissension will go with me to the grave.

You friends who thought of me with love, consider and believe that there is no good I can now accomplish, powerless and hapless as I am. So do not wish for the return of better happier days; and, because I have been heavily punished here on earth, pray that I may receive a share of eternal peace.

246. Gebet (Prayer)

O my Lord God, in thee I trust. O beloved Jesu, save me. In cruel prison, in fearful affliction, I long for Thee; in lamentations I cry aloud to Thee; despairing in the dust I implore Thee to hear and save me.

The rest was silence. One of the saddest entries in Schumann's diary records his joy on completing these last five dismal songs. We can only conjecture what personal meaning he found in them. The first begins 'I am going away'. The last ends 'Save me'. Soon after their completion came his mental breakdown, his attempt to drown himself in the Rhine, and his incarceration in the asylum at Endenich, where in July 1856 he died.

5 · POSTLUDE

From Clara Schumann's diary.

I saw him [in the asylum] that evening. He smiled at me, and – with a great effort, for he had lost control of his limbs – he put his arm round me. I shall never forget that.

Then he became restless, and you could hardly understand anything he said.

Just once I distinctly heard him say 'My . . .', and I'm sure he wanted to add 'Clara', because he was looking at me very affectionately. Then he said 'I know.' . . . – 'you', I expect he meant.

His last hours were peaceful. His head was beautiful in death, the brow serene and gently rounded.

APPENDIX I

Posthumously published early songs

	Title	Poet	Date	Edition
1	*Die Sehnsucht*	Ebert[1]	1827	Universal Vienna 1933
2	*Die Weinende*	Byron	„	„ „
3	*Erinnerung*	Kerner	1828	„ „
4	*Kurzes Erwachen*	„	„	„ „
5	*Gesanges Erwachen*	„	„	„ „
6	*An Anna I*	„	„	„ „
7	*An Anna II*[2]	„	„	*Collected Works*, 1893
8	*Im Herbste*[3]	„	„	„ „ „
9	*Hirtenknabe*[4]	Ebert[1]	„	„ „ „
10	*Der Fischer*	Goethe	1829	*Zeitschrift für Musik*, 1933

[1] Not 'Ekert', as misprinted in 1933 and subsequently.

[2][3][4] The music of these songs was later used in, respectively, the slow movement of the F sharp minor piano sonata, Op. 11, the slow movement of the G minor sonata, Op. 22 (both c. 1835) and the *Intermezzo* Op. 4, No. 4 (1832).

APPENDIX II
Schumann's Health

The evidence of the songs is plain. Schumann never again reached or even approached the level of his 1840 masterpieces. The songs of 1849 are a decline; the later ones a descent, first steep and then precipitous. It would be very surprising if the music as a whole showed a different pattern; nor does it, by general consensus. Other composers of comparable stature are believed to mature in their music; Schumann appears to deteriorate. A favoured explanation is mental illness, e.g. schizophrenia. However, there seems to be no very clear evidence of any mental condition before the final breakdown which would account for a deterioration. On the other hand there is much evidence of a constitutional tendency to ups and downs of mood, with physical or psychosomatic illness, especially in the depressive phase of 1843–4.

Expert testimony in recent times has come from Dr Eliot Slater and Dr Alfred Meyer, two eminent specialists in the fields of psychiatry and neuropathology respectively. Their conclusion from a clinical standpoint, after a study of the biographical and other data, is that the diagnosis most conformable with the facts is early syphilis culminating in dementia paralytica (v. *Confinia Psychiatrica*, Vol. 2, No. 2, 1959). But Dr Dieter Kerner (*Krankheiten grosser Musiker*, 1963) offers the alternative explanation of arteriosclerotic psychosis. The layman can only speculate. But the musical evidence presented in this book seems to support a theory of progressive disorder from 1849 onward.

APPENDIX III
The Sources

It is not now possible to establish beyond all doubt the sources from which Schumann took his song-texts. Then as now, poems were printed in various journals in varying texts before being collected in book form, and were still subject to revision in subsequent editions. But if there are no absolute certainties, there are exceedingly strong probabilities. Thus, there is the clearest textual evidence that certain of the Heine settings of 1840 were taken from the 1827 first edition of the *Buch der Lieder*, and no other source; and the reasonable assumption must be, since all but one of the Heine songs were written in the same few months, and all but that same one are found in *Buch der Lieder*, that that volume was in fact the main source. In such ways, most of the sources have been established beyond reasonable doubt, unless otherwise indicated (by a question mark).

To help with verification, the following list of poets and translators concerned with Schumann's song-texts is arranged to lead back to the known or putative source-book. Thus Burns' poems are shown under that name, not the translator's, because the source is entitled *Burns' Poems, translated by Wilhelm Gerhard*; conversely the Moore poems, though listed under that name, are cross-referenced to Freiligrath, because their source was a volume of the latter's poems.

The references are to the numbers of the *songs* in this volume. The list is also annotated to show (*) poets known to Schumann whether in person or in correspondence, and (†) poets known for their liberal or radical views (see p. 4).

* Andersen, Hans Christian (1805–75)
trans. by Chamisso, q.v.: 93–96
trans. by Anon. (in *Andersens Werke*, Leipzig 1847): 162.
Anon., 165, 202.

Arnim, Ludwig von (1781–1831)
ed. *Des Knaben Wunderhorn*, q.v.

† Béranger, Pierre (1780–1857)
trans. by Chamisso, q.v.: 91–92.

* Bernhard, Lily (fl. 1840, friend of Clara Schumann)
? private communication: 113.

* Braun, Ferdinand (fl. 1841, in correspondence with Schumann)
? private communication: 209.

Brentano, Clemens (1778–1842)
ed. *Des Knaben Wunderhorn*, q.v.

* Buddeus, Julius (fl. 1850, friend of the Schumanns)
? private communication : 189, (?) 202, 207.

† Burns, Robert (1759–1796)
Gedichte von Robert Burns, trans. W. Gerhard, Leipzig 1840: 15, 21, 24, 25, 30, 31, 33, 34, 39.

† Byron, Lord (1788–1824)
Lord Byrons sämtliche Werke (by various translators, including Schumann's father August, edited by him in Zwickau 1821–7)
Vol. I trans. J. Körner: 26, 184–6
Vol. XXVII trans. K. Kannegiesser: 27
(see also Fanshawe).

Camoens, Luis de (c. 1524–80)
trans. by Geibel, q.v.: 143.

* Candidus, Carl (1817–82)
? private communication: 208.

* Chamisso, Adalbert von (1781–1838)
Gedichte, 1st–4th edns, Leipzig 1831–7: 40, 82–97.

* Christern, Carl (fl. 1840, Hamburg correspondent etc. of *Neue Zeitschrift für Musik*)
? private communication: 43.

Des Knaben Wunderhorn
trad. poems ed. Arnim & Brentano, Heidelberg, 1808: 157, 160.

* Eichendorff, Joseph Freiherr von (1788–1857)
Gedichte, 1st edn, Berlin 1837: 49–61, 109, 110, 191.

Fanshawe, Catharine (1765–1834)
wrote 'Riddle on the letter H' attrib. to Byron q.v.: 27.

† Follen, Adolf (1794–1855)
Alte christliche Lieder, etc., Eberfeld 1819: 218 (Latin text).

† Freiligrath, Ferdinand (1810–76)
Gedichte, Berlin 1838: 28, 29.

Fröhlich, Abraham (1796–1865)
Fabeln, Aarau, 1825: 112.

* Geibel, Emanuel (1815–1884)
Gedichte, Berlin 1840: 104–107
Volkslieder und Romanzen der Spanier, Berlin 1843: 140, 141, 143–7, 154–5.
? private communication: 142.

Gerhard, Wilhelm (1780–1858)
translator of Burns, q.v.

Goethe, Johann Wolfgang von (1749–1832)
Westöstlicher Diwan, 1819: 13, 16, 17, 19, 187
(and see Willemer)
Gedichte, 1815: 163, 201
Faust, Part II, 1832: 170
Wilhelm Meister, ? Paris 1840: 171, 176–83.

Halm, Friedrich, (pseud. of Eligius Freiherr von Münch-Bellinghausen, 1806–71)
Gedichte, Wien 1850: 205.

* Hebbel, Christian Friedrich (1813–1863)
? periodical/private communication: 38.

*† Heine, Heinrich (1797–1856)
Buch der Lieder, Hamburg, 1827: 2–11, 18, 32, 35, 45–48, 62–81,
Taschenbuch für Damen, Tübingen 1829: 135.

Heyse, Paul (1830–1914)
Der Jungbrunnen (short stories), Berlin 1850: 210
? periodical: 235.

*† Hoffmann (von Fallersleben), August (1798–1874)

Gedichte, Leipzig 1834: 136, 164, 204
Gedichte, Breslau 1837: 148, 150, 153, 158
Kinderlieder, Leipzig 1843: 149, 151, 152, 161.

Immermann, Karl (1796–1840)
Gedichte, Stuttgart 1830: 137.

Kannegiesser, Karl (1781–1861)
translator of Byron, q.v.; see also Fanshawe: 27.

Kerner, Justinus (1786–1862)
Gedichte, Stuttgart 1826
(or *Dichtungen*, Stuttgart 1834–1841): 114–27.

† Kinkel, Gottfried (1815–82)
Gedichte, 2nd edn, Stuttgart 1850: 223.

Kletke, Hermann (1813–86)
Gedichte, Breslau 1836
(or *Deutschlands Dichter*, ed. Goedeke, Berlin 1844): 159.

* Körner, Julius (1793–?)
translator of Byron, q.v.: 26, 184–186.

Kulmann, Elisabeth (1808–25)
Gedichte, 3rd–5th edn, Leipzig 1844–7; 6th edn, Stuttgart 1851: 228–34.

* L'Egru, Ch. (fl. 1850)
? private communication: 188.

* Lenau, Nikolaus (pseud. of Niembsch, Edler von Strehlenau), (1802–50)
Gedichte, Stuttgart 1832, 1838: 212–17, 224–7.

* Lorenz, Wilhelmine (fl. 1845 – Oswald Lorenz was sub-editor on the *Neue Zeitschrift für Musik*)
? private communication: 44.

Mary, Queen of Scots (Mary Stuart 1542–68)
poems attributed to her, trans. Vincke, q.v.: 242–6.

Miranda, Francisco Saa de (fl. 1550)
trans. by Geibel, q.v.: 140.

Moore, Thomas (1779–1852)
trans. by Freiligrath, q.v.: 28, 29.

Mörike, Eduard (1804–75)
Gedichte, Stuttgart 1838: 138, 139, 167, 221, 222.

* Mosen, Julius (1803–67)
Gedichte, Leipzig 1836: 14.

* Müller (von Königswinter), Wolfgang (1816–73)
? private communication: 236.

* Neun, Wielfried von der (pseud. of Wilhelm Schöpff, 1826–1916)
private communication: 193–200.

Padilla, Pedro de (fl. 1580)
trans. Geibel, q.v.: 147.

Pfarrius, Gustav (1800–84)
Waldlieder, Köln 1850: 237–9.

Platen, August Graf von (1796–1835)
Gedichte, Stuttgart 1828: 203.

* Reinick, Robert (1805–52)
Lieder eines Malers, Düsseldorf 1838: 98–103.

* † Rückert, Friedrich (1788–1866)
Gedichte, Erlangen 1834–8: 12, 22, 23, 36, 37, 41, 42, 128–34, 172–5, 190
Moosrosen (periodical), Tübingen 1826: 169.

Schiller, Johann Friedrich von (1759–1805)
Musenalmanach, 1798 (or *Gedichte*, Leipzig 1800–3): 192
Wilhelm Tell, Tübingen 1804: 166, 168.

Schlegel, August (1767–1845)
translator of Shakespeare, q.v.: 1.

Seidl, Johann (1804–75)
periodical (?Aurora, Wien) 1840: 108.

Shakespeare, William (1564–1616)
Twelfth Night, trans. Schlegel & Tieck, Leipzig 1841 (sic): 1.

† Strachwitz, Moritz Graf von (1822–1847)
Neue Gedichte, Berlin 1848: 211.

Tieck, Johann (1773–1853)
translator of Shakespeare, q.v.: 1.

† Uhland, Ludwig (1787–1862)
Gedichte, Stuttgart 1815 (10th edn 1843): 156, 240, 241.

*† Ulrich, Titus (1813–91)
periodical *Deutscher Musenalmanach*, Berlin 1851: 219, 220.

Vicente, Gil (c. 1465–1537)
trans. Geibel, q.v.: 144, 146.

Vimioso, Conde dei (fl. 1520)
trans. Geibel, q.v.: 141.

Vincke, Gisbert Freiherr von (1813–1892)
translator of poems attrib. to Mary, Queen of Scots
? private communication: 242–6.

Willemer, Marianne von (fl. 1815)
wrote some of the poems in Goethe's *Westöstlicher Diwan*, e.g.: 20.

* Wolff, Oskar Ludwig (1799–1851)
? private communication: 206.

Zimmermann, Georg Wilhelm (1794–1835)
? periodical: 111.

INDEX A

The Songs

(Songs with titles are indexed by title; others by their first words. Main page references are shown in bold type.)

(Main page references are shown in bold type.)

(Main page references are shown in bold type.)

INDEX A THE SONGS

(Main page references are shown in bold type.)

INDEX B
General